Celebrating the Dawn

"Through the window of science we see the Dawn of the Age of Enlightenment."

Maharishi before a picture of his teacher, Guru Dev.

Celebrating the Dawn

Maharishi Mahesh Yogi
and the TM Technique

Epilogue by Maharishi Mahesh Yogi   Written by Robert Oates, Jr.

G. P. Putnam's Sons
New York

Transcendental Meditation, TM®, the Science of Creative Intelligence, SCI, and World Plan® are service marks of World Plan Executive Council—United States, a non-profit, tax exempt educational
Organization.

SBN: 399-11815-2

Library of Congress Cataloging in Publication Data

Oates, Robert M
    Celebrating the dawn.

    1. Transcendental Meditation.   2. Mahesh Yogi,
Maharishi.   I. Title
BF637.T68017   158.1[B]   76-14884
ISBN 0-399-11815-2

PHOTO CREDITS
All photographs in this book are the property of Maharishi International
University with the exception of those on the following pages: page 28 David
Boss; page 35 Vernon Shibla, New York Post; pages 68 (left) and 77 Bill
Deknatel; page 81 E. Streichen, Shostal Assoc.; pages 111 and 137 Fairfield
Ledger; page 115 Myron Feld; pages 120 and 126 Allen Cobb.

Editorial and Publishing services provided by
COBB/DUNLOP, Inc., New York

PRINTED IN THE UNITED STATES OF AMERICA

Beyond Relaxation to Enlightenment

In the spring of 1975, Maharishi Mahesh Yogi took one month to fly rapidly on a five-continent tour of the world. The purpose of that tour was to bring out a new understanding about the nature of man.

The Transcendental Meditation Technique had already been widely accepted as a means for relaxation.

Maharishi went out to tell people about the Dawn of the Age of Enlightenment.

As this book goes to press, nearly a million people have begun the Transcendental Meditation Technique in America alone. The number learning the technique is increasing rapidly. Five years ago forty thousand people were beginning every year. Now the number is forty thousand a month.

Most of these new students come to learn the Transcendental Meditation Technique for a very simple reason. They have heard it is an effective way to relax and escape from tension and stress. And the TM Technique does work to relieve stress, of course. In fact, it works so well it has become the standard for many imitative "relaxation techniques." Television shows and book stalls have recently showcased a number of unsupported claims that other methods work "just as well as Transcendental Meditation."

But thinking about the Transcendental Meditation Technique as merely a method of relaxation misses the essential point about the practice. The point is that the TM Technique brings about rapid progress in the quality of life at every level. It is true the first research on the technique focused on the deep physical relaxation it brings, relaxation deeper than that produced by any other technique tested by independent researchers. More recent studies, however, have centered on the more fundamental effects of the

The TM Technique works so well it has become the standard for many imitative "relaxation techniques."

Much more than
relaxation is
promised by the
ancient
understanding
about man's
consciousness
that produced
this technique in
the first place.

practice. Hundreds of these studies, conducted at universities and independent research centers, have established two important facts (see Part Two of this book for a review of the research). First, the Transcendental Meditation Technique not only brings relaxation to the body; it also progressively improves the functioning of both the nervous system and the brain itself. Second, as the technique improves the functioning of these basic levels in the human system, it brings parallel—and cumulative—benefits to all aspects of an individual's life.

People who practice the Transcendental Meditation Technique for any length of time soon notice there is much more going on than simple relaxation. Physical health improves, mental abilities increase, personal relationships become more rewarding—the whole range of life seems to be positively affected. And the reason Maharishi went on his 1975 tour, the reason he has begun to emphasize the concept of "enlightenment," is to call attention to the fact that this personal growth is not haphazard or accidental. It is an integrated pattern of progress beginning at the level of human consciousness, continuing on through the other aspects of life, and heading toward a cumulative goal—the state Maharishi terms enlightenment.

The word "enlightenment" as Maharishi uses it needs some definition. To most people, the word simply means a state of having correct factual knowledge about a subject. Using the term in roughly this sense, historians call the eighteenth century an "Age of Enlightenment," referring to the flowering of rational thought led by Voltaire, Montesquieu, Rousseau and others. But when Maharishi uses the term he means something quite different. He is not talking about improving *what* we think about, or the type of logic we use. He is talking about improving the mechanism that does the thinking. He is talking about improving the nervous system, the mind, the consciousness that is the basis of all our thoughts.

"Enlightenment is the normal, natural state of health for the body and mind," Maharishi says. "It results from the full development of consciousness and depends upon the perfect and harmonious functioning of every part of the body and nervous system. When one is using the full potential of the mind and body in this way, every thought and action is spontaneously correct and life-supporting. This is life free from suffering, life lived in its full stature and significance."

Ideas such as these about consciousness and enlightenment are new to most people, of course. They can seem abstract and philosophical instead of concrete and practical. For this reason the plan of this book is to approach these concepts from three different angles.

Part One of the book takes the form of a travelogue on Maharishi's 1975 world tour, and imbedded within the narrative is a series of interviews with Maharishi. These interviews present a theoretical understanding about the relationship between the Transcendental Meditation Technique and the state of enlightenment. Part Two takes these ideas, theories passed down by the tradition of teachers from which Maharishi comes, and examines them in the light of modern scientific research. Part Three allows experts in seven different fields to discuss the impact of the Transcendental Meditation Technique in their own terms.

Although the connection between the Transcendental Meditation Technique and a state of enlightenment is not yet widely understood, man has been expecting some such breakthrough for quite awhile. He has begun to expect more from his consciousness.

Until recently most of the energy, creativity and intelligence of Western man has been used to increase material wealth and expand technology. We have succeeded beyond the wildest dreams of our ancestors in freeing ourselves from the "external" problems of poverty and toil. But this turns out to be only another stage in our progress. We have sought comfort and leisure, and what we found is that comfort and leisure simply provide a basis for more meaningful searching. Now our attention has begun to turn inward. And in a scientific age, when apparent miracles are daily occurrences, it's really no surprise that laboratory experiments have succeeded in isolating a technique for the rapid expansion of conscious capacity. What has happened is that scientific expertise has "caught up" with ancient knowledge.

It shouldn't be surprising that this "discovery" of the Transcendental Meditation Technique was appreciated first for its surface values. Relaxation may not be the most fundamental benefit of the technique, but in an age of stress and tension, relaxation is a desperate necessity in itself. And as Maharishi points out, some such benefit should quickly appear from any effective technique for enlightenment.

"If we are proceeding toward a light," he says, "then at every step the light should increase."

With the practice of the Transcendental Meditation Technique, this "light" may first appear as relief from stress and tension. But relief from tension is hardly the end of the process. The Transcendental Meditation Technique does not fit neatly into any of our familiar categories of thought, and it certainly cannot be confined under such labels as "relaxation technique" or "non-medicinal tranquilizer." Much more than relaxation has already been shown by the scientific research on the TM Technique. Much more than relaxation has already been noticed by the large number of people who have been practicing it. And much more than relaxation is promised by the ancient understanding about man's consciousness that produced this technique in the first place.

It is time to hear what Maharishi means when he says we are living through the Dawn of the Age of Enlightenment.

Contents

The TM Program: Some Basic Facts

Detailed information available from local centers of The International Meditation Society (also listed as The Transcendental Meditation Program).

The Transcendental Meditation Technique is an easy, natural mental technique. It involves no concentration or effort and can be learned easily by anyone.

Not Religious—The Transcendental Meditation Technique is not a religion or philosophy. It requires no particular lifestyle, and it is enjoyed by people from all walks of life.

Dissolving Stress—The Transcendental Meditation Technique allows the body to experience a revitalizing state of rest and relaxation measurably deeper than the deepest point in sleep. This level of rest and relaxation "dissolves" fatigue, stress and anxiety, and increases energy.

Refining the Nervous System—The Transcendental Meditation Technique allows the mind to experience peaceful levels of relaxed inner wakefulness. This refreshing experience allows the brain and nervous system to develop more refined levels of functioning, thus enlivening the mind's capabilities.

Improvement of Life—The refreshing effects of deep rest and refined mental activity bring benefits to all aspects of life. Physical health strengthens, the mind's capabilities increase, psychological attitudes improve, and social interaction becomes more rewarding.

Scientific Research—Hundreds of research experiments, performed independently at universities and research centers in more than twenty countries, have demonstrated (1) the reality of the experience during the Transcendental Meditation Technique and (2) the validity of the benefits that come in all areas of life outside the meditation period.

The Course of Instruction—The Transcendental Meditation Technique is quickly and easily learned in a sequence of four two-hour lessons over four consecutive days. The initial session is personal instruction, one-to-one, so that each student is guided to a correct experience of meditation the first time. The next three sessions are group meetings involving other students who have begun individually on the first day.

Course Fees—The course fees are the major source of financial support for the World Plan Executive Council, a non-profit educational organization established by Maharishi Mahesh Yogi to further the teaching of the Transcendental Meditation Program throughout the world. Under a system that is audited independently every year, these fees help support the local centers, as well as the state, national and international levels of the World Plan Executive Council. Further support is always needed, and donations to the WPEC are tax-deductible.

The current fees in the United States are:

Adult	$125
College Student	$65
High School Student	$55
Jr. High School Student	$35
Family	$200

Seven Goals of the World Plan

A World Plan has developed to make the Transcendental Meditation Program available to all people. It is a plan to establish one teacher training center for every million people and train one teacher of the TM Technique for every thousand people. There are already more than three hundred World Plan Centers in America alone, and more than fifteen hundred world wide. The aspirations of the World Plan are summed up in these seven goals:

1. To develop the full potential of the individual

2. To improve governmental achievements

3. To realize the highest ideal of education

4. To eliminate the problems of crime and all behavior that brings unhappiness to the family of man

5. To maximize the intelligent use of the environment

6. To bring fulfillment to the economic aspirations of individuals and society

7. To achieve the spiritual goals of all mankind in this generation

"Go and tell the world
no one has the right to suffer any more."
—Maharishi

Traveling with Maharishi: An Action Portrait of Knowledge

This section of the book is a "teaching chronicle," a record of the world tour Maharishi took in 1975. It has been handled as a sequence of narrative scenes (covering the tour and a few incidents setting the stage for the tour) interspersed with a series of interviews with Maharishi. During that month Maharishi went very carefully into a theoretical picture of the nature of enlightenment. He then analyzed the impact of individual growth toward enlightenment on the governmental, economic, educational and social problems facing the world today. Part One presents a distillation of that teaching.

As an exercise in editorial judgment this section posed some interesting challenges, mostly because Maharishi is without interest in personal publicity. It is virtually impossible, for instance, to persuade him to talk about himself or his biographical background. There are a couple of reasons for Maharishi's personal reticence. In the first place, he considers himself to be solely a teacher. To him, it is what he is teaching that is important, not the facts of his personal life. It is almost possible to say his life *is* his teaching—he works a seemingly endless succession of eighteen-hour days and seven-day weeks. In the second place, Maharishi doesn't take personal credit for what he is teaching. The Transcendental Meditation Technique, as he often points out, is nothing new. It has been preserved for thousands of years by an unbroken tradition of teachers in northern India. Maharishi's contribution has been to present it in a systematic form that is scientifically verifiable.

For these reasons, the first part of this book has not been written as a biography or personality portrait in the usual sense. It is simply hoped that by hearing Maharishi talk in the context of the energetic activity of the tour, the reader will gain some sense of his thoughts as a living, practical reality. The aim is to present an action portrait of knowledge.

> Maharishi considers himself to be solely a teacher. To him, it is what he is teaching that is important, not the facts of his personal life.

The Foundations:
Rest is the Basis of Activity

It is hardly a
usual occurrence
for a man to go
on television and
announce the
Dawn of the Age
of Enlightenment.

Maharishi has just arrived. He is backstage with the show's host, Merv Griffin, and the taping is scheduled to start in a few minutes.

As several of us step out into the wings to wait, the spacious stage is a scene of brightly lit activity. Glittering backdrop screens are sliding sideways into position. Two large cameras are wheeling gracefully through practice maneuvers around a small group of chairs and props. A well-dressed lady is covering one of these chairs in light blue silk, and stage hands are bringing in flowers and small trees to function as scenery. These last aren't the usual preparations for an interview show. But then, it is hardly a usual occurrence for a man to go on television and announce the "Dawn of the Age of Enlightenment."

The show will be seen by thirty million people. Merv Griffin, it turns out, is an open, friendly man when you meet him informally, and this is just how he seems on television. People like him. To most of the viewers who watch him regularly, he is a familiar and comfortable personality, almost a friend in the home.

To most of these same people, on the other hand, Maharishi Mahesh Yogi will be a totally new sight.

The show's preparations have been completed by now. The house lights have been turned off and the stage curtain is drawn. As thirty million people tune into the show, this is what they see:

Merv Griffin walks out on stage, turns his back on the camera and joins the applause coming from the audience. Another man follows him out, a man with long hair and a white beard. He is dressed in white silk and he carries an armful of flowers. There is a large smile on his face and he answers the applause by sweeping his eyes slowly through the audience. It is obvious he is enjoying himself.

Many of the people in the live audience are teachers of the Transcendental Meditation Technique, teachers Maharishi has trained personally. Their applause is warm. They know him well. And if most of the people at home are not so familiar with him, if they are wondering why Merv Griffin is bringing Maharishi Mahesh Yogi onto his show, that question gets answered right away.

"I think I'll just make everybody comfortable," Merv Griffin says as he sits down. "I'll start off by saying that I practice the Transcendental Meditation Technique."

He sits back smiling to wait for the applause to die away.

"I started nine days ago," he continues, "and I've never felt better in my life."

The show is off to a rolling start, and Merv Griffin keeps the pace moving.

"Clint Eastwood is the man who got me started," he says.

"It's helped my tennis game," he smiles.

"The Transcendental Meditation Program," he continues, "is being taught in many public school systems. It's being used by businesses, by hospitals, by athletic teams, by the military. It's being funded for various projects by the state governments of Pennsylvania, Massachusetts and New Jersey.

"And last week in Detroit," says Merv Griffin, "a judge sentenced a young drug offender to four years on the TM Technique. Twice a day."

There is laughter and applause, and for the first time Maharishi speaks. "This is the judgment of the Age of Enlightenment," he says. "A man is sentenced to develop his full potential by law."

It's a good transition point, and Merv Griffin moves on to cover some basic facts.

"We should clear up a couple of misconceptions right away," he says. "The Transcendental Meditation Technique doesn't have anything to do with religion, does it?"

"No," Maharishi says, "it's a technique, a practical way to enjoy deep rest and enliven the mind and body."

"And it doesn't encourage you to be passive?"

"No, no. Rest is the basis of activity. The Transcendental Meditation Technique increases the ability to be active and be successful in activity. Not only does the mind become more vital and dynamic, but the physical system performs better."

"And Joe Namath passes better?"

"This is what I hear. Many great athletes are enjoying the Transcendental Meditation Technique."

Merv Griffin's attitude seems to be totally positive, and the interchange is sprightly and informative. For those of us backstage who have

17

A venerable
actress, a
practicing
psychiatrist, an
established
politician—and
perhaps the most
enthusiastic of
these meditators
is Merv Griffin
himself.

been traveling a month with Maharishi, the program feels like a fitting mass media climax to our world tour. The trip so far has stretched from India throughout Europe and across North America. The agenda has tended more to dignified meetings than prime-time television. There have been large symposia in the major halls of three continents, interspersed with meetings between Maharishi and university leaders, corporate executives and heads of state. After such impressive, if somewhat solemn, occasions, the quick glitter of television is a sudden change.

Just behind where we are standing, in a small room in the wings, technicians watch the show four times over, punching camera angles out to the nation with illuminated buttons. Out front on the large, mostly empty stage, the huge cameras glide and turn around the small raised set. On camera, Merv Griffin begins to bring out his other guests. All of them practice the Transcendental Meditation Technique.

One is Grandma Walton from the TV show, "The Waltons." She is Ellen Corby, a lady perfectly cast for her part as a reassuring no-nonsense, grandmotherly type.

"I spent three and a half months on a course taught by Maharishi several years ago," she says. "Looking back, they were the best months of my life."

Another guest is Dr. Harold Bloomfield, a psychiatrist. He is the clinical Director of the Institute for Psychophysiological Medicine in San Diego, California, and co-author of the best-selling *TM: Discovering Inner Energy and Overcoming Stress.*

"The Transcendental Meditation Technique is the fulfillment of psychiatry," says Dr. Bloomfield. "More research has appeared on the benefits of the TM Technique in the last five years than in seventy-five years working with all other techniques for improving mental health."

The third guest is Arlen Gregorio, a State Senator in California serving his second four-year term. A good-looking man with a shock of hair swept across his forehead, Senator Gregorio is chairman of two of the more important committees in the California Senate.

"At first my staff thought I shouldn't talk about the fact I practice TM," Senator Gregorio says. "But it's an important experience for me and I feel people should know about it. I have only missed two meditations in two years and three months. I can't afford not to do it."

A venerable actress, a practicing psychiatrist, an established politician—and perhaps the most enthusiastic of these meditators is Merv Griffin himself.

"This is a hectic business I work in," he says. "It feels so good to just take the phone off the hook and meditate for fifteen minutes. And when you come out, you feel so, you feel so . . ."

"Fresh," says Maharishi.

"Fresh!" says Merv Griffin. "And I wish I could find words to explain how easy it is."

"It's easy because it's natural," says Maharishi. "The mind naturally settles down to that quiet level of relaxed alertness. And we know from science that that level is the state of least excitation, a field of perfect order."

As Maharishi talks, one camera often focuses on his hands as they move and dance with each point.

"It's so natural," he says. "It doesn't take any practice or anything. That's why more and more people are enjoying the Transcendental Meditation Technique. More than one million people have now learned the technique. That's why we find the Dawn of the Age of Enlightenment."

The Dawn of the Age of Enlightenment—there isn't much time in a fast-paced hour to explore such a startling idea in any detail. Television can provide an instantaneous introduction for millions of people. More complete information, however, is often communicated in other ways—through private conversation or the printed word.

Maharishi discusses enlightenment with Merv Griffin; the number of people starting the TM Technique tripled after this show.

"**A** beautiful time is coming for the world," Maharishi says after the show. "The Age of Enlightenment will be a time when there will be less sickness, less crime, when problems will be fewer. It

THE COMING
AGE

will be a time when life will be happier, more harmonious. Progress will be more, success will be more, life will not be a struggle."

In an Age of Enlightenment, most problems will simply disappear?

"Yes, yes," Maharishi says. "People will remember that there *was* a time when the hospitals were filled, the jails were filled, when doctors were always worried and lawyers were up late at night unable to rest. They will remember, but all this will be a tale of the past."

That seems quite unlikely, doesn't it? The state of the world today is discouraging.

"Yes, the idea of an Age of Enlightenment must seem an unbelievable thing, like telling a dream to someone. There is so much crime everywhere, all this inflation and depression at the same time. Talk of an Age of Enlightenment seems just inconceivable."

Why talk about it then?

"It's a scientific phenomenon we are witnessing. There has now been so much research proving the benefits that come through the Transcendental Meditation Technique. Health improves, the mind becomes more clear, behavior keeps on getting better. And this is happening with so many people—over a million people by now. It's not impractical idealism we are talking about, high-sounding moral values with no basis. This is something that has been verified subjectively by so many people, something that has been verified objectively by all these hundreds of experiments. It's possible now for life to become better. It's possible. It doesn't matter how long the world has been in darkness; now we can see the first rays of the Dawn."

A statement like that seems so optimistic. The history of mankind has been considerably different. It has always been full of suffering and struggle.

"This has been the story. Man has lived with problems and suffering throughout the ages. History does not record a time when man was free from suffering, and so life was declared a struggle. 'Life is a struggle'—it's a very common axiom in English."

And this hasn't been true?

"This *has* been man's experience. And being his experience it also became his established understanding. Life is a struggle. To err is human—as if man is born to make mistakes."

But if that is the experience of life, how can it be argued with?

"The thing is, life has been lived on a very wrong basis. But now it's not necessary any longer. Life is not meant to be lived in dullness, idleness and suffering. Now science has verified that man need not suffer as he has in the past. All that has been missing is the knowledge of how the full potential of life could be developed."

Does this mean we should stop trying to handle our problems—stop working on crime and pollution and so forth? All we have to do is meditate?

"When problems are there, then they must be dealt with. It's like a boil on the skin. When the boil comes up it must be treated on its own level, the doctor must operate on it. But a wise physician would also advise taking some internal medicine for the blood to become purified. Do something to stop the tradition of boils from coming up. In the same way, all people should be given the knowledge of the full potential of the physiology—how to live full physical health, full mental health, and on that basis derive the maximum from life."

But if there is such knowledge, why haven't we known it? Where has this knowledge been?

"It's difficult to understand. When the nature of life is to grow, why hasn't it grown to full potential? The answer is that life started to grow only on the horizontal level. Progress was thought to be only on the horizontal level. Man has always been searching, but in an age of science there have only been the joys of technological progress and material development. Something has been missing. The vertical expansion of life was overlooked. The requirement for inner growth was overshadowed."

And the Transcendental Meditation Technique can fill this need?

"This is what the research tells us. It is a technique—like the use of a lever—a means to do something previously found impossible. As long as it was not known, nothing could be done. But now we have it. It's no longer necessary to be satisfied with the information one reads in psychology that a man commonly uses a small portion of his mind. No. This is a technological age, and now a technique has been verified that can unfold full potential, a natural technique to take our awareness to that full value of energy and intelligence deep within, and from there incorporate it in our daily lives. It is this that will allow the whole world to live the best that life has to offer. It is this that will allow us to make obsolete the old understanding that life is a struggle and to end suffering for mankind in this generation."

When people hear this, what are the questions they usually ask?

"Really only one: how can such a simple thing have such a profound effect? This is why we are fortunate to live in an age of science. It is through the window of science we have seen the Dawn of the Age of Enlightenment."

The few words in this sentence cover a trip backward in time, almost two years exactly. It is now mid-April, 1973. The place is La Antilla, a small resort village on the Atlantic coast of Spain. The setting is a lecture hall, late at night, with one thousand people listening to a talk by Maharishi. At this point the world tour is far in the future, but for many of those who will eventually be led to that Merv Griffin Show, including me, this is one of the beginnings. It is here in this isolated little town by the sea we have first seen Maharishi in person.

The evening's lecture is just coming to an end. The video equipment used to record Maharishi's formal talks has been turned off, and the bright lights around him are fading. Most of the people are beginning to file out of the hall but Maharishi has asked a number of us to stay behind to hear the plans for tomorrow. He has just announced we are going to have another test.

We have all come to La Antilla for a course training people to become teachers of the Transcendental Meditation Technique. The course has been going on for months now, and Maharishi has arrived recently to handle the final stages of the teaching himself, and to approve each student individually. With a thousand people here, representatives of more than twenty countries, Maharishi faces quite a task.

Before undertaking the job, however, Maharishi decides one more challenge would be good for us. He announces there will be an extra test. This comes as a late-night surprise for most of us, since we have just finished several days of final examinations, but watching him laugh and joke about it takes some of the edge off. His plan for the test is somewhat unusual. Rather than having another written exam, he wants everyone to go through a two-on-one oral grilling. The idea is to dig out any weak spot in any area of our studies.

We move up to fill the open seats in the front of the hall. Maharishi is sitting in front, dressed as always in a white silk "dhoti," a wrapped garment typical of Northern India. He has a microphone in front of him—a bow to utility—and some flowers nearby as a touch of life. As we all get settled, Maharishi begins to explain his reasons for this *final* final test.

"It's such a beautiful opportunity we have," he says. "This knowledge is so precious, so delicate, and this is our chance to master it, to own it completely."

It's a good thought, but it probably would have sounded better earlier in the evening, when we weren't so tired.

"Maharishi," somebody says from the back with a late-night tone in his voice, "we just *finished* our tests on all this material."

"Good," Maharishi says. "Good. And now this will be another time. And every time the people take a test they become more confident of what they know. The thing is, a man might know the material but when he comes in for testing he gets so *nervous.*" He enjoys a hearty laugh, as if the very concept of being nervous were a totally preposterous idea.

"But they will be tested in fire this time," he goes on, "and when they are through here anything they find out in the field will seem easy by comparison. And we must be strong. If a man is not ready, we must not pass him. He will have another chance to pass in three days. And if he still is not ready, there is no hurry. When he does pass, we must know his knowledge is thorough."

There is no arguing with his logic, even if it does seem a little rigorous. But the plan raises a question. How are we going to get one thousand people through the testing tomorrow night—tonight, that is—in the five hours between six o'clock and eleven? Several people raise the point.

"It'll be all right," Maharishi says. "We have how many, one hundred and fifty people here? You can be tested during the day by the people on the teaching staff. Then you will combine, two together, and test the rest of the people tomorrow night. It will go well."

It all sounds easy when he says it, but as we leave the hall, some of us are still a trifle dubious. The whole process has to start in less than eight hours.

After the rigors of the rest of this course, however, the addition of this last minute hurdle is not really surprising. Although the village of La Antilla is a lovely vacation spot—a small, irregular white-washed town settled in the sand and looking out to one of the world's most beautiful ocean views—the course has turned out to be something other than a vacation. Before we came here, most of us knew Maharishi only from his video taped lectures on the nature of consciousness. But soon after we arrived we found out he is not merely a teacher of theoretical knowledge. He is also an eminently practical man, a stickler for organization and thorough study. Under his direction, classes are conducted morning, afternoon and evening, six-and-a-half days a week, and the final testing program is only the culmination to a series of intermediary tests given at every stage.

By now, however, only this final examination is at issue. And when the morning comes we find that contrary to our late-night expectations, the two-stage endeavor lifts off smoothly. The performance of Maharishi's staff under pressure has been impressive: detailed test outlines have appeared overnight, and one thousand soft theater seats have disappeared from the lecture hall, replaced by seventy-five cloth-covered examination tables. Testing begins at ten for the first tier of course participants, and most of them have passed by mid-afternoon. Then, teamed up in pairs, these people start to interrogate the rest of the course participants at six.

With Maharishi sitting up in front supervising the mechanics it's quite an intense scene. A long line stretches all the way outside the lecture hall onto the sand, and staff members guide individual testees from the door to open tables. Seventy-five people at a time field questions that switch rapidly from one area of the learning to another: What are the physiological parameters of the fourth state of consciousness? Can you explain the mechanics that allow the mind to experience more refined aspects of thought? What are the basic steps to check the correctness of a person's meditation?

If any weakness shows up, any hesitation, there is a series of sub-questions to probe more deeply into that area. Nor is a correct answer enough by itself. If either examiner feels the student is unsure in his reasoning, the student is asked to come back again in three days.

It's a long day for the testers—the same people who started at ten in the morning are still pushing at eleven at night—but somehow the long hours don't lead to fatigue. Examinations are usually dreary events, but the confrontation character of this particular test makes it seem something of a shared adventure. By the time the last of us exit onto the moonlit beach, we enjoy a comforting sense of weary camaraderie. We indulge ourselves in mock-heroic talk as if we have just passed a trial at sword's point instead of simply handling some pointed questions.

Yet it seems likely Maharishi was aiming at something other than our entertainment when he called for this test. There was one point he repeated during the course more often than any other. Nothing will be more important to us as teachers of the Transcendental Meditation Technique, he said, than maintaining the purity of the teaching procedures. This knowledge has been lost before.

The Transcendental Meditation Technique is thousands of years old, but until recently it has been overlooked, forgotten, even in India. Now that science has re-established the technique's validity, Maharishi intends to preserve the teaching in its purity.

The accuracy of teaching procedures has become a major issue now that thousands of people have come to help Maharishi. And this help is a necessity to meet the goals of the Transcendental Meditation Program. Maharishi began as one man teaching alone, but even when he came out of India the first time, his stated purpose was quite startling: "to end suffering in the world in this generation." Since there were three and a half billion people in the world at that time, he was clearly setting himself quite a task. At one press conference after another he was asked an obvious question, a question that seemed to have no answer.

"How can you hope to reach all these people?" they asked him. His answer was simple.

"I'll multiply myself," he said.

In the years since, that's just what he's done. Modern technology, especially video tape, has been one multiplier, and a continuous series of teacher training courses like this one in La Antilla has been another. Through the tapes, his lectures on theoretical background knowledge have been made available in many parts of the world simultaneously. The teachers have passed on the practical technique.

"Training all these teachers is so necessary," Maharishi says later. "All we need to do is make this knowledge available to the people and all will enjoy."

Could we talk about the Transcendental Meditation Technique itself?

"The Transcendental Meditation Technique is a simple, natural procedure," Maharishi says. "It can be learned easily by anyone. We take

One thousand course
participants join
Maharishi for a "class
picture" on the
teacher training
course in La Antilla.

In La Antilla the sunset is one of the daily glories of life.

fifteen or twenty minutes morning and evening and let the mind settle down to a state of least excitation. In this way, the mind and body gain deep rest.

This is a purely mental technique?

"Yes, we just sit in a chair and close the eyes and begin."

But how can a mental technique bring physical rest to the body?

"For the simple reason that the mind is responsible for the activity of the body and, looking from the other side, the activity of the body and nervous system is responsible for the state of the mind. If the mind wants to run, then the body runs. And if the body becomes a little tired, then the mind decides to sit. Mind and body work together. So, with the Transcendental Meditation Technique, the mind settles down to a state of least excitation, a state of restful alertness, and due to that the body gains deep rest. What this rest does is dissolve stresses and strains deposited in the system."

But isn't the sleep we get at night good enough to take care of stress and strain?

"People thought that the rest they naturally get in the night is enough. But it hasn't worked that way. Whatever activity we undertake, it leaves some deeper stresses that are not dissolved during a night's sleep. All these stresses are like clouds that hide the sun. Our full potential is there but there are resistances to its full utilization in daily life. Scientific experiments indicate that the Transcendental Meditation Technique provides a fundamental and integrated level of rest, and this deep rest dissolves these stresses and strains. The cloud that was hindering the full use of our creativity and intelligence begins to wither away."

And this process is natural? If that's true why do we need a technique to bring it about?

"Everyone is born with the spontaneous ability to speak, but we have to learn how to speak. Otherwise, even though the child speaks, all he will say is, 'Um, um.' The same way, even though the expression of our full potential is natural, we have to learn how to channel it. It's spontaneous for the water to flow down from the lake, but when we want to bring it to our field, we channel it through a pipeline. There is an area deep within the mind where thought starts, and that area is a reservoir of immeasurable energy and intelligence. When we allow our mind to settle down to that pure level, we open a channel to that reservoir."

How can we open such a channel?

"It's the natural tendency of the mind. Once we give the mind the correct angle it will settle down automatically to more refined levels. As the mind experiences finer aspects of the thinking process, it experiences more refined levels of awareness. This makes the mind more and more awake. And when our awareness has gained maximum wakefulness, the next step of refinement transcends the field of thinking. We attain a field of 'pure' awareness. The mind is awake within itself, but without a thought."

"People thought that the rest they naturally get in the night is enough. But whatever activity we undertake, it leaves some deeper stresses that are not dissolved during a night's sleep."

29

That seems to be a contradiction. How can the mind be awake if it is not actively thinking?

"It's a phenomenon we witness at the start of every activity. We see a runner who is about to run, but has not yet started. He's so full of liveliness inside, yet he's steady, not active. This is like the state of least excitation of the mind—the mind is awake but without a thought. We can call it pure wakefulness, pure consciousness, pure intelligence."

But isn't it hard to make the mind settle down like this? It's hard to concentrate.

"The Transcendental Meditation Technique is unlike any practice of concentration. Concentration is static, but the mind wants variety. The Transcendental Meditation Technique is a dynamic, spontaneous process."

What does one think about then?

"Thinking *about* things is also not the process of the Transcendental Meditation Technique. Thinking about something is contemplation—one's attention goes from meaning to meaning, but all on the conscious thinking level of the mind. It is like floating on the surface of a pond. The Transcendental Meditation Technique is not a horizontal mental activity. It is vertical. It is like diving to the depths of the pond."

But what do we do to make the mind settle down like this?

"We don't have to do anything. We simply make use of the natural tendency of the mind to go toward a field of greater happiness. What we find is that the basic state of pure consciousness has another aspect. It's also a state of pure happiness—concentrated happiness. It is a state of pure bliss consciousness. And so the Transcendental Meditation Technique is a dynamic process that allows the mind to move in the direction of greater charm and satisfaction. This is why no concentration is needed. The mind does not need to be trained to enjoy more. The mind takes that direction spontaneously, once it is given the correct angle."

What if a man doesn't accept these explanations? Will the Transcendental Meditation Technique still work for him?

"Of course. Once we have taken a ticket and gone into the plane, we are going to be taken to our destination."

It's not a matter of faith?

"Believing or not believing doesn't matter. That is why we call the Transcendental Meditation Technique a technique. It's a mechanical sort of thing and produces the required effect whether we believe in it or not. Very naturally the mind settles down to that state of pure consciousness."

La Antilla has come undone. For two and a half months it has been one of the quietest communities imaginable, an isolated little town occupied almost entirely by people who specialize in the production of silence twice a day. But today the place is alive with activity. For two-thirds of us, it's moving day.

Two planeloads are leaving, one for America where hundreds of new teachers are returning to begin their activity, and another to Switzerland, where Maharishi is moving into the new facilities for international headquarters. The disorder in the dusty streets is magnificent. Buses for both planes are leaving at the same time. Most of the possible combinations for misplaced luggage and misdirected passengers come about as people dash in crazy circles exchanging addresses, hugs and hopeful glances. There isn't enough space on the buses that arrive, and animated, arm-waving entreaties with amused Spaniards produce first a rickety truck to carry excess luggage and then, in an hour, a fleet of ten taxis from a neighboring town. The taxi windows are rolled down and the rest of the people pack themselves in, five to a Fiat.

As the last of this unlikely caravan rolls out of town about noon, Maharishi is still in the lecture hall holding a series of quiet individual meetings with new teachers who are not scheduled to leave until the next day. He has been there since nine thirty, smiling and talking softly with one and then another while outside the happy turmoil built in a crescendo. He was up all the night before, too, working until five thirty in the morning in similar individual conferences to clear up all personal questions before the departure.

This is the first day I get a chance to spend a lot of time with Maharishi outside of the lecturing situation. The first surprise is the way he manages to keep working in the confusing circumstances of a travel day. Most of us let our minds go out of control in the excitement and disorder, but Maharishi doesn't seem affected. After working in the hall for an hour after the caravan has left, he steps into a car with three staff members, including the national leader of the World Plan in America, Jerry Jarvis. While the car hurries through the rolling Spanish countryside on the way to Seville, Maharishi uses the ninety minutes for a discussion of the possibilities of the new headquarters site in Switzerland. The Swiss World Plan Executive Council has purchased two hotels and made them available for an international center.

The car arrives at the main door of the airport while the last of the teachers and staff members are climbing into the charter. Maharishi walks through the terminal and enters the plane just at flight time. A last-minute difficulty develops—the plane is overloaded and some luggage has to be taken off—but Maharishi and Mr. Jarvis are already busy working together to outline advanced courses that are to be conducted in America. Their conference ends only as we land in Zurich two hours later. During the slight delay at the gate, a new series of individual discussions begins with teachers who have made the trip up from La Antilla. These conferences continue on the tram ride to the terminal and on the walk down the hall to the lobby.

The trip is going forward, but Maharishi is working continuously, fitting endless demands into odd corners of time. And for all the activity he never appears to be rushed about anything. You can see it in the way he walks down the terminal hallway, moving with an easy, flowing motion that speaks of composure and serenity. He glides from topic to topic, from meeting to meeting, in the same comfortable way, never wasting a moment but never seeming to strain either.

As soon as we arrive in the lobby, Swiss efficiency makes clock-work of our luggage retrieval, and soon we are loading into the spacious, gleaming buses. An hour's ride takes us to the city of Lucerne, and at this point the tone of this once hectic journey takes a sharp turn toward the fairy tale. The rest of the trip will consist of a two-hour cruise down the Lake of Lucerne and then a mountain railway ride halfway up the face of a mountain to the small village of Seelisberg.

The sun has gone down as we arrive at the lake and the boat is waiting, glowing with light. It is a sleek, white, double-decked cruiser. There is enough room to handle two hundred of us easily. Bread, cheese and fruit juice have been provided by the welcoming staff from Seelisberg.

While the passengers eat, the ship slides away from the dock, eases down a long inlet, and turns out into the dark silence of Lake Lucerne. The night is warm for a May in Switzerland and a breeze comes to clear away the last of the jangle left from our La Antilla departure. Above the lake on both sides, great grey mountain shapes interrupt the stars, and high in the sky, a little behind the ship, a full moon rides down the long lake with us. There's nothing to do but enjoy one of those moments that couldn't be fantasized any better.

A couch has been set up for Maharishi on the second deck facing forward, with rows of benches laid out in front of him. A microphone has been wired into the ship's public address system. The circumstances seem fitting for a picture of the beauties of life when it is lived at full potential.

"We should enjoy two hundred per cent of life," Maharishi says. "One hundred per cent of the inner life and one hundred per cent of the outer life. And only when the inner life is developed to its maximum extent does outer life attain its full glory."

Maharishi adjusts a light shawl he is wearing. The refreshing breeze is one of the current joys of the "outer life."

"The inner life and the outer life are not separate," he continues. "They are two aspects of the totality of our existence. After the inward stroke of meditation, one comes out to engage in outer activity with greater energy, more intelligence and improved efficiency. This is the glory of enlightenment. Once we have that inner fulfillment, the field of activity becomes more substantial and rewarding at all levels. It is this that brings harmony between the inner and the outer glories of life."

Maharishi pauses for a moment.

"It's a very great knowledge about life," he says."This is why we can only keep on saying, Jai Guru Dev."

Jai Guru Dev—"Jai" means thanks, more or less; "Guru Dev" means "illustrious teacher." This is the way Maharishi refers to the man who was his teacher, the man who revived the TM Technique on a wide scale.

It is typical of Maharishi to mention Guru Dev when speaking of the benefits of the Transcendental Meditation Technique. Guru Dev was one of the most influential teachers in India's recent history. His full title in India was Swami Brahmananda Saraswati, and he sat in the seat of the Shankaracharya of Jyotir Math, a position of spiritual leadership for all of northern India. He was the first man deemed worthy of holding this seat in one hundred and fifty years. For the thirteen years that Guru Dev sat as Shankaracharya, from 1940 until his death in 1953, Maharishi was both his student and his close personal aide. It was then that Maharishi learned the knowledge he now teaches to the world. This is why his response is always the same when people thank him for his contribution: "Jai Guru Dev." The honor goes to Guru Dev and the long tradition of teachers who have preserved this knowledge for thousands of years.

Maharishi's lecture, and the pleasant evening, seem to make our two-hour voyage down Lake Lucerne pass very quickly. Soon the ship settles up against a landing. A mountainside jumps up sharply out of the water. The moon provides the light for the short walk to the mountain railway and then we wait to take our turns riding the two steeply angled cars that shuttle up and down the midnight slope. It's been a long day, and by the time everyone gets to the top of the slope and walks to the hotel, the thought of bed seems very good indeed. In a short time the reception area is empty.

On the way upstairs I pass Maharishi's room. Soft light is coming from his open door. He is dictating a translation of one of the ancient works central to the Shankaracharya tradition.

"The goal of the Transcendental Meditation Technique is the state of enlightenment," Maharishi says later. "This means we experience that inner calmness, that quiet state of least excitation, even when we are dynamically busy."

But activity and quietness seem to be opposites. Isn't it necessary to sit and close the eyes in order to enjoy the peaceful effects of the TM Technique?

"It's only in the beginning days of meditation that one has to meditate in order to experience that silent, quiet level of the mind, that state of pure consciousness. As we continue to alternate the experience of meditation with daily activity, the value of that pure consciousness is infused into the mind.

THE STATE OF
ENLIGHTENMENT

The pure level of consciousness becomes stabilized in our awareness. And when that pure level—the state of least excitation—is a living reality even during daily activity, this is the state of enlightenment. This is life free from suffering, life when every thought and action is spontaneously correct."

But how is it possible for the mind to experience two different states at the same time?

"This is the question. How can the mind be both active and silent? How can one have the state of least excitation in the midst of all activity? What we find is that it is the natural ability of the nervous system to live one hundred per cent of the inner value of life, and one hundred per cent of the outer value. It is only stresses and strains which restrict this normal functioning of the nervous system."

Then it would be necessary to dissolve stress in order to experience the state of enlightenment.

"Yes. And it brings very practical value to life. Even if we forget about 'enlightenment' for a moment—maybe that state seems to be inconceivable—still it is our daily experience that the whole value of life is very little if we are tired, if we are stressed. If we think of a morning when we have not rested well in the night, then we feel so groggy and everything just collapses into dullness and inertia. The *world* is the same as on the other days, but our appreciation of the world is so much less. And with the Transcendental Meditation Technique we have a natural and effective means to dissolve even deeply rooted fatigue and stress. This is the way to unfold full value of life. Even in the first days of meditation we find that our eyes seem to be a little more open, our mind seems a bit more clear. Our feeling towards our friends seems to be more harmonious. And then, as the practice is continued every day, a time will come when we will start living life free from *all* stresses. We cleanse the awareness of all stresses and strains, leaving the conscious mind completely free in its pure value."

Does this mean that evolution toward enlightenment is automatic as stresses are released?

"Yes. When all stresses are gone, the whole appreciation of life is so much greater. Then the value of every perception, every thought, every action, every feeling will be supported by the full value of that pure awareness. This is enlightenment. It is like the ability to maintain contact with a bank even while out in the marketplace."

Maintaining contact with a bank—can that analogy be made clearer?

"Maintaining that pure awareness, that bliss consciousness, can be compared to having great wealth. If one is *not* aware of having great wealth in the bank, and one has only five dollars in the pocket, then there is some pinch about spending even one dollar for a rose. A man could say, 'Ah, the rose is so beautiful, but now there are only four dollars left in the pocket.' There is some pinch to the feelings. But if the awareness is open to the great wealth in the

Holding one of his favorite props, Maharishi clears up a theoretical point.

bank, a dollar is spent for a rose and the man is only faced with the joy of having a rose. No pinch is there. And this is one's experience in the state of enlightenment. When that pure state of silence and bliss is stabilized on the level of one's awareness, every activity is supported by that peace and joyfulness. Every activity is the expression of the fullness of life."

This would be the experience of the state of pure consciousness at the same time as daily activity. But it's still not clear how the mind is capable of maintaining this pure state in a permanent manner outside of the meditation period.

"What we find is that this ability depends on the condition of the body and nervous system. We have said the mind and body work together. This is true in every state of consciousness. When the body is tired, for instance, the mind doesn't function very effectively. The metabolic rate changes, the brain wave patterns change, and due to that the mind experiences dullness and inconsistency, and then the sleep state of consciousness. Or, if there is another specific type of physiology—brain waves are different, the metabolic rate is different—then we experience dreaming, the dream state of consciousness. And with another type of physiology, a different type of physical activity, the waking state comes up. Waking, sleeping, dreaming—all these three states of consciousness have corresponding styles of physiological activity. The mind and body always work together. Like that, the Transcendental Meditation Technique produces its own style of physiology. Due to that particular style of activity in the body, the mind experiences the state of least excitation, a fourth state of consciousness."

This is referring to the research on the Trancendental Meditation Technique showing very low metabolic rate, orderly brain waves, and so on?

"Yes. Blood chemistry changes, blood pressure changes—the body and nervous system are functioning in a particular manner and due to that, consciousness has that value of restful alertness, of least activity, of pure consciousness."

During meditation, then, the body is operating in a certain way, and this correlates to the pure state of consciousness—a fourth state. But the question is still how to experience that level of silence at the same time as activity?

"What happens is that during the Transcendental Meditation Technique, the mind experiences the fourth state of consciousness. That experience takes the nervous system to a particular style of functioning. As we repeat our meditations, this inspires the nervous system to function in that new style more and more. It's the nature of life. Something is more fulfilling and life goes for it."

The nervous system gets used to functioning in this way?

"It gets into that habit. This is how the experience of pure consciousness is infused into the conscious thinking level of the mind. It's like the principle of dying a cloth. We take a white cloth, dip it in yellow color and then put it to the sun. In the sun the color fades away, but it doesn't fade away completely. Dip it back in the color, put it back to the sun, and more of the color remains. Just like that, we meditate morning and evening, dipping the mind in that pure awareness and then exposing it to action. In action, the value of pure awareness fades, but it doesn't fade away completely. Meditation and action—this is the procedure which stabilizes that pure awareness. This gradual and systematic culturing of the physical nervous system creates a physiological situation in which the two states of consciousness exist together simultaneously. And once it's done, it's done forever. Once the cloth is color fast, it doesn't fade."

And then the nervous system maintains the ability to contact the state of least excitation even while functioning in the waking state of consciousness?

"Or in the sleep state. Or in the dream state. And in this is eternal freedom for every human being, like having the full wealth of the bank in our pocket at all times. There are changing values on the surface of the mind and then there is that non-changing steady state of the mind deep inside. And this is not just in fanciful thinking, but in the transformation of the physiology to maintain that pure state of consciousness in a permanent manner. And the research shows that with the Transcendental Meditation Technique, progress begins in this direction right from the first day of meditation. All the studies are there to indicate that a man develops inner stability and at the same time increases in his ability to adapt to the environment. The nervous system becomes more stable even under stressful stimuli. What we notice from this is that we seem to have our feet more on the ground. We are finding stability. We are finding more contentment within ourselves. We are experiencing the growth of that pure level of consciousness."

And all that is necessary to experience this growth is to meditate?

"What is important is the *alternation* of the Transcendental Meditation Technique with daily activity. Rest and activity—this is the way to grow to enlightenment—to live life free from suffering, to live life in bliss consciousness. Now with this knowledge there is no reason why every man cannot enjoy life at full potential, why he cannot experience unshakeable peace and joy in the midst of great, successful, dynamic activity."

It's after midnight but the meeting seems nowhere near an end. Maharishi and a group of faculty members and editors are working on the catalogue for Maharishi International University. They have been working on it since about nine o'clock. In fact, they have been working on it, on and off, for much of the six weeks since we came to Seelisberg.

Evening meetings like this are a regular feature of our routine. They are large gatherings attended by most of the two hundred people who work on the headquarters staff. Usually they take place in a spacious hall in one of the two hotels made available to us here by the Swiss World Plan Executive Council. The room is grand, two stories high, with filigreed columns and a figured ceiling. Maharishi sits against one of the long walls on a slightly raised platform designed to serve as a set for his frequent video taping sessions. Occasionally he will lecture at these sessions but more likely he will attend to whatever topic is at hand, drawing on the help of all those who wish to participate.

The topic at hand tonight is the catalogue. The planning for the new university is still in the concept stage, and Maharishi and his co-workers are using the catalogue composition as a means to think out the school's structure. At this point, they are putting together a section that relates M.I.U. to the Science of Creative Intelligence—the theoretical course of study that explains the mechanics of the Transcendental Meditation Technique.

"We should read that back," Maharishi says.

" 'The essential function of Maharishi International University,' " reads the secretary from her notes, " 'is to serve the educational needs of all areas of society through the Science of Creative Intelligence.' "

"Good," Maharishi says. "And then?"

"There should be a definition of SCI right here," says one of the editors.

"Yes," Maharishi says. "It should say, 'SCI provides knowledge of the nature of creative . . . SCI provides knowledge of the nature, origin, growth and application of creative intelligence in life. This new science. . .'—What should we say here?"

"Maharishi, will the reader know what we mean by 'creative intelligence'?" asks someone else.

"They will find it out in a few pages. By now they will be interested. Only what should come next?"

"Something like, 'This new science arose from the discovery of a fundamental source of intelligence in every man'?"

"Good. 'This new science arose from the major discovery that there exists a fundamental . . . that there exists in every human being an inexhaustible and fundamental source of intelligence, energy and happiness.' "

There's a pause and then a suggestion from one of the editors.

"I think we should mention how this source expresses itself outwardly," he says, "how it affects daily life."

"It would be good," Maharishi says. "How should it be?"

"It could read, '. . . an inexhaustible and fundamental source of intelligence, energy and happiness . . . that expresses itself in the life of the individual as orderly thinking and skill in action.' "

"And we should mention personal fulfillment," says Maharishi. "The concept of fulfillment is very important. So we should read that back."

The work goes on. After midnight, however, my capacity for concentration begins to dwindle. I first noticed Maharishi's constant attention to his work on the trip up from La Antilla, but I still can't adjust to his schedule. We have come to one of the most monumentally beautiful spots in the world, but Maharishi rarely even steps outside to take a look.

Seelisberg is a tiny village etched into the side of a steep, green mountain face. There is a breathtaking view of Lake Lucerne almost straight below, augmented by one hundred eighty degrees of Swiss mountains in the middle distance. The most impressive of these mountains is Frohnalpstock, right across the lake, an imposing force pushing itself up into a great, bare, rounded top, with rivers of trees flowing down the crevices in its face.

In this esthetic atmosphere a tremendous amount of work is being performed by a group of people from all over the world. After two decades of nearly constant travel, Maharishi has settled here to consolidate the world-wide growth of the Transcendental Meditation Program. By now he has trained nearly ten thousand teachers. These teachers operate the local centers in more than one hundred and twenty countries, freeing Maharishi to remain in one place, produce new teaching materials and plan for the future. It is work that requires people with both talent and expertise. Maharishi is surrounded by a growing number of specialists—scientists, writers, artists, designers, computer specialists, electronic engineers, filmmakers, television crewmen and other experts in necessary fields. The expense of all this talent would be prohibitive except for the dedication of the people involved. A large part of them work on a completely voluntary basis, footing their own bills. The rest accept only room and board.

Maharishi works with them video taping lecture series, on pamphlets and other published material, on translations of ancient writings, and on major new projects such as M.I.U. He enjoys working under the pressure of deadlines, and his general attitude toward all projects was summed up earlier in the meeting this particular night. Someone asked when a certain set of posters should be started.

"We want to *finish* soon," he said. "It doesn't matter when we start."

Still, despite this sense of urgency, his approach is painstaking on every project, and he often encourages group participation. Getting the set ready to make a videotape, for instance, he can take an hour conferring with his video people, making many suggestions himself and trying all the possibilities others come up with. Working by committee can sometimes be slow, but in this situation it has a couple of advantages. First, the people who have come to work for Maharishi get to know his thinking in detail. Second, he learns the technicalities of modern specialities—of video production, for instance, or of typesetting and design.

He is, after all, a monk, a man who has chosen the recluse way of life. Watching him work easily with Westerners in coats and ties, one tends to forget the great cultural leap he has taken. When he left India for the first time in 1958, his knowledge of Western technology was sketchy at best. Although he had taken a degree in physics from Allahabad University in northern India before joining Guru Dev, his thirteen years with that great Shankaracharya were spent in relative seclusion. So were the first two years after Guru Dev's death in 1953.

In the eighteen years since then, however, Maharishi has focused on a union of ancient wisdom with modern expertise. This work has been greatly enhanced by the stability here in Switzerland. The experts are coming to Maharishi, and he works with them constantly in patient sessions aimed at both accomplishment and mutual education.

It is work that produces fascinating new directions, compelling offshoots of this fertile combination. It is probable that many more of us would have gone to bed earlier this night, for instance, except for the thoughts that are forming as the M.I.U. catalogue goes forward. At this particular point, the definition of a university is being expanded in a most surprising way. At M.I.U., the student will not only gain factual knowledge, and be tested for that intellectually. He will also practice the Transcendental Meditation Technique for rapid personal evolution, and be tested for *that* physiologically. An M.I.U. student will grow in his physical and mental capabilities, as well as in his knowledge.

The secretary is reading back some earlier work.

" 'In addition to the usual academic measures of progress, therefore,' " she reads, " 'the M.I.U. student will be given the opportunity to *objectively* validate his improvements in health, intelligence and breadth of awareness. These objective validations will be on the basis of laboratory measurements of metabolic rate, blood chemistry, brain wave patterns, responsiveness of the senses and other indications.' "

"Good," Maharishi says. "And here it should say, 'Through these physiological measurements, M.I.U. will set standards for the stages of progress, for the steps of human evolution. It will then be . . . It will become known that enlightenment is not only a concept in the mind of man, but also a reality . . . a living reality that his body can reveal and his behavior express.' This is good?"

"It needs to be nailed down," says a writer. "A summation."

"Yes. A summation. Then it should read, 'Enlightenment will no longer . . .' wait a moment. It should read, 'In this way the value of enlightenment will be lifted from the shadowy misinformation of past ages into a modern scientific reality.' "

A university that will validate enlightenment in scientific terms—few ideas sum up Maharishi's goals more succinctly.

Maharishi poses for a formal portrait amidst the mountain peaks above Lake Lucerne in Switzerland.

*Spring in Switzerland;
from a meadow above
and behind Seelisberg
looking over to
Frohnalpstock*

43

"Maharishi International University will be a beautiful reality," he says. " 'Maharishi' means 'great seer'. What we will find is that every student at M.I.U. will graduate as a 'great seer' in his own right."

The basic course at M.I.U. will be the Science of Creative Intelligence?

"Yes. Every student will study SCI and then he will study every discipline in the light of SCI. It is intelligence that studies every discipline, and with SCI we have a means to study that intelligence itself."

How did the Science of Creative Intelligence develop?

"In teaching the Transcendental Meditation Technique around the world these last fifteen or twenty years, we found that the teaching has developed into a science naturally. We have found that every aspect is systematic and verifiable, capable of being understood on the basis of physics, physiology, chemistry and mathematics. So we now see the Transcendental Meditation Technique as a practical aspect of this new Science of Creative Intelligence."

But the Transcendental Meditation Technique is a personal experience. How can a personal experience be a science?

"The procedure we have adopted to experience the field of pure consciousness is a very automatic one. The activity of the mind settles down automatically and that state of pure consciousness is produced. This experience is gained in a systematic, natural manner and is therefore repeatable. More than a million people have begun to say, 'Yes, it really is a state of restful alertness for the body and mind.' And we were encouraged to call this knowledge a science in a more profound sense when scientists found that physiological, psychological and sociological changes produced through the practice of the Transcendental Meditation Technique are very systematic; that is, they are repeatably verifiable through scientific experiments, which are the objective means of gaining knowledge."

And the Science of Creative Intelligence is the theory that accounts for these practical results?

"Yes. All activity is based on intelligence. The Science of Creative Intelligence studies what that basic level of intelligence is, how it unfolds into activity, and how its full potential can be developed in one's awareness."

What is meant by "creative intelligence?"

"The word 'creativity' we take to mean the cause of change present everywhere at all times. 'Intelligence' is a basic quality of existence shown in the purpose and order of change. This means that 'creative intelligence' is the energy (or creativity) and directedness (or intelligence) at the basis of existence."

You are saying that there is "creative intelligence" behind all the activities of man?

Maharishi enjoys a quiet moment in Seelisberg, Switzerland.

"The experience
of pure
consciousness, of
pure intelligence,
makes our mind
more lively. This
is the practical
value of it. It will
enrich every
aspect of life."

"There is creative intelligence behind everything we experience in creation."

How can we know that?

"It's just at the level of common sense. It is obvious there is something deep within physical values which is the cause of change and progress. We see order in creation. There is some intelligence working at every level of existence, some orderliness at the atomic level, at the molecular level. There is obvious orderliness in the sequence and progression of life. Everything is growing, and growing in a very orderly way: an apple tree produces apples, a banana tree produces bananas; the apple tree doesn't grow guavas. Some order is there, some intelligence is there."

But if this level of intelligence is deep within the physical values, how does it express itself at the physical level?

"We can take the example of a plant, a rose. A rose has a stem, some leaves, a flower; it is green somewhere, red somewhere; it has all this variety of expression. But deep within the plant is the essential constituent: the sap. The stem and petals, the colors of green and red, are all the expressions of the colorless sap. First there is that field of the sap, and then there is the process of the sap becoming a leaf, a stem, a petal. Like that, there is the field of pure intelligence deep within, and then its transformation into progressive values of creation."

The sap is within the plant. If the level of intelligence is within the physical values, how can it be reached?

"This is our joy to say. It's not necessary for any man today to remain only partially exposed to the value of life, to be caught up either on the outside or the inside. With the Transcendental Meditation Technique the mind naturally settles down deep within and gains that field of pure consciousness. This is that field of pure intelligence which permeates all aspects of life. It's possible now for that pure value of consciousness, that field of pure intelligence, to be established as an all-time reality in the awareness, and then a man can behave from that level where everything springs."

Everything comes out from the level of pure consciousness?

"Yes. There is the sap, and then come the leaves and petals. There is that pure field, an unmanifest field, from which the intelligence starts to work. From there come all the manifestations, all the infinite variety in creation."

This is hardly obvious. How can all the different values in the universe come out of one undifferentiated field?

"We can think of an example. An oxygen atom and a hydrogen atom in one state show the properties of gas. In another they combine and exhibit the properties of water. In yet another they have the properties of solid ice. Even though the properties of gas, water and ice are quite dissimilar, the essential constituents of oxygen and hydrogen never change. In the same way, there is that pure level of creative intelligence—unchanging, unmanifest, absolute, unbounded—and then come all the relative levels of growth and change."

And a man's awareness can open to that unmanifest level?

"In a very automatic way. And the experience of pure consciousness, of pure intelligence, makes our mind more lively. This is the practical value of it. A man begins to meditate and right away he notices his mind is more clear, he doesn't make as many mistakes."

His mind starts to develop more of the value of pure intelligence?

"It's like dying the cloth. The mind begins to inherit that pure intelligence. All values of our action and aspirations become richer. This is why the saying has become popular, 'Water the root to enjoy the fruit.' A gardener knows that by watering the root of a tree, all the branches and leaves and fruit will be enriched. The root of life is that unmanifest value of pure intelligence. To water the root, we take our awareness to this level of pure creative intelligence, and the value of that will get infused into the nature of the mind. This will enrich every aspect of life. It will enable a man to think, to speak and to act in such a way that every thought, word and action will accomplish the maximum in life. Water the root. This is the way to do less and accomplish more."

This is one of the last of the evening meetings I'll be attending here in Seelisberg. I'm going back home soon, back to the East Coast to teach the Transcendental Meditation Technique. If this will be one of the last meetings, however, it promises to be one of the best. In the first place, some of the prospective M.I.U. faculty members are seated near Maharishi. They are beginning one of their discussions about the theories of modern science, and these discussions always bring a fascinating glimpse into the mechanics of nature. In the second place, several of the people on the kitchen staff are standing near the door. Often that means a birthday celebration is planned for the evening. Their presence brings pleasant visions of a festive dessert not far in the future.

Exploring nature intellectually will come first, however. Maharishi is putting a lot of attention into the theories of modern science. For fifteen years, he has been saying that this entire teaching is scientific. Now that the benefits of the Transcendental Meditation Technique have been verified by laboratory experiments, he is eager for the validity of the theories behind these practical results to be established as well. In an age of physics, it isn't necessary to be metaphysical. Maharishi wants the mechanics of consciousness to be as clear to a scientific age as the mechanics of the lever.

To encourage the growth of this systematic expression of his teaching, Maharishi often surrounds himself with groups of scientists, mathematicians

47

These discussions are an integration of the best thinking from East and West. They are a cooperative effort of leading representatives of two of mankind's great bodies of knowledge.

and philosophers, engaging them in a series of wide-ranging discussions. Many of these experts have indicated they will become faculty members at Maharishi International University. They are frequently joined by scholars of international reputation who are drawn to Maharishi because of his knowledge about the nature of consciousness. These distinguished visitors include Professor Brian Josephson, the Nobel Laureate in physics from Cambridge University in England; Dr. John Lewis, Professor of Planetary Sciences at the Massachusetts Institute of Technology; and Dr. George Sudarshan, Professor of Physics at the University of Texas. Dr. Sudarshan's discovery of one of the four "weak forces" operating at the sub-atomic level was one of the major breakthroughs in the recent history of quantum mechanics.

These meetings are an important contribution to the modern world's search for an accurate picture of reality. The richness of this contribution comes from the fact that the discussions are an integration of the best thinking from East and West. They are a cooperative effort of leading exponents of two of mankind's great bodies of knowledge: the ancient subjective wisdom about man's inner nature and the modern objective understanding about the outer material world.

In the past it has been difficult for these two schools of thought to talk together usefully. Two things have changed now. First, Maharishi has opened up traditional knowledge for logical comparison with the thinking in other sciences by structuring his teaching in a systematic way as the Science of Creative Intelligence. Second, modern scientists have brought their understanding of the workings of nature to an extremely subtle level. The finest mechanics of nature are beginning to be understood. And when these widely disparate approaches are compared, the results might seem surprising to a casual observer. At fundamental levels the two schools seem to be describing the same processes.

The discussion this evening is of special interest. It concerns Maharishi's statement that there is a pure, silent, unmanifest level at the basis of the world we see around us. On the face of it, this seems an improbable idea—that there is an invisible, untouchable, "unmanifest" field at the basis of all the "real," "manifested" things we see; that there is an unbounded field of pure "creative intelligence" that manifests into all the specific, bounded objects in creation. Ideas like that sound suspiciously like saying "nothing" is the basis of "everything." They certainly don't sound like common sense.

In the world of modern science, however, there are many theories that don't much commend themselves to "common sense" either. In physics since Einstein, for instance, space and time have started to melt together, matter and energy often seem interchangeable, and the whole of our everyday "reality" seems to be disappearing like fog in the sun. And one of these new theories, an established part of modern quantum mechanics, is a brand of "uncommon" sense that seems to be peculiarly appropriate to Maharishi's teaching. This is the theory of the "vacuum state."

The main idea of the vacuum state, an idea that physicists can experimentally prove to seven decimal places, is that, as a matter of fact, "everything" *does* come out of "nothing." The vacuum state is said to be absolutely empty of every "real" thing. Not even one small particle of light—one photon—exists in the vacuum state. On the other hand, the vacuum state is also said to be the source of everything that *is* real. The reason is that although the vacuum state is empty of everything in a *real* sense, it contains everything in what the scientists call a *virtual* sense. A photon of light isn't really there, it's *virtually* there, "almost" there. Given the right conditions, these virtual, non-existent photons pop out of the vacuum state into the "real" world like pop corn jumping out of the pan.

"Something" from "nothing," the "real" from the "virtual," the "manifest" from the "unmanifest"—these are clear parallels with Maharishi's teaching about the pure field of life. If "common sense" doesn't hold at the fundamental level of the universe, if the nature of reality is really quite different from the way it seems in daily life, at least these two pictures seem to be quite similar.

On this evening, a presentation about the vacuum state is made by Dr. Lawrence Domash, a Professor of Physics at Maharishi International University. As he talks, Dr. Domash is careful to avoid any implications that are not yet proved. He doesn't say Maharishi's idea of the "unmanifest field of life" is the same as the physicists' idea of the "vacuum state." He uses phrases such as, "It seems that ancient wisdom and modern science are converging on similar pictures of the nature of reality."

Dr. Domash has a gift for making abstract ideas readily understandable, and his presentation on the vacuum state begins a lively discussion. It's started by Dr. Geoff Clements, a physicist trained at Sussex University in England.

"An important quality of the vacuum state," he says, "is that it is the simplest of all the states in which the universe can exist. It is the state of least excitation, the easiest state to describe mathematically."

"What do you mean by saying it's the simplest?" someone asks.

"It's like the surface of a lake. If the lake has no waves, if it's just flat, it's easier to describe exactly than if it has many waves on it."

Maharishi listens to this exchange, and then sends the discussion off in a new direction.

"In meditation," he says, "when the mind settles down to that simplest state, to that unmanifest level, this has the result of enlivening the mind. It widens comprehension. We have some philosophers here. The question is, why does knowledge of the simplest state help us comprehend all the more complex phenomena?"

There is a slight pause after his question and activity over by the door

"The simplest
building block is
the field of all
possibilities. The
value of knowing
the simplest thing
is the value of
knowing the
infinite."

brings a pleasant reminder that dessert is coming to complement this discussion. Two serving carts are wheeled in as Dr. Jonathan Shear begins an answer to Maharishi's question. Dr. Shear is Professor of Philosophy at M.I.U.

"The complex is structured of the simple," he says. "To know a complex whole, you must know the simple parts and the way the parts relate to each other."

Maharishi nods. "This is good," he says.

Dr. Domash is about to add something when the two carts are wheeled out into the space between Maharishi and the rest of the group. One cart carries four cartons of ice cream. The other has a big cake with two candles. With timing dictated by the half-life of ice cream, it's time for the birthday party.

"Two people have birthdays today," says one of the young women who have ushered in the carts.

"Good," Maharishi says. "We should sing."

The two honored celebrants walk up to the front and the whole audience indulges itself in a round of "Happy Birthday." Maharishi encourages these birthday celebrations now and then. Notwithstanding all the organization and efficiency he is creating, the group here is still like a large family as much as anything else.

In a few minutes of cutting and scooping, the home-made cake and ice cream are ready, and filled plates are distributed hand-to-hand throughout the hall. The dessert goes down well and quickly, and as this interlude draws to a close, the vacuum state becomes lively again. Dr. Domash picks up where the discussion left off.

"The vacuum state is not only the simplest state," he says, "but the physicists know that it also contains within it the possibilities of all the more complicated states."

"So the simplest building block is the field of all possibilities," says Maharishi. "This is important. What it means is that the value of knowing the simplest thing is the value of knowing the infinite."

Dr. Eliot Abravanel, Professor of Medicine at M.I.U., has not quite finished his dessert. But he puts his plate aside to take a microphone and contribute a thoughtful question.

"It's not intuitively obvious to me why you have to constantly reduce all complicated states to the simplest state," he says. "Why can't you just start any place, since all states contain the possibility for infinite variation?"

Dr. Shear gives an answer.

"The simplest state is the field of all possibilities," he says. "Other states have to return there before going on."

"But why is that?" asks Dr. Abravanel.

"Think of an example," says Dr. Shear. "Imagine a flat surface marked up into squares. Imagine that each of these squares is the top of a stick that can be pushed up into the air. Now if none of the sticks is pushed up, if there is just a simple, flat surface of squares, then any combination of raised sticks is possible just by raising the sticks you want. But if some of the sticks are already pushed up—if you have a complicated situation to begin with—then you'll have to push those sticks down before you can get your new situation."

"This is the point," Maharishi says. "You would need something to stop the momentum of the more complicated state. Only the simplest state is the field of *all* possibilities."

As I sit here, the thought occurs to me that the lecture hall itself has been in a complicated state—an informal party as a background to an abstract discussion about the nature of reality. The situation sums up much about Maharishi and his methods of operation. His attitude seems to condense itself into five words: enjoy yourself and keep working.

Turning back to one of the basic ideas, Maharishi sums up the discussion so far.

"We know the simplest state is the state of least excitation," he says. "Every other state is more complicated, more excited. And from the angle tonight, we know the philosophy of science is not complete until we know this simplest state of least excitation. And to know it means to *live* it, to have this state of least excitation of consciousness stabilized on the level of our awareness, to have it as a living reality in our consciousness. Only then can we recognize the basis of all in every part. Only then can we see the totality in every fragment."

Dr. John Richter, another philosopher from M.I.U., adds a one-sentence summation.

"When you can recognize the truth," he says, "you can recognize the truth in anything."

"Beautiful," Maharishi says. "Perception of the truth in everything is the goal of philosophy. And the truth is that the complex is the expression of the simple. Have the simplest state established on the level of your awareness, and truth reflects from every object of your perception."

For me, this whole evening has been a pleasant and fruitful way to spend time. Dessert never hurts, and hearing ideas evolve is one of my favorite avocations. And the fact is, working around Maharishi is a pleasure most of the time.

Being here at this international headquarters, however, I find one thing is missing. Even as this discussion goes on, it crosses my mind again. It's been three months since I completed the teacher training course, and I still haven't had a chance to teach. While working on organizational matters is useful, I feel as if it's time now to go out and share the information I've learned.

As this train of thought passes, the empty plate in my lap loses its fascination, and I look up again. Maharishi is laughing.

"With the
awareness
established at
that basic level
then every
projection of
awareness will be
lively in the spirit
of all the laws of
nature."

"No, no," he says. "We should *say* it. We know they are the same."

"But Maharishi," says Dr. Clements. "We can't actually prove yet that the state of least excitation and the pure state of consciousness are the same thing."

"But we *know* it," Maharishi says. "We know it from our experience in meditation. We know it from the ancient records of enlightened men. We are the world's leaders in this field, and if we know a thing, it would not be good to keep it to ourselves."

Maharishi the teacher takes over from Maharishi the theoretical explorer. A big smile lights the room.

"If we are the leaders, why should we wait for someone else to find it out and then we have to *quote* him?"

He's laughing again.

It will be hard to leave.

"The physicists have counted some very interesting qualities of the state of least excitation, the vacuum state," Maharishi says. "One characteristic is that it is the field of perfect order. There is no entropy at that level, no disorder. Another quality is that it is the simplest state, and that it is everywhere, all-pervading, unbounded. The state of least excitation is there within all the more excited states. And another quality—it is an unchanging field, an eternal field, and yet it is the source of all change. All fluctuations come out from there. It is the home of all the laws of nature, the source of all the forces that structure the different excited states of nature."

This is all description from physics?

"Yes. Quantum mechanics, quantum electrodynamics. The vacuum state is an eternal field, a field of perfect order. It is the source of the more excited states. And through the Transcendental Meditation Technique, the mind will reach that state of perfect order, the state from which all the laws of nature originate. And this will be the way to educate a man so he will not make mistakes."

No mistakes? Why would this prevent a man from making mistakes?

"A mistake means a violation of some law of nature."

First, then, what does the phrase "law of nature" mean in this context?

"In a scientific age, quite a lot is known about the laws of nature. Scientists are concerned to find the laws of nature that govern the universe. An apple fell, Newton started to think about gravity, and all the mathematical calculations came to describe gravity. And even if we have not yet discovered them all, different laws are there to govern all creation—to bring out the red and green of the rose, the growth and development of a tree, the progress and

evolution in all nature. And the thing is, if we violate some law of nature, if we make a mistake, suffering is the result. If a man eats something wrong, then he feels sick."

So obviously we should try not to violate any of these laws.

"Of course. But what we find is that it's not possible to know what all the laws of nature are."

Why not?

"There are too many. There is an infinite number. It's just not possible to know all the laws that govern the growth and development of a rose, or all the laws that govern our breath when we are sitting here, or on a mountain or in a desert. This is why it is necessary for a man to establish his awareness on that level of perfect order, the home of all the laws of nature."

What does that accomplish?

"With the awareness established at that basic level, then every offshoot of awareness, every projection of awareness, will be lively in the spirit of all the laws of nature. Even without knowing the laws intellectually,

"The correct formula is to regulate one's life in a way that thinking is spontaneously in accordance with all the laws of nature. Then a man will not make mistakes."

action will be spontaneously right, unmistakably right."

You say spontaneously right. But can action always be spontaneous? Isn't it necessary to think out a course of action before going ahead?

"Often it's just not possible. It's the same as with the laws of nature. Every man has so many phases of his activity, so many areas of love and relations, and every aspect has to be first class. It just can't be done on the basis of thinking and planning for every area. Maybe a man wants to say something—he could spend his whole life wondering if what he wants to say is intellectually right, grammatically right, socially right. There is a proverb: Look before you leap. It makes sense but it has its own limitations. I want to pick up a flower—but there could be a hundred points in favor of picking it up, a hundred points in opposition. It's just not possible to act all the time on the basis of intellectual discrimination. The correct formula is to regulate one's life in a way that thinking is *spontaneously* in accordance with all the laws of nature. Get in touch with the home of all the laws of nature, that pure field of consciousness, of creative intelligence, and then a man will not make mistakes. This is the state of enlightenment. All thinking and behavior will be in the direction of evolution naturally."

Errorless behavior has hardly been typical of man so far.

"This is so. We have heard that man is the master of his own destiny. But what we have experienced is different—often what we want doesn't happen. This is because any time we violate some law of nature, roughness and entropy are created—disorderly influences come up—and suffering must result from that. We may not know what law we violate, but ignorance of the law is no excuse. If we make a mistake, we have to bear the consequences."

Cause and effect.

"It's very simple. And now, in an age of science, there is no reason why every man cannot act in a manner that is spontaneously right. There is no reason why every man should not enjoy the support of all the laws of nature. If you are a house guest of your friend, then everything in the house is available to you. If we want the full advantage from a bank, then we just have to make good acquaintance with the president of the bank. All that is necessary is to allow the mind to become familiar with that state of least excitation, the state of perfect order. Then the entire field of creative intelligence will be supporting every impulse of our activity. That pure field of creative intelligence stands by to support the individual intelligence, and we know that it is very natural to get in touch with that pure level. Even if we study the behavior of atoms, we find that they all naturally settle down to the state of least excitation whenever the environment will allow."

But then, when a man is established at that level, doesn't he ever use his ability to discriminate intellectually, to think and analyze?

"Yes, yes. The ability to analyze is a great joy on the intellectual level. If one owns the whole mechanics of the laws of nature, it's a very great joy to be able to see through one's own doings, to understand the whole performance of creative intelligence. But what I am saying is that living that value of righteousness—experiencing it as a reality in daily life—is not on the basis of one's ability to analyze."

It depends on the level of consciousness, on establishing that home of all the laws of nature in our conscious awareness.

"This is the thing. Life is not a thing just to be thought about. It is to be lived in fullness."

But what about a man with negative desires. Wouldn't this help him to do wrong things more effectively?

"No, no. The nature of every law in creation is to support evolution, to support growth. Naturally, when the mind is in contact with the home of all the laws of nature, every action becomes progressive and life-supporting. One can't go wrong even if one wants to. All the research is there to show that a man begins the Transcendental Meditation Technique, and very quickly he begins to be more tolerant, more sociable. All these weaknesses—these feelings of irritation and hostility—begin to fall away. This is what the research shows. When the deepest value of life is vibrant in our awareness, then that translates into positive behavior spontaneously."

Chapter Two

Back to India:
Starting at the Beginnings

It's a question of education, of bringing a new understanding into a confused world. It will take some time. Maharishi is going to start by going on a world tour.

Time has traveled again, a year and a half in the more normal direction this time. I've been traveling, too, a long round trip to America and back. It's March, 1975, and I'm standing in the lobby of the Park Hotel in Vitznau, Switzerland, just across the lake from Seelisberg. While we wait for Maharishi to come downstairs, I say hello to a lot of old friends I have missed more than I realized.

I wasn't thinking much about missing them when I was back home because I was having such a good time. Teaching the TM Technique is an enjoyable activity, and the real joy lies in one simple fact. It works. Not to say this was any great revelation, of course. I already knew that the Transcendental Meditation Technique worked for me, that it worked for my friends and relatives, that it worked for all those anonymous people who appear in the scientific studies. Still, to be with another person when he has his first experience of pure consciousness, that's a new type of enjoyment altogether. After starting the program, newcomers return for meetings the first three days and their smiles get bigger each day. Even though most of the important benefits of the Transcendental Meditation Technique build up over time, most people notice some effects right away. The reports they give have an innocent charm.

"My assistant says he has worked for me for fifteen months and today was the first time he ever heard me whistle." An advertising executive told me that.

"I got an 'A' on my spelling this week." An eleven-year-old boy said that.

"I lost five pounds in a week and I wasn't even dieting." It was my mother who said that.

It's easy. Anybody can do it. All aspects of life start to improve. A teacher of the Transcendental Meditation Technique says these things over and over every week in his lectures, but somehow when it's time to do the teaching it's a beautiful surprise every time.

It works.

I had just become comfortable with the teaching, as a matter of fact, when the time came for a change in our introductory lectures. We had been emphasizing rest and relaxation, as well as the development of full human potentials. Now, Maharishi had decided to sum these ideas up in one startling word. On January 12, 1975, he had inaugurated the "Dawn of the Age of Enlightenment."

As a change in terminology, using the word "enlightenment" has surprised a lot of people. As a stage in the teaching, however, Maharishi sees it as a logical development. Seventeen years of work around the world have laid the foundation. Now it is time to let people know what "life free from stress" can really mean. It's a question of education, of bringing a new understanding into a confused world. It will take some time. Maharishi is going to start off by going on a world tour to generate some public awareness, a tour to announce "The Dawn of the Age of Enlightenment."

Right now, however, a more prosaic excursion is on the agenda. It turns out that, given a chance, Maharishi does have one activity which will take him away from his normal routine of working in small meeting rooms or working in the lecture hall. Now and then he likes to go out and work on a boat ride. He wasn't able to do it often in Seelisberg because the trip to the docks took too long. Here at the Park Hotel, however, there's a landing right out back and Maharishi has been going out a couple of times a month in a long, bubble-top excursion boat. He's going out today with twenty-five scientists, writers and temporary "editorial assistants" to do some hurry-up work on the latest booklet of scientific research charts. This booklet has to be revised and expanded every six months to take care of the flood of new studies appearing all the time. The people responsible for this new edition want to have it ready when Maharishi leaves in three days for India on the first leg of his tour.

About forty of us are going on the ride and when Maharishi comes downstairs he leads us down the hall and out the side door of the building. The day is sparkling clear, and the air's spring crispness seems to go well with the neatly clipped garden outside and the carefully sculpted mountains across the lake. Maharishi moves down to the boat and steps across lightly.

"It looks to be a good day for boating," he says when we're ready to go. It's virtually his last conversational comment on the ride. He has been putting a lot of his attention recently into an analysis of the research.

"We could not have done better than to inspire such research," he says as we pull away from the docks, "and to make it available for the people to see."

These results are
the first evidence
of what
Maharishi has
said all along—a
harmonious mind
has a harmonious
effect on its
environment.

The boat is long and narrow, and the bubble top lets in a welcome panorama of light, lake and mountains. While most of the people work two and three together proofing and revising the charts and copy, Maharishi meets with several of the scientists up in the bow to discuss one of the most interesting new studies to be included in the booklet. It was this study, in fact, which triggered his decision to begin talking of an Age of Enlightenment. It is the first study to indicate the benefits of the Transcendental Meditation Technique can extend to a whole society. It shows that as the number of meditators in an area reaches the level of one per cent of the population, the crime rate in that area falls. Dissolving stress in individuals appears to lower the stress level in the society as a whole.

This new research is hardly conclusive at this point. Any study that covers whole communities is hard to pin down exactly, of course—there are so many factors floating around that are hard to control. And in this particular case the correlation seems so unlikely—how can a few people meditating in their own homes have an effect on their community at large?

Still, the results so far have been encouraging. They were first noticed in twelve smaller cities throughout the United States, cities such as Ames, Iowa; Ithaca, New York; and Chapel Hill, North Carolina. These were cities where the population of meditators reached one per cent in 1973. Official figures showed that the crime rate in these cities decreased an average of almost nine per cent in that year. This decrease contrasts with a national *increase* in crime of six per cent, as reported by the FBI, and an increase of nearly eight per cent in twelve cities that were selected because of similar size and population groupings to the cities where one per cent of the population is meditating.

These first reports gained considerable credence when the FBI's 1974 crime report for the fifty largest American cities appeared. The San Francisco-Oakland area became the first metropolitan region to go over the one per cent level in meditators in 1974, and it is also the only large city on the FBI's list to show a decrease in crime for that year.

For sociologists these figures might seem to be an inspiration to do research in a new direction. But for Maharishi the news has been a spur to direct action: a tour to announce the Dawn.

"It's a very important indication to have on a scientific basis," he is saying to the group in the front of the boat. "What it means is that when just a few people begin meditating morning and evening, their brains begin to function in a more orderly way. Then, as they move around in the society, they tend to make the whole society more orderly."

His quick acceptance of this research might seem surprising, but it is necessary to remember that his understanding of the Transcendental Meditation Technique long pre-dates any scientific investigation. Maharishi was teaching for ten years before scientists began to validate the benefits of the

Transcendental Meditation Technique just for individual meditators. He didn't wait then and he isn't going to wait now. These preliminary results are the first objective indications of what he has said all along—a harmonious mind has a harmonious effect on its surroundings. He is going out to tell the world there is no time to waste.

This up-coming tour will be the first extended trip he has taken in more than two years. His time is free for such an educational endeavor because the movement has flowered administratively. This round-the-lake working excursion is only a small fraction of the activity here at international headquarters. The work has outgrown Seelisberg—design and printing facilities have remained there—and with nearly four hundred people here full time, day-to-day administrative details are taken care of through settled routines.

Moreover, as the organization has increased in efficiency, the acceptance of the Transcendental Meditation Program has also been increasing in the world at large. More and more often in the past year, governments, businesses, school systems and other institutions have begun programs teaching the Transcendental Meditation Technique. After years of work, the technique is being accepted at leading levels of society. Maharishi's tour at this point will be building on success instead of simply breaking ground.

The world-wide scope of the movement will also make the trip an easy one. The local World Plan centers will take care of all the planning and accommodations in each area. And fittingly, the first stop on this five-continent tour will be India, the first home of this knowledge. Maharishi has rarely been there in recent years. He seems so comfortable in the swift technological culture of the West that it is something of a surprise to remember that for him, going to India is going home. He left partly because he wanted scientific validation of the fact that it's easy to enjoy rapid progress toward full potential. That validation is available now. It will be interesting to see how his homeland reacts to his return.

And it looks as if the pamphlet will be ready in time for his departure. The staff has been out here working for several hours now, and most of the details seem to be in place. It's getting late as the boat turns back. The sun is setting behind us, flashing gold across the surface of the lake and up into the windows of the hotel. The backdrop is the deep green immensity of the Swiss Alps. It's an intriguing thought: the next mountains we see will be the Himalayas.

"It is so encouraging that only one per cent of the population can benefit the whole society," Maharishi says. "It's only a small number of people causing the imbalance and negativity that are a threat to the peace and happiness of the whole society. All that is needed is a small percentage of people moving about with more orderly thought, more orderly

behavior, and that is good enough to counteract all these sources of negativity."

*That may be, but when the one per cent study is first seen, the
reduction in crime seems more like a miraculous event than a logical
conclusion.*

"A man who has never seen an airplane sees one in the sky and thinks
it is a miracle. But the phenomenon is not a miracle once we understand the
principle. It's just common sense—if we want to have a good influence on our
environment, we have to have a good influence developed within ourselves.
The light bulb is able to influence the surroundings just by being what it is
within itself. This is why, when we think of improving the environment, we
always think of improving the individual."

*If you strengthen individuals you could strengthen the differences
that divide societies already.*

"It's true that the field of differences is one of life's great values. Every
society is composed of many different people with different likes and dislikes,
different levels of understanding and levels of emotion. And it is vital that
these different values be maintained and strengthened. But it is also vital that
as differences are strengthened, harmony is also strengthened."

How can that happen?

"It is the nature of life. All diversity exists on the basis of an
underlying unity. There is the field of diversity, not only in people but in all
creation. But there is a unity underlying all these individual existences. It is
this basic level of unity—that unbounded, unchanging field of pure consciousness—that is contacted when the mind settles down to the state of least
excitation. When this basic value is applied to life, individuality is made
stronger, but at the same time it brings together the growing differences to
make a strong society. It's like the sap in a plant. When the sap strengthens the
individual petals, at the same time it strengthens the unity of the petals. The
flower blossoms in its full glory."

*So the Transcendental Meditation Technique is a way to end self-
ishness?*

"What we find is a man becomes more and more *reasonably* selfish.
The Transcendental Meditation Technique doesn't minimize the self—it
expands the self. Everything becomes as dear to a man as he is to himself. It's
not a question of becoming self-less, but of becoming self-full."

*And a fully developed individual can live in greater harmony with
his neighbors?*

"Very naturally. And this is the goal of society. The social order
should be for the enrichment *and* the integration of all differences. Any
society which, for the sake of social values, undermines the value of the
individual, or any society which is dedicated to enriching the interest of the
individual but is not able to uphold the interest of society as a whole—that

Maharishi leads the way from the Park Hotel down to an excursion boat on Lake Lucerne.

Instead of working in the lecture hall, now and then Maharishi likes to go out and work on a boat ride.

The Park Hotel from Lake Lucerne; in Switzerland, even the commonplace partakes of fairy tale.

organization of society is lacking in merit."

Why does a society tend to lose its integration in the first place? Speaking of crime, for instance, what is its original cause?

"Crime means mistakes, and mistakes mean weakness. Just weakness—the inability to fulfill a desire. A man is weak, he can't accomplish what he wants, and his suffering can be the seed that grows into aggression and criminal behavior. Weakness is the basis of *all* suffering and problems in life."

What about the influences of the environment? Don't you think criminal behavior and other problems of the individual are often caused by negative influences in the environment?

"We can't blame everything on the environment. There could be a thousand different causes, but the basic thing is that the man is weak—he is not able to handle the situation. He has not enlivened that ability in his nervous system which is capable of handling any situation in a peaceful way, and not only in a peaceful way, but in a way to derive maximum benefit."

But many people feel that to change individuals, you must change society.

"Yes, and society will also be changed by individuals. Angels will not drop from the heavens to improve society. When individuals can think better, work better, be more creative in any situation, they will structure a more harmonious society. Otherwise, who is going to improve society? The ideal is all right, but who is going to do it? And it's so weakening to a man to blame his environment. Man gets in the habit of making mistakes. And if we say, 'To err is human,' then if I make mistakes I am only human. And this makes a man bold to make mistakes. What we want is to create a situation where a man will be disallowed to make mistakes. That law is cruel that allows a man to make a mistake and then punishes him for it."

Laws allow *people to make mistakes?*

"When the law-making bodies can make any law, why not make a law so the source of all crime is eliminated? When you can make a law to punish a man for beating someone, why not make the law so the tendency to beat someone doesn't arise? The government should institute a program whereby every heart will be full of human values and every mind will be at full potential. Every man should be given that technique whereby he will be able to open his awareness to that field of pure consciousness, the field of all possibilities, and then to act from there. No man should be victimized by circumstances. A man is not born to make mistakes. He is born to be the master of nature."

It would take a long time to reach all the people, especially to teach the Transcendental Meditation Program to those who have already fallen into criminal behavior.

"There are courses in the Science of Creative Intelligence to be used in prisons and to bring people back from drug abuse. They have proved very beneficial. It has been proved scientifically that the ability to cope with the surroundings and circumstances increases with the practice of the Transcendental Meditation Technique. But what really gives us confidence is the information about one per cent. Just a few people in higher consciousness will take all the people to higher values of life."

But is one per cent enough to structure an ideal society?

"Not that with one per cent all suffering will end. But what we see is what the scientists call a 'phase transition,' a definite change in the trends of society from suffering and disorder toward harmony and peace. And the thing is, one per cent won't stay one per cent. Rapidly it will grow to five per cent, to ten per cent. It is a snowball set rolling and it is just going to roll on and on. This is why I thought to go to every continent and shout aloud, 'A better time is coming for the world.' This is the generation when we can efface the word crime from human literature, when 'To err is human' will be a blemish washed from human life. Now it is within our grasp to create an ideal society."

"When individuals can think better, work better, be more creative in any situation, they will structure a more harmonious society."

65

A dream-like
voyage seems to
move not only
East but also
backward in
time, away from
the sparkle and
clash of the West
toward something
older, simpler,
more basic.

Embarkation day has come up with Swiss perfection. Crisp air and clean blue skies greet Maharishi as he steps out of the hotel at about ten. Nearly everyone on the international staff is there to greet him also, and to wish him a good journey.

For many of these staff members, the departure scene stretches out the hour or so it takes to drive to the airport in Zurich. Everyone has brought flowers along—flowers substitute for handshakes with Maharishi—and as he emerges from the car he soon has them all. There is a short walk to the passport gate and the group stops in an impromptu circle. Maharishi spins slowly and hands the flowers out again one by one.

"Jai Guru Dev," he says. "Jai Guru Dev."

The first flight is a short one to Frankfurt, Germany. There's a wait of two hours, spent mostly in a private VIP lounge provided by the airline. Traveling with Maharishi is going to be a very different experience than being with him at headquarters, and it is here in this small airport room that we first feel that difference. At headquarters he is usually surrounded by many people, but on this trip there are only nine.

It's basically a functional group. Two professionals have come who will help make presentations with Maharishi. The two are Dr. Lawrence Domash, a physicist from Maharishi International University, and Dr. Byron Rigby, a psychiatrist from Guy's Hospital in London. Also in the group are a film maker, an audio specialist, and a designer to work with Maharishi on the spot as the need for printed materials arises. Among the several remaining members of the party there is also a writer to chronicle the journey—I'll be going through three continents before stopping off in California with my family.

It's strange to see Maharishi out again amidst the plastic and chrome of modern architecture after being with him for so long in the more aged and sedate hotels around Lake Lucerne. And this is only the beginning. The next two or three weeks promise a kaleidoscope of varied settings. Even this first leg of the journey should provide many new sights, because we are starting our global trip with the longest leg first. We will be flying nearly half way around the world, from Frankfurt to Delhi, India, and then driving straight on eight hours by car into the foothills of the Himalayan mountains. We are heading for the academy Maharishi has established near Rishikesh. He wants to begin this world-wide tour to stimulate action toward the Age of Enlightenment with a day of peaceful solitude.

Near flight time we leave the lounge and walk down the long corridor to the plane. As soon as we step into Air India's 747, there is the feel of another world. It's not just the hostesses draped in saris but also the people taking the trip along with us. There are some European businessmen, and a few American tourists, but they are a minority scattered in a setting of brown skins, dark eyes and shining black hair. India is coming to meet us.

It's mid-afternoon by the time the plane takes off. We are headed east, toward the night. Most of us haven't slept in two days keeping up with the frantic pace of Maharishi's final preparations, and as soon as the meal is finished many of the long seats, with their arm-rests raised, have tired bodies stretched out along them.

The windows darken quickly as we race away from the setting sun, and a dreamy sort of sleep floats in like a mist. Now and then a voice drifts by, speaking of places that seem to ring in some old memory. First it's the Danube River and Vienna; they fade into suspended quiet and then the Black Sea and Istanbul materialize; even deeper silence ensues and then that drops away to become the valley of the Tigris and Euphrates. A dream-like voyage seems to move not only East but also backward in time, back away from the fast sparkle and clash of the West toward something older, simpler, more basic.

And then the plane is down on the ground. This is Kuwait. It's the middle of the night and we will sit here for an hour to refuel. There is time to go up and see Maharishi.

The forward door is open into blackness. Kuwaiti workmen are filing into the plane, dressed in dirty coats and haphazard headscarves, carrying buckets and small tools. Maharishi is past the door, up toward the front. He is out of his seat, leaning with one elbow on the seat back and chatting to a newsman from a small newspaper.

"It's a five-continent tour," he is saying. "We are just going around to stir the air."

Air seems a good idea and Maharishi moves down the aisle and out onto the landing of the stairway that leads to Kuwait. It's here that one of the members of the flight crew catches up to him after leaving the cockpit. The man is a meditator whom Maharishi himself initiated years ago. Standing out on the landing blackness, back-lit weirdly by powerful light towers, they take advantage of the coincidence with an animated conversation featuring eloquent gestures and many smiles. A crowd has gathered at the door, clogging the aisle, watching Maharishi. One lady pushes her small son forward.

"Hier ist ein grosser Mann," she says.

Here is a great man.

Maharishi gives the crewman a flower and then turns back inside. Kuwait is starting to fade away. It's time to take off.

It's time to sleep.

For groggy Westerners with body clocks awry, the scene at Delhi airport the following morning is a jumble of unlikely impressions. Out the window of the arrivals building a farmer is plowing his field behind two yoked cattle. Inside, the general effect of a mid-American bus depot is enlivened by birds flying around and singing. We are in India but we are not

One India; the rural roads still fill with living traffic from early morning until after dark.

really there yet. This is India heavily influenced by the West, a confusing mixture of cultures.

We drive into Delhi and stop at a hotel to pick up Jerry Jarvis and his wife Debbie. They have also just arrived, coming the opposite way twenty-eight hours across the Pacific from California. Even before our cars have pulled away again, Maharishi and Mr. Jarvis are immersed in discussion.

Our four-car caravan drives through the modern elegance of Delhi and out onto the road to Rishikesh. It is here that we finally seem to find India full strength. The urban influence is less pronounced, and the road is a living ribbon, a flowing exhibition of life in northern India. Both lanes are clogged with people—people on foot, on carts pulled slowly by water buffalo or cattle, on bicycles, on bicycle rickshaws and motorcycles, people in cars and buses and trucks, people using anything that will move them down the road. They are all ages and both sexes and they are all slim and dark with brown-black limbs extending from the white garments wrapped around them. A different way to be alive is streaming past us.

After hours of watching this cultural revelation, darkness comes, the lights go on, and the crowds begin to thin out. We are heading now for the Ganges, for a small pontoon bridge across that sacred river. We are heading for still another India, for the region of the Himalayas where the possibilities of human life have been kept as if stored in the individuals who have lived their reality.

It's after ten when the tires begin to crunch the gravel of the Ganges bed. There is a gate to the bridge, a small cabin for an attendant who records each car as it passes, and then we are on the far side of the river and heading into forested hills. The road now is just a path hacked from the forest, and the cars lurch and side-slip slowly around the gnarled turns, headlights spilling light into the trees and undergrowth. My previous trip with Maharishi, the one from La Antilla to Seelisberg, had ended like a fairy tale in the Swiss Alps. This trip ends as a jungle adventure of some minor stature, with elephants blocking the road, cars bogged down in mud, and tigers glimpsed amidst the trees.

In the darkness we miss a turn-off, then double back and jounce down the small road to a stop. As we get out of the cars, we can see small flames coming toward us. The people are running, twenty or thirty of them, both Indian and Western. It's been years since Maharishi spent much time here.

He steps from the car and several people walk before him, lighting the way down the path. The path curves, goes through a bowered gate, over a small footbridge and leads up to the door of the house where Maharishi will stay. A small candle-lit procession follows him, and many old friends find each other in the wavering light and pass smiles back and forth.

The group files into the small main room of the house to share a few brief words of welcome, and then Maharishi goes to rest. The remaining new arrivals move on to another house where we enjoy a meal that seems just right, a satisfying conclusion to a long journey.

And then, cup overflowing, the beds are soft and the blankets warm.

"Travel shows how striking are the differences we find in the world today," Maharishi says later. "Science and technology have done so much to integrate the world. Take a jet plane and you can travel halfway around the world in one day. And all the vast communications network—newspapers, telephones, radio, television—the whole trend of the time is conducive to integration. The days are gone when a man can live in isolation—world-wide thinking enters every home. And since this is true, it's only natural for the hidden values of the integration of life to come up now, for the technology to rise to the surface that is making all individuals into universal individuals."

Is there any real value in the sort of technological progress that has

> "This knowledge is nothing new. We only brushed off the dust deposited on this ancient technique and now it is expressed in a systematic way."

EAST AND WEST

"It's very necessary that life is not wasted in narrowness of vision, in narrowness of thinking. One must think great things, do great things."

"It's very important. The age of science has brought some comfort to life, some knowledge of the laws of nature. But still there has been a lack. There has been material evolution, but evolution to fulfillment—evolution toward life at full potential—has not been available. In fact, the fast pace of technology has often brought more stress and strain to the quality of life. Progress has often been at a cost to life, the cost of stress and tension—to say nothing of evolution toward fulfillment. So a new science was needed, an understanding of the integration of life, and now East and West have come together to give expression to this new science."

But wouldn't this knowledge be just as effective without recourse to scientific language?

"Certainly. In the beginning days, we taught the Transcendental Meditation Technique purely on the subjective level of the experience people had when they started meditating. A man begins to experience that state of pure consciousness and what he finds is that this influences life on all levels to such a degree that the whole value of life is transformed. And then, when the scientists became interested, their research was helpful. In a modern world, scientific language has proved to be a good way to communicate. But really, this whole knowledge is nothing new. Nothing useful is new under the sun. We only brushed off the dust deposited on this ancient technique and now it is expressed in a more systematic way. The original knowledge comes from the ancient Vedic literature, validation comes from modern science, and now we feel ourselves to be on a very solid footing."

What is the "Vedic literature"?

"The Vedas are a very great source of knowledge. The word 'veda' means knowledge. The Vedic literature is the most ancient record of man's experience on earth."

And descriptions in this ancient literature match the descriptions of modern science?

"The expression is different, the vocabulary is different. But even before the age of science, even before this knowledge of the vacuum state, for instance, it has always been known that silence was at the basis of life. There has been this huge literature saying that if we could allow our minds to experience the silent, unmanifest field of life, great benefits would come. There is a story in the Upanishads, one of the branches of the Vedic literature. The story is about a master and his disciple. The master said to his disciple to bring a fruit of the banyan tree. The disciple brought the fruit and the master said to break it open. He broke it and the master said, 'What do you see?' The disciple said, 'Many seeds.' The master said, 'Break open a seed and tell me what you see.' The disciple did so and said, 'Hollowness.' 'Hollowness,' said the master. 'This hollowness is the unmanifest value of the whole tree. It's from this hollowness that the whole tree has come up.' "

And this level of hollowness is to be equated with the vacuum state?

"We can say so. Even before the scientists discovered that all aspects of the universe come out from the vacuum state, this understanding was there. Only now it is given a systematic expression in the Science of Creative Intelligence. And so long as there was no technique for bringing this level to our conscious awareness, the scientists thought of it as a vacuum. But when it dawns on the awareness, it dawns as the fullness of life. The awareness then is unbounded."

Unbounded awareness? What is meant by that?

"It's like that awareness of the untold wealth in the bank. In that state of pure consciousness—where the mind is awake but without a thought—no boundaries are there. There is not even the finest boundary of a thought. So we say the awareness is unbounded. It is infinite. And life aspires to expand its territory of influence to encompass this infinity and make it a living reality in daily life. If this unboundedness is not being lived within the value of every thought and action, then life feels cramped. This is the seed of all frustration and suffering."

The experience of pure consciousness is the experience of unbounded awareness?

"Yes. And as one practices the Transcendental Meditation Technique morning and evening, the influence of that unboundedness creeps in life more and more. Suffering is only there when our vision is narrowed down in small boundaries. When we open our awareness to unboundedness, then that narrowness is neutralized. One becomes a man of greater comprehension. One sees a bigger horizon, as if one has gone up on a hill."

Is the phrase "going up the hill" an analogy for a higher state of consciousness?

"This is what it means—developing that wide-angle vision, that ability to maintain unboundedness even while focusing on the small boundaries of daily life. It's very necessary that life is not wasted in narrowness of vision, in narrowness of thinking. One must think great things, do great things."

Scientific theory says that the vacuum state is also unbounded, infinite. So we have scientific theories and ancient teaching. Which provide the most important guidelines?

"They are complementary. When we have it from physics that the infinite, unbounded level of all possibilities does exist, and when we have it from the ancient tradition of masters that there is an easy way to establish our awareness on that universal level, then naturally we want to live that state. The tradition is so important—we feel comfortable when we know that others have gone this royal road of fullness before us. Naturally it makes us want to move in that direction. And then, when scientific experiments show us that we are moving in the right direction, we are satisfied. We only feel bold to keep moving ahead."

It's a day for rest and quiet. From here it's five continents in five weeks, and every minute of rest now will make a difference in some frantic future activity.

There couldn't be a better place or time than this hilltop setting on March 9, 1975, for finding peace and serenity. The academy is a sanctuary for quietness and the day is so perfect it seems pre-arranged.

A late morning begins with a walk to the Ganges. The academy sits on a bluff overlooking an arc of the river and most of the visitors walk down the steep path to bathe. Then comes breakfast and a walk around the grounds. There are sixteen acres here—lush, wooded land leased to the World Plan Executive Council for ninety-nine years by the Indian government. The rental is approximately ten dollars a year, collected only for legal purposes.

Maharishi used the academy for teacher training courses during the early 1960s, until the courses outgrew the facilities. European courses were then established, while Indian courses have continued here. There are accomodations for one hundred and fifty people, all rooms with private baths, as well as a lecture hall and dining hall. The most unusual sight is a low line of "bunkers" coming up from the ground only a few inches, with tiny ventilation windows spaced every few feet. These are small meditation rooms built underground to withstand the heat of the summer.

It's a very complete facility, surprising this far into India's traditional countryside. The candle-lit arrival the night before turns out to have been only the fortuitous result of a fuse blowout; the entire grounds are wired for electricity from a small transformer fed by power lines arching across the river. Even in the Himalayan foothills, Maharishi is all for technology. He's all for beauty, also, and the natural attractions of the setting have been enhanced by man-made streams, small fountains and banks of flowers. Adding the beauty of the weather—the slight excess of warmth from the sun is filtered by the trees to provide perfect comfort—the whole day has the feel of meditation, an interlude of lively comfort.

In the middle of the afternoon, Maharishi comes out of his room and moves up to the roof of the house. He sits there alone for more than an hour, overlooking the Ganges. Then at about five o'clock he comes down, walks across the grounds, and enters the large, rounded lecture hall. There are about one hundred and fifty people here, mostly visitors to the academy, sitting on the carpeted floor in front of a low stage. The late-afternoon light is turning pink and gold, settling softly into the hall through a window-wall at one end. Maharishi begins to speak in the musical sounds of the Hindi language, his mood matching the peace of the moment.

Since I can't understand him most of the time, I find myself caught up in his actions, his manner. His hands dance lightly through a continuous flow of gestures, fingers sometimes waving like leaves in slight puffs of air. Every movement is graceful, yet pointed and strong. And the feeling that comes from him as he speaks is rich and full, inspiring a lively and contented enjoyment.

His happiness while teaching is one of the first memories I have of Maharishi, a memory that goes back to the first video-tapes I saw of him. He has been saying the same thing for nearly twenty years now—changing languages and vocabulary when necessary—but each link in the logic retains an eternal freshness and beauty for him. His appreciation comes out in spontaneous smiles and laughter. This profound love he has for the teaching is one indication of its validity—"Beauty is truth and truth beauty."

"It was good to talk to the people just now," he says. "Now my thoughts are consolidated for the eleventh."

In two days, Maharishi will preside at a public presentation in Delhi. He has titled the meeting the "Inauguration of the Dawn of the Age of Enlightenment for the continent of Asia." Similar meetings are scheduled for the other five continents. The idea behind these "inaugurations" is to focus attention on a new phenomenon, to make an educational session into a public event. Visibility is important. The more people who know about this new development and come out to help, the faster an Age of Enlightenment can arrive.

In serving this need, the Delhi inauguration promises to be an effective day of symbolic communication. Objective validation will be represented— there will be speeches by many prominent businessmen, educators and scientists—and enlightenment will come just as strongly from a more intimate, personal source. The current Shankaracharya of Jyotir Math will be in attendance.

The presence of the Shankaracharya will be of interest in two different ways. In the first place, the Shankaracharya of Jyotir Math is the most respected spiritual leader in all of northern India. His participation will add immense prestige to the inauguration ceremony. In the second place, it will be good to see Maharishi together with the man who is Guru Dev's direct successor as Shankaracharya. The two men have rarely seen each other in the twenty years since Maharishi left Jyotir Math to begin his teaching. As a matter of fact, the residence at Jyotir Math—the place Maharishi spent thirteen years with Guru Dev—is actually not far from here. Dirt roads make it a two-day journey, however. The Shankaracharya will be coming down to Delhi by train early on the morning of the eleventh.

"It will be a good day," Maharishi says now. "It is a necessary step. The Dawn is coming, but if the people go on sleeping, then they won't enjoy it. So it's necessary to go around and give them a gentle shake, tell them to come on and enjoy the Dawn."

We sit quietly in the candlelight for a while, and then Maharishi asks someone to play a recording of some Vedic chanting. When it is done he comments briefly on what we have heard. His summation is one of the basic observations in his teaching—the idea that evolution is natural, that it is inherent in the nature of life to evolve. He sits quietly again for a moment and then turns to Dr. Domash, the physicist, with what seems to be quite an unusual question, a question he may have been saving for awhile.

"And what about metals?" he asks. "Do scientists say that metals evolve?"

Dr. Domash looks surprised for a moment.

"They do, actually," he says.

"And how is it?"

"It's a very slow process that goes on during the cycle of birth and death that stars go through," Dr. Domash says. "You want me to explain it?"

"Yes, good."

"To get iron, for instance, you have to start with the simplest atom, hydrogen. Hydrogen is converted to the next most complicated atom, helium, in a fusion reaction in a star. Then that star explodes and joins the clouds of gas in space. Eventually the gas condenses into a new star and fusion this time brings about heavier elements. Then another explosion and another condensation—it takes four or five cycles of different stars to produce iron. It *is* a process of evolution. They call it 'stellar evolution.'"

"And this evolution seems to be through the process of rest and activity," Maharishi says.

"You could say that," Dr. Domash says, smiling. "Stars come and go. It's just a very long cycle."

Maharishi sits quietly again, and several of us look upward to see the magnificent view of stellar evolution provided for us. It's the right place and the right mood to think about the process of evolution that runs through all of natural creation.

After a few moments, Maharishi looks up with a smile.

"It was good to come here, even for a day."

A breeze stirs the leaves into harmony with the Ganges rushing over the rocks below.

"It makes a difference," he says. "It makes a difference."

EVOLUTION
IS EASY

"The tradition is so important to us" Maharishi says. "Guru Dev's teaching came out to be so perfect. It is his knowledge that is leading us on to the Age of Enlightenment."

But if his teaching is so effective, why is India still a developing nation? The Transcendental Meditation Technique seems to have failed to make India dynamic and progressive.

"It's not the Transcendental Meditation Technique that has failed in India."

But don't most people there meditate?

"There is a lot of talk of meditation, and many people practice one technique or another, but the whole field is one of confusion. The idea is there, but the simplicity has been lost. Evolution is natural to life, but people in India began using effort and concentration and it all became tedious and unnatural. The whole understanding about spiritual development was lost."

Even now some people from India say that it's only by struggle and asceticism that a man can make any progress.

"These people are sold out to austerity. They think nothing can be gained without austerity, but they are mistaken. Struggle does not belong to the nature of life. One has to struggle only when he does not know how to grow without struggle. People who practice austerities often maintain that it is the desire to grow that makes a man unhappy. All desires can not be satisfied, they say, so if you keep on desiring more and more, you must remain unfulfilled. Therefore, they say that desires should be cut down."

This isn't correct?

"It's against our common experience in life. Satisfaction and progress come from the fulfillment of desire. If we want something and we get it, we feel satisfaction. And every step of fulfilled desire raises our standard of desiring to something a little higher. These steps of increasing satisfaction are the steps of progress, and progress strengthens a man. This is why the path of

The park-like grounds of the academy near Rishekesh sit on a bluff overlooking the Ganges.

75

First we meditate
and then we find
we are gaining
clearer vision of
life. We don't
have to change
anything. We find
ourselves
changing.

austerity and effort often produce a kind of dullness — it brings no satisfaction from the experience of the steps of progress."

But the idea behind a life of austerity is that it is necessary to renounce the world—to live life by some standard of purity—in order to make progress.

"No, no. This is what they call putting the cart before the horse. What we do is bring light to dispel the darkness—not that we should try to remove darkness in order to come into the light. First we experience the state of pure consciousness, and *then* we find we are gaining clearer vision in life. We don't have to change anything. We find ourselves changing. The Transcendental Meditation Technique is a preparation for activity. Otherwise, by simply abstaining from the activity of life, one merely falls into a state of idleness and inertia. That whole direction is unsatisfactory. The goal is not separation from life. The goal is union with the basis of life, that level of pure consciousness."

Then it is not necessary to live a reclusive life in order to evolve?

"No, it is not necessary to live a monk's life. It is not necessary to have any sense of detachment or renunciation, to abstain from life, to ignore the responsibilities of life. A man in the world, his life full with feelings of love for others and of accomplishment in society, such a worldly life is also there for freedom, for eternal freedom. Accomplishing all that they might stand for, yet all the people could very well rise to that great height of evolution where they will be glorifying the outer values of life by the light of pure consciousness."

Then to go back to the topic of suffering—if suffering is not caused by worldly life and an excess of desires, what is the cause?

"The cause is weakness—this is what we have said. Weakness is the basis of all suffering and problems. When one is incapable of fulfilling a desire, this inability causes frustration and fatigue, and this in turn increases weakness. Life continues in suffering."

Again, there are some people who say that actually suffering is just an illusion, that it has no reality in itself.

"No, no. The suffering is a very concrete reality. One can't say that no one is experiencing fear and heartaches and suffering. But what is unreal is the basis of suffering."

Because the basis of suffering is weakness?

"Yes. Just the inability to fulfill a desire. The mind is out of touch with that unbounded potential, the field of all possibilities. And it is the gift of Guru Dev that now, in this generation, we are witnessing a revival of that precious knowledge that leads to contact with the true nature of the self."

And this is not a long and difficult process?

"No. It's ridiculously simple. The thing is, the level of unboundedness, the state of least excitation, is just a man's own consciousness. And a man's consciousness is what he *is*. It's natural for a man to live what he is. This has been the error through the ages. People started to try, and they got out of the naturalness of evolution. Techniques involving effort and discipline were taught, and it was thought to be a very long process. But now is the time to clear away all this rubbish from the past. Consciousness—that pure field of intelligence—is one's own intimate phase of life. Something so close and intimate should not be hard to experience as a living reality. There is no question of having to *do* something to have this experience."

But isn't meditating doing something?

"The Transcendental Meditation Technique is a way to undo the doing. It allows the mental activity to become less and less, and soon activity takes the form of no activity. The whole process is natural. This is why this is such a great knowledge about the nature of life. And it's a very complete knowledge. The whole thing is there—the procedure to gain the experience and the knowledge about the experience."

Part of this knowledge is the selection of "mantras." Every student is given a mantra when he learns the Transcendental Meditation Technique. How important is it to have a suitable mantra?

"It's very important. It's vital. This is why the tradition of knowledge is so important. A mantra is a thought we take for its sound value only. It is a sound that is a vehicle to allow the mind to settle down very naturally to the state of least excitation."

But why is any particular sound important?

"We know from physics that everything is waves—sound waves, light waves. Everything is vibration. Physics also tells us that progressively finer levels in creation have more power—atoms have more power than molecules. For this reason it is extremely important that a suitable sound—a suitable vibration—be used so that as it is experienced by the mind in its finer states, more and more powerful effects of a life-supporting nature will be produced. If the sound is not stable, then unstable influences will increase."

Does everyone have his own mantra?

"Different types of people have one mantra, and other types another. But there is not one mantra for every person. The mantras we know from our tradition of masters. It's a very great science of life—the effect of sound on consciousness—and we just follow their teaching. I teach the teachers and they teach the students."

And a person shouldn't try to meditate with just any sound he wants?

"It's not good to take chances with the mantra. No one wants to play with his life. But the knowledge of mantras is an ancient knowledge. There is nothing experimental about it. It's a very great gift of life that Guru Dev has given us. It's all his teaching and this is why it's taught in his name. As teachers of the Transcendental Meditation Technique, we only think of ourselves as loudspeakers of this great tradition."

We are back in Delhi, back in India's national capital. It's about nine o'clock in the morning and Maharishi is stepping into the first of several of the tiny, black, English-bred cabs that will take us on the short trip to the auditorium. It's time to let Asia know about the Dawn.

New Delhi provides a beautiful backdrop for the ride, with vistas surprisingly spacious and dignified. Wide avenues lead through streets landscaped like parks and much of the architecture is monumental in scale. Unlike the road to the academy, the streets here are uncluttered, and light traffic swings smoothly around the large traffic circles at every intersection. It is becoming obvious that India is a land of contrasts.

The cabs drop us at the side of a massive building, the Vigyam Bhavan, a building used by the Indian government for large official functions. Maharishi leads the way into the auditorium. It's a wood-paneled hall seating twelve hundred people. Each member of the audience has his own desk with earphones available at every seat for simultaneous translation. All the seats are taken and people fill the aisles and the space in front between the seats and the stage, sitting on the ground in a way that seems natural here. The audience is mature and well-dressed, a cross-section of Delhi's establishment.

The stage is crowded with seating arrangements. The left side is set with cushions and cloth. Just off center to the right is Maharishi's couch with a large picture of Guru Dev above and behind. To the right of that are several more couches and chairs. The middle of the stage is empty, a space waiting for the arrival of the Shankaracharya.

Maharishi climbs the stairs to the stage and is joined by about forty traditionally robed pundits—specialists in the Vedic literature. This is India, and Maharishi has the twelve hour program started in a ceremonial manner familiar to the audience, with chanting from the Vedas. The program is then introduced by the moderator, Mr. Gulzari Lal Nanda, a retired political leader who has held several cabinet posts in the Indian national government and twice been the interim Prime Minister. His remarks are brief, and then it is time for Maharishi to speak.

"It is my great joy to be able to say that a good time is coming for the world," he begins. "Suffering will be missing. Problems will be missing. It will be our task today to analyze how it is that the scientific age is rising to become the Age of Enlightenment."

His tone is clear and direct, his gestures short and decisive.

"Today we can say it," he goes on. "I have been teaching the Transcendental Meditation Technique around the world for seventeen years, and never until now did it occur to me that this technique would bring an Age of Enlightenment. But now we have the information that only a small percentage of the world's population is necessary to bring about the Dawn. It's a very beautiful time for the world."

He continues for most of an hour, speaking alternately in English and in Hindi. His speech is built around the scientific reasoning he has used in the West. Phrases such as "vacuum state," "physiology, psychology and sociology," "state of least excitation," and "field of all possibilities" appear even in the Hindi portions of his speech. It occurs to me that it must be a surprise for this Indian audience to hear such technical talk in such a setting.

It is nearly eleven in the morning when Maharishi pauses briefly and looks offstage. Several men are walking in with a chair made of intricately modeled silver, and they set it down in the center of the stage. It shines brilliantly in the glare of the powerful television lamps lighting the stage. The Shankaracharya should arrive soon.

Maharishi speaks again for several more minutes, and then a small disturbance breaks out at a side door. A crowd of people backs into the auditorium. They separate to form an aisle, and then wait quietly as the figure of the Shankaracharya emerges from the shadowed hall. He is a powerful, imposing man wearing a rich, orange-colored dhoti. He carries a staff wrapped in orange in his left arm.

As he ascends the stairs to the stage, Maharishi rises with a garland of flowers in his hands. He moves to the Shankaracharya and places the garland over his head. The Shankaracharya stops and with his one free arm, in a decisive gesture, he removes the garland and places it on Maharishi. It is a special moment and it brings a wave of applause from the audience.

This is Shantanand. The name means "The Bliss of Peace." He walks deliberately across the stage, flanked by five members of his ashram, and sits down in the ceremonial chair of the Shankaracharya. His people gather around him, two standing at his shoulders, two sitting at his feet, one slightly to his right. Once settled, the group moves very little, a silent tableau at center stage.

There is a brief ceremony of welcome and Maharishi resumes his seat on the couch to express his joy at the presence of this great spiritual leader. Then he resumes his opening address. In just a few minutes his main theme emerges again: enlightenment can be understood in terms of scientific theories, and it can be verified by scientific experimentation. Two eminent representatives of the ancient Vedic wisdom are now on the stage, and still the discussion is structured in modern technology and objective verification. Even for a Westerner, the contrasts of the scene are surprising. For the Indian audience here—even though this is Maharishi's homeland—the presentation must seem even more startling.

When Maharishi speaks in the West, of course, his personal appearance is a surprise in itself. In a way, this surface unfamiliarity serves a purpose, however. His listeners know immediately that Maharishi is outside their normal routine, and that he is probably saying something they don't normally think about. His appearance prepares them for new thoughts.

If Westerners are
surprised to find
there is any way
at all to develop
consciousness,
people in the East
are surprised to
hear that it's easy
and natural.

In India, on the other hand, the situation is reversed. People here are used to monks dressed in the traditional manner. They are not only used to seeing them but also to hearing their ideas. Based on these preconceptions, the audience here this day is probably expecting mystical talk and an urgent challenge to take up the austere path of discipline, self-sacrifice and renunciation of the world. What they are hearing, instead, are scientific explanations and joyful invitations to enjoy the fullness of life. The whole approach is dramatically new.

Thus it is that wherever Maharishi goes, even when he returns home, his teaching comes as a new understanding. If Westerners are surprised to find there is any way at *all* to develop consciousness to its full value, people in the East are surprised simply to hear that it's easy and natural, that anyone can do it. The West hasn't thought much about consciousness, the East hasn't thought much about technology—and both have needed the coming of a scientific age to clear away the confusions.

When Maharishi is done, the Shankaracharya gives a short talk. He speaks in deliberate, measured phrases in a voice that is full and clear, a voice with a tone of relaxed authority. From the translation it is clear he is happy to be here. He spends a few minutes in praise of Maharishi's world-wide accomplishments, success he terms unprecedented in the recent history of mankind's search for enlightenment. Then he supports Maharishi's main point in simple language. Meditate morning and evening, he says, and begin to enjoy the energy and happiness available within.

By the time he finishes, it's nearly noon. The World Plan Center here in Delhi has next scheduled a series of five symposia that will run throughout the afternoon. Maharishi wants to sit with Indian experts and explore the meaning of an Age of Enlightenment in five areas: government, education, business, science and health. The two couches to his left have already filled with specialists in the field of government. They are all meditators who are here to speak on their experiences and give recommendations on the application of the Transcendental Meditation Program to governmental problems. Members of the Indian national parliament have signed a proclamation endorsing Maharishi's Inauguration, and this is read out as a means to get the first symposium under way.

As the afternoon continues, a succession of scientists, educators, business executives and doctors all make contributions. It was only two years ago that a delegation of Western teachers came to India to begin the teaching of the Transcendental Meditation Technique in earnest. Judging by the speeches we hear this afternoon, the work has been successful. Support for Maharishi's activities is now coming from influential people in many areas of society.

The last of the symposia concludes just after six. While most of the audience and the other speakers break for dinner, Maharishi goes upstairs to

*Another India: New
Delhi is a showcase of
parks, wide avenues
and monumental
buildings such as
these governmental
offices.*

conduct a press conference. More than one hundred and fifty media represen-tatives from all over the country have come to cover Maharishi's first formal appearance in India in many years, and the conference lasts over an hour.

After the conference Maharishi returns to the main hall. He arrives just before the Shankaracharya. Both men take their seats and there is a moment when the Shankaracharya looks down at a wristwatch on his left wrist, a watch with an orange wrist band to match his dhoti, and then looks over to Maharishi. They both smile: technology and enlightenment.

It's a pleasure watching them together. Maharishi, of course, is a deeply religious man, a monk who took his vows many decades ago. He rarely makes a show of this personal side of his nature—usually he is surrounded by scientists, technicians and teachers—and seeing him onstage with the Shankaracharya seems to bring the spiritual core of his life into clearer focus.

It also adds meaning to the decision Maharishi made two decades ago not to *teach* his religious beliefs. He has taken the ancient technique of Transcendental Meditation and presented it to the world by itself as a means to strengthen the body and nervous system. He knew when he started what science has proved by now—as fatigue and stress dissolve and people begin to feel better, they naturally begin to act in a more harmonious and life-supporting manner. Maharishi emphasizes technology to reach a profoundly human goal. He wants all people to spontaneously live their lives in greater accord with the teachings of their own religion. By coming together to inaugurate the Dawn of the Age of Enlightenment, Maharishi and the Shankaracharya are only giving expression to one basic idea: the human nervous system is capable of evolving rapidly toward a state where life is lived at full potential and in accord with the highest aspirations of human life.

The ceremonies for the day finish with another short speech by the Shankaracharya. His conclusion is in verse, a poetic declaration he has composed in ancient Sanskrit to honor Maharishi and the Dawn.

When Maharishi rises, his face is radiating happiness.

"Today," he says, "we have successfully inaugurated the Dawn of the Age of Enlightenment for all of Asia."

"In today's society," Maharishi says, "there are so many problems and hindrances on the surface level of life. This is the difficulty. What is needed is to remove these surface problems and then, when the stress is a little bit less, automatically the deeper values of life will come up for each person in his own terms."

This is why religious concepts are not taught in the Transcendental Meditation Program?

"The thing is, religious teaching has not yet brought about an Age of

> "What is needed is to remove the surface problems and then, when stress is a little less, automatically the deeper values of life will come up for each person in his own terms."

Maharishi presents a message compounded of scientific verification and smiling invitation to the audience in Delhi.

A UNIVERSAL APPROACH

83

"Personal
development is
no longer a
fantasy or only a
metaphysical
reality, but it can
be seen in
measurable
terms—
physiologically
psychologically
and
sociologically."

Enlightenment. Religious language doesn't belong to an age of science. I respect religious language, but it's not the language of the scientific age."

You are a monk, a man who has devoted himself to a religious life. Doesn't it seem that teaching a simple technique and using a scientific approach is taking you away from the main focus of your life?

"No, no. We teach the Transcendental Meditation Technique, which is universally applicable. It brings about betterment in a man's life—he has less of stress, his mind is more clear, his health gets better. And what we know is that this improvement is coming from the deepest level within. We teach a technique for reaching that basic level. Every religion comes from some basic level, a universal level, and that level is also the basis of all science, all art, all the variety of life. That level is the basis of all good, all progress. It is on that level we function. In itself it is not a religion, or science, or art. But it has its effect on all. People of all religions say religious life improves when stresses and strains are removed with the practice of the Transcendental Meditation Technique."

So it changes religious life?

"It doesn't change it, just makes it more effective, more rich. Every momentary experience of that pure, crystalline, unbounded level of life is so purifying for the whole nervous system. The whole daily routine is purified."

And to accomplish that, a scientific approach is good enough?

"Yes. The development of the individual has been talked about in every age in the language of that age. Now we have created for ourselves a scientific age, where it is possible to investigate all the values of consciousness in an objective way. And the research shows that the Transcendental Meditation Technique does produce that kind of brain functioning which is capable of enriching not only the mental activity, but also the connection between mind and body and the relation between an individual and his environment. The personal development one gains day after day is now no more a fantasy or only a metaphysical reality, but it can be seen in terms of measurable qualities—physiologically, psychologically and sociologically. It is on physical terms, on the level of the very practical, concrete values of life."

In the teaching of the Transcendental Meditation Technique there is no list of "do's and don'ts." There is no specific moral code taught by which people are supposed to judge their behavior. Why is this?

"This is what we have said before: our behavior depends on what we *are.* The whole field of our activity depends on how limited or how broad we are in our awareness. Our behavior, our feeling, our perception—these are all just the channels of application of our awareness. We teach a technique whereby a man may broaden his awareness."

But still, when there are no specific teachings about how to act, aren't people encouraged to persist in wrong actions?

"No, no. It's important that we don't do something we *know* to be wrong. Not that we waste our life analyzing whether it is right or wrong to take this step, or to say this word. No. But if we *know* something is wrong, why do it? It's simple. And as we continue to practice the Transcendental Meditation Technique, naturally our thinking will be more right, our actions will be more right."

In the teaching of the Transcendental Meditation program, there is also no teaching about the after-life. Why is that?

"The Transcendental Meditation Technique is concerned with life, not after life. It's a waste of time to think about after life. As long as life is with us, it's better to live it than waste it thinking of when it's gone."

Then what will be the role of religious teachers in the Age of Enlightenment?

"The role of religious leaders will be the role of success."

We are headed today for Benares, a city that is reputed to be the oldest in the world. This is a statistic that is hard to verify, since Indian chronology is notoriously inexact. Indian historians are said to be more concerned with eternal truths than specific events.

Our flight between Delhi and Benares sweeps over a small portion of India's immense central plain. The scale is staggering—Delhi is a thousand miles inland, for instance, and only seventy feet above sea level. Watching this vast flatness unfold below, it is easier to understand the mystique of the Himalayas far to the north. Even in geography, the contrasts of India are striking.

We arrive in Benares at mid-morning. Several of the ubiquitous black cabs are waiting to take us through the city to Benares University, where the local World Plan Center has scheduled a full day of activities. As we drive through the downtown section, the appearance of the city gives credence to its reputation for age. In contrast to the carefully planned grandeur of New Delhi, Benares has a feeling of organic decline. Dusty streets wind between soiled one- and two-story buildings that seem to huddle together for mutual support, and traffic is once again a chaotic tangle of pedestrians, bicycles and bicycle rickshaws engulfing the isolated cars and trucks.

In the midst of this activity, Maharishi's car stops. He steps out and walks down a small side street with two of his Indian staff members to visit one of the most famous temples in India. By tradition this is not an excursion for Westerners, so several of us take the few minutes to walk through the crowded streets down toward the Ganges.

As we approach this holy river, which has followed us across the plain from Rishikesh, the street widens out like a fan and cascades downward in a series of broad stairways and landings to empty at last in the waters. Each landing is filled with barkers angling for tourists, barbers squatting under small umbrellas, and a few beggars leaning against the walls. Cattle hunker down on several of the landings, hiding from the sun in the shade of the walls—even in March the air feels of summer coming.

After a few minutes immersed in this intense world, we walk back to the cars. Maharishi has returned and the caravan continues on to Benares University. It's ten minutes to the campus, where wide streets and spacious grounds open out into a welcome feeling of light and air. We arrive at the University Guest House and carry our luggage upstairs. As we come back down, the inviting sound of Maharishi's laughter reaches out to us from the main room. He is sitting inside, talking with a number of people from the local World Plan Center. We come in and stand to the side for a few minutes, and I don't think I have ever been happier to be around him. After the crowding and confusion of the city streets, Maharishi's joy and serenity have a clearly soothing effect. It's becoming more obvious to me why people enjoy just being with him, why they like to sit quietly in his presence.

Maharishi, of course, is focused on his work. He finishes up the meeting and is driven off to the first of three lectures. It is to the faculty of the university, a talk he delivers in a packed five-hundred-seat auditorium. Next, sitting on a brightly decorated platform in the late afternoon light, he speaks to about twenty-five hundred students who have gathered on a lawn in the midst of a lush garden. Then, after dinner, he goes to the medical school and speaks to both the faculty and students in one of the steeply sloping lecture halls typical of a medical classroom anywhere.

These three talks are among the most challenging I have ever heard him give. He comments on this himself several times during the day. When Maharishi first began his teaching years ago he expressed himself in reasonably soft terms, offering the possibility for enlightenment to those individuals who would like to try it. Since the research has become so convincing, however, and since the World Plan has advanced to the stage where teaching large populations has become feasible, his tone has become very direct. "It's possible now to bring the world out of problems and suffering," he says, "and it is the responsibility of society's leaders to make this program available to the people."

Here at Benares University, he is speaking to a very receptive audience. The city of Benares is India's most famous center of scholarship on the Vedas—India's ancient literature—and Benares University has become the first school in the country to establish a Center for Yoga, a center devoted to scientific research on ancient techniques for developing human potential.

Westerners usually think of "yoga" as a set of physical exercises or postures. In fact, the word yoga means union (it is the forerunner to the English word "yoke") and it embraces many different types of techniques, including physical postures, breathing exercises and various forms of mental practices. Any technique aimed at bringing about a union between man's surface, excited states of consciousness, and the state of least excitation of consciousness deep within, could properly be called a technique of yoga. There are many such techniques and the question is basically one of relative efficiency—which technique works the fastest for the most people? Here at Benares University, a start has been made on investigating these questions. India is beginning to take its own heritage seriously.

Since the people here are already beginning to think about a science of enlightenment, Maharishi doesn't have to go through a lot of groundwork. He has a technique which anyone can use to achieve this state of union quickly and easily, a technique backed up by hundreds of research studies exactly like the people here are planning to begin now. In a sense his appearance fulfills the purposes of the Center for Yoga in one stroke. At the conclusion of each talk he challenges both students and faculty not just to begin the Transcendental Meditation Technique, but to take a teacher training course immediately and begin to work to bring the entire continent of India rapidly to the Age of Enlightenment.

"Benares University is known as 'The Capitol of Knowledge,'" Maharishi says. "It was established to allow the light of life to go out from here. Give me your time for a teacher training course and we'll make this ideal a living reality. We'll make Benares University the sunshine of the nation."

The response during the lecture is enthusiastic. The applauding audience picks up the challenge almost like audiences at political rallies. More importantly, the enthusiasm is translated immediately into concrete action. Working in a small conference after the speeches with senior members of the faculty, including the heads of the medical sciences department and the Center for Yoga, Maharishi sets up a teacher training course to be given on campus starting a week hence. He assigns one of his most capable teachers to the course. In Benares, always the leader of Vedic scholarship in India, ancient knowledge is becoming a practical reality again.

It's a satisfying day, watching Maharishi get this practical, energetic response. I wondered how India would react to him this time, and this is one answer.

"**T**he activity at Benares University was very gratifying," Maharishi says. "The Science of Creative Intelligence is being taught in many universities now. It's so important that this knowledge be made available through every school, because it is obvious that for decades, for centuries, something fundamental has been missing from educational systems. Education has been facing so many problems. The quality of life that is expected in an educated man does not seem to develop."

What do you think the problem has been?

"Education has
concentrated on
expanding the
amount of
knowledge
without doing
anything to
expand the
container of
knowledge—the
consciousness of
the student."

"If we look at the present system of education, what we see is that it excites the thirst for knowledge without ever satisfying it. A man studies his field for years, but what he finds is the more he knows, the more he finds a larger field of the unknown unfolding before him. The more he knows, the more he doesn't know. What is growing is ignorance of his subject. The man is left in despair because he is unable to satisfy his thirst for knowledge. This is from one angle. From another angle, present education teaches all the different subjects, but the learners are not prepared to enjoy the learning. Why do so many students leave education at an early age? Children should want to run to the school, but if a student is dull, he is afraid. Every morning his mother has to say, 'Now come on, take this book and go to school.' But the student is not very clear-minded, he is afraid. All this pressure comes from outside—from home and society—and it pushes him into school and what he does is revolt against the teacher, revolt against the teaching, revolt against everything. Knowledge is not fulfilling, education is not attractive."

But why not? What is missing?

"Education has concentrated on expanding the amount of knowledge without doing anything to expand the container of knowledge."

The container of knowledge?

"By that we mean the consciousness of the student. You see, if we look into the process of gaining knowledge we find that there are two sides to it. One side is the object and the other side is the subject—there might be a rose, for instance, and then the man who views the rose. The present system of education provides the knowledge of the objective field, but what it misses is the knowledge of the subject, the knowledge of the *knower*. And when the knower is in ignorance about himself, then any knowledge he has can only be nonfulfilling. The whole structure of knowledge is baseless."

You are saying that the consciousness of the student is the basis of knowledge?

"Very obviously. When the mind is dull, when the knower is sleepy, then knowledge is something different than it is when one is wide awake. Knowledge is different in different states of consciousness. We could see a beautiful rose when we are in the waking state of consciousness, but if the consciousness changes and we experience the dream state of consciousness the beautiful rose could become a banyan tree. Yet another state of consciousness, the sleep state, and nothing is there at all. No experience. Knowledge is different in different states of consciousness."

So an educational system must do something to raise the level of consciousness of the student.

"Of course, the field of consciousness is that field where all knowledge gets deposited. This is why we say consciousness is the home of all knowledge. If we want to know about a rose, we look at it and the image of the rose goes to the retina of the eye and then moves on to sit on the level of

"If one knows the
ocean, then one
knows the basis
of all waves. If
one knows pure
consciousness,
then one knows
the basis of all
knowledge."

consciousness. All these impulses of information enter our senses and reach deep within to be deposited on our consciousness. Knowledge is *structured* in consciousness. And if knowledge is structured in consciousness, then obviously education must do something to bring the knowledge of our consciousness to our awareness. Otherwise, why build something if you don't dig the foundation? Why have an educational system if the education is going to be baseless?"

How does the Science of Creative Intelligence fill this need?

"It provides theoretical knowledge about the field of pure consciousness and a practical technique to experience that pure field directly. This puts the student in touch with the source of thought, the home of all knowledge, and then both sides of the process of knowing are open to the students' awareness. The object and the subject are both available. Consciousness is developed at the same time as knowledge is gained. Education expands the container as well as fills it. The point is, the development of pure consciousness is very important to any student. It's like the pure surface of a mirror without any dust. On that pure surface knowledge is reflected in its purity."

This would account for the research showing that students do better in school.

"Yes, there are many scientific studies to show that with the Transcendental Meditation Technique, intelligence goes up, memory improves, the students get better grades. And then education becomes interesting, because it is success that is interesting. If a man is walking, he keeps on taking steps and soon finds that he has gone a mile. Good. One mile covered. But if he is walking and somehow the globe moves with him, then he is in the same place all the time. Soon he will stop walking. Because it is success that is interesting. It is success that is charming, that is enticing. A man who meets with success just doesn't bother with anything. It doesn't matter if he is criticized, it doesn't matter if he is honored, but with every step of success, the charm increases, and the man just keeps moving forward in the steps of evolution."

Still, it would never be possible for a student to master all the knowledge in all the fields of education.

"No, no. But it's possible to enjoy the *fruit* of all knowledge, to structure the *home* of all knowledge in our awareness."

What is meant by that?

"If one knows the ocean, then one knows the basis of all waves. If one knows pure consciousness, then one knows the basis of all knowledge. From that pure level, that level of stillness—like the ripples rising from the still surface of the ocean—all thoughts arise. So on that basis, one becomes at home with all knowledge. And this is the highest goal of education. Every teacher wants his students to enjoy life in as high a state of consciousness as possible, and now it is possible to create the physiology and psychology such that every student can think and act from the level of enlightenment. When the Science of Creative Intelligence is taught in all the schools, then this will be the call of education—that all people should live life in the waves of happiness and fulfillment. Students will develop within themselves that source of all thought and then they can study anything. They'll really enjoy what knowledge is. No student will fall back. And the Ph.D. of tomorrow will be more than just a specialist—a mathematician or physicist or doctor. He'll be a universal man."

This morning's meeting promises to be an exciting one. We are back in Delhi and, by two-continent coincidence, the same week Maharishi decided to come to India, the Indian government has decided to hold a three-day hearing on the topic "Yoga and Science." The meeting is in one of the upstairs meeting rooms in the Vigyam Bhavan, the same building Maharishi used three days ago.

Although the agenda was already full, the conference organizers have opened up half an hour for Maharishi to speak at ten thirty. We arrive at ten fifteen and enter the large semi-circular room. There is a dais along the flat end of the room and Maharishi is ushered to a seat at the head table on that platform. In the concentric circles of seats facing the dais there are over three hundred people, an audience made up of scientists, educators and members of the government's ministry of Health and Family Planning. Apparently India's awakening interest in her own heritage is not confined to Benares University.

As we settle down to listen, however, it soon seems that enlightenment is not making much headway in these hearings. Misinformation and mystic triviality have dominated the field for centuries, and these proceedings seem not to have escaped the general decline. We catch the end of a vague talk by a man who says he once saw someone bend metal without touching it, and the moderator projects an air of resigned clock-watching as he introduces the next speaker. If anyone in the room expects to hear striking new ideas today, it's not apparent at this point.

Maharishi sits on the dais waiting quietly for his turn. Since he does not appear on the printed agenda, it seems likely that many of the people don't know who he is. It feels as though he will have to tone down his talk to reach the soporific level of these proceedings, and I find myself wondering how he will begin—with health, perhaps, or the idea of stress release. When his turn comes, however, I find he isn't thinking that way at all.

"It is a great joy to see how quickly the Age of Enlightenment will come," he begins, "when a powerful government like that of India is prepared to take action."

There's a certain stirring in the room. Eyes seem to focus a little and the moderator looks sharply down the row of speakers toward Maharishi.

"The age of science," Maharishi continues, "has advanced enough in this historic generation of mankind to point out for us the locality from which all laws of nature are controlled. This is the vacuum state, the state of least excitation. And when the science of yoga is there to make this state a living reality on the level of our consciousness, then this is the Eureka! for an Age of Enlightenment."

Maharishi is smiling, but he's speaking in his strongest tones, cutting into the dullness collected in the room.

"On what basis am I saying these things?" he continues. "I am not talking in the air. This is not just some mood of good will. Everything I am saying is on the basis of more than a million people practicing the Transcendental Meditation Technique around the world by now. Everything I am saying is on the basis of all these hundreds of scientific experiments that have been conducted so far. And what I am saying is that if the government will just come along, if we can establish the Transcendental Meditation Technique everywhere in society, within one year I can promise the beginning of an ideal society, the beginning of an ideal nation in India."

By now the room is alive with whispered conversations and waving hands. Maharishi moves ahead with a pointed analysis of India's difficulties and the solution available at the level of consciousness. By the end of his speech the level of interest in the room is manifesting itself obviously. In the tightly packed schedule of the hearing, however, there is no time for discussion. With the room still buzzing, the next speaker steps up, an elderly yogi with a written statement. In flat, dull tones he speaks out the conventional wisdom: yoga takes years of discipline and effort to produce results; it is the path for those who choose to renounce society, not for those who wish to improve society.

The meeting soon breaks for lunch. It seems a shame that with such an influential audience, there was no time for questions and discussion to follow up Maharishi's presentation. He has come on this tour to stimulate action, especially among responsible leaders in society, but it takes more than half an hour to break down centuries of preconceptions.

Back at the hotel someone asks Maharishi if he was upset with the yogi who had presented the standard ideas.

"No, no, we don't mind," he says. "There must be differences when there is a whole galaxy of yogis. What was a joy was that I got a chance to say what I wanted to say."

Most of us seem a little subdued, but Maharishi doesn't appear upset. He's laughing and talking about the afternoon's appointments. But there comes a moment when he stops and looks over to the man who had arranged his speaking engagement at the hearing.

"There will be another time to talk this weekend?" he asks.

"No, Maharishi," is the reply, "the schedule is full."

"Yes," Maharishi says. His palms are drumming lightly on the table in front of him.

"Maharishi," says someone else in the group. "I have today's schedule. It says that this afternoon there is supposed to be a general discussion at 4:30."

A big smile answers that.

"A discussion?" His hands tap the table again.

"This is a very good thing. I should *be* there."

In a few minutes, he goes into his own room for a private meeting, and a number of us head out for a lunch that seems suddenly more appetizing. Enlightenment may get a hearing after all.

Three hours of waiting build our expectations again, but by the time we arrive at the Vigyam Bhavan it's apparent the machinery of government is still grinding slowly. We arrive at four thirty but no move to discussion is at all evident. A seemingly endless series of speakers is shuttling up and down from the dais and each of them is limited rigorously to five minutes by the moderator. Too many speakers have been scheduled and the moderator's often stated goal is simply, "This meeting will end promptly at six."

Limiting this particular group of speakers to five minutes does not seem unwise, actually. The level of contribution has slipped again toward stories about men who can stare at the sun without blinking, or perform alchemy on base metals. A cynical attitude toward the whole proceeding becomes more and more understandable. Finally, the moderator calls on a man with an M.D. after his name. A tall, fiftiesh man in a grey suit strides up to the microphone and gives vent to the frustrations of many in the audience.

"I came here to hear a conference on 'Yoga and Science'," he says with emphasis. "And what I want to know is, where is the science?"

Applause breaks out in many parts of the room.

"Where are the research papers?" the doctor goes on. "If yogis can turn stone into gold, then for heaven's sake, give a demonstration and the finance minister will rush up and embrace you."

Some life stirs again in the room, but the moderator moves on without comment.

"It's ten to six," he says. "One more speaker is scheduled, and then the Maharishi would like to have a few words."

There are only a few minutes left when the final speaker finishes. Maharishi mounts the dais and sits down behind the microphone. It is hard to see what he can accomplish in just a few minutes.

"My purpose in coming now," he says, "is that perhaps I have spoken things this morning that were beyond comprehension, or that sounded impractical. And so I was very glad to hear the doctor just now saying that what is needed is scientific proof. There is almost nothing that can't be measured today, and it's my joy to say that all the benefits of the Transcendental Meditation Technique have been tested and proved in the great laboratories of the West."

As Maharishi is speaking, several of the people from the Delhi World Plan Center are moving around in the audience, passing out the new research booklets. People reach for them eagerly, and turn the pages as Maharishi talks. With some credibility established, he sits back comfortably in his chair.

"There is no longer any doubt about it," he says, "and so I have come back for discussion with all the great minds assembled here. If there are any questions, I would be glad to deal with them."

The voices of three people who stand immediately are drowned out by the moderator.

"Maharishi!" he says in a startled tone. "It's six o'clock now. The meeting is coming to an end."

Maharishi turns to the moderator, but the microphone still picks up his words.

"Such an illustrious audience gathers only rarely," he says. "It will be so fascinating to go into the scientific basis for this teaching. Because the conclusion is that we can create an ideal world."

The moderator looks over his shoulder at several of the other officials sitting on the dais.

"I don't know if this is possible," he says. But some action is clearly going to be necessary. The meeting is starting to come apart. A number of people in the audience are still standing, trying to call out questions. Many more have left their seats to walk down toward the front to speak to Maharishi privately if possible. Apparently an objectively verified technology for evolution seems to be what most of these people are interested in. With the noise level in the room rising rapidly, Maharishi turns back toward the microphone.

"Then if this is not a good time," he says, "we can work something out. We should have a special session with both the scientists and the yogis. We must not lose this opportunity to go deep into this subject. I am staying at the Ashoka Hotel and we can meet there tomorrow."

"Yes, good," the moderator says quickly. "Very good. So now this meeting . . ." The microphones go dead in the midst of his adjournment, but his announcement is superfluous anyway. The hearing has effectively broken up already. Much of the audience is milling in front of the dais and Maharishi is talking with those who can get close to him. And the real measure of the interest Maharishi has generated comes that evening and all the next day. The meeting room at the Ashoka Hotel is continuously overcrowded with visitors, most of whom are ready to act. One of the more important is a woman who is the President of the Indian Federation of the United Nations Association. She not only plans with Maharishi how to use her UN contacts, but offers to give a speech on the Transcendental Meditation Technique at the European Conference for the Women's International Year, where she will be chairperson.

Another government representative, an official in the education department, comes both days to outline the procedures the government could employ to train teachers of the Transcendental Meditation Technique in every province of the country. A large group of scientists and medical doctors, including the government's advisor on Yoga and Health, and the Director of the National Institute of Neuro-Sciences, spends the better part of an afternoon with Maharishi. By the end of the meeting there is a schedule for a ten-day "think tank" session later in the summer, to which each of the men here will invite his most respected colleagues.

In addition, two important educators are here, men who each operate a string of private secondary schools. One man's schools specialize in Indian culture, and the other is nationally famous for his innovative educational approaches.

"Why can't we teach the Transcendental Medication Technique in the schools?" this latter gentleman wants to know.

"We can, we can," Maharishi says. "The courses have been structured to teach children physics, literature, chemistry—all subjects in the light of the Science of Creative Intelligence."

"Can you start with children of eleven and twelve," the educator asks, "so that when they graduate they will be ready to teach this material themselves?"

"Of course. The Transcendental Meditation Technique is so easy, from the age of ten the children can do it."

"To an educator, this is tremendously challenging."

Maharishi smiles broadly. "Very challenging," he says. "The scientific research is beyond doubt. Now it is the duty of society's leaders to take action."

"I am ready to do what you want," the man concludes. "We can use my schools as a starting point."

Once again the response is positive and action-oriented. India has been slow to start, but the progress is coming more quickly now. Maharishi is showing India to herself in the mirror of technology.

"It is good to see the governments becoming interested in this field," Maharishi says later. "Governments face so many problems, and the history of governments is so disappointing."

Even modern governments are disappointing?

"All governments today have such beautiful constitutions. The constitutions are ideal, but the achievements are not up to the dignity of the constitutions in any part of the world. With all the power, with all the

THE TM TECHNIQUE AND GOVERNMENT

"If the people
begin to perform
action from the
level of perfect
order, then their
actions will be
more orderly.
Then the
legislature will
make more
orderly
decisions."

national resources, with all the good will of the people, with all the highly intelligent experts assembled to handle every field, yet no government has been able to create a society free from suffering."

Governments do try different programs to solve specific problems.

"Yes, and it's the experience of every unit of government, of every member of a legislature, that with all the good will and expert minds, still the results of these actions are not so profound as they are intended. And many times, whatever the government wants, it brings opposite results. There is some progress, some success here and there, and these small areas of success keep the government breathing. Otherwise the situation is that any sincere leader must die of heart failure. The leaders may be so conscientious but the problems are so many."

Presumably you would want to see every government install programs in the Science of Creative Intelligence for all its members, to upgrade the abilities of the individuals running the government.

"This is from one angle. It is the individual that matters. Every department of a government is handled by individuals and it all depends on the ingenuity of the individual, on the comprehension of the individual, on the reaction of the individual to the need of the nation. And it goes without saying that if the individuals of an organization are alert and fresh in their thinking and full of heart, then anything they would like to achieve will be easier to achieve. This is one angle, but it is not the most important one."

What is?

"We have to ask why it is that governments can't achieve their aspirations, and what we find is that it's the total influence of all the people in the nation that makes the difference. Success or lack of success by the government is just an indication of how people are behaving in their private lives in that country."

You mean even the people outside the government—how they act affects government action?

"If the people in the country are disorderly, only the fruit of disorderly action will come to the nation. If the people create chaos in society, then this can only result in chaos in government. So much that comes to a nation comes through the organization of a government, and if the people are chaotic, the government itself will be chaotic, making wrong decisions, delivering wrong things to the people. The government is like a channel produced by the activities of the nation, and through that channel flows what the people in a country deserve."

But what if a government is corrupt?

"Then it reflects the total corruption of all the people in the nation. The government is innocent always—it can only deliver what the people deserve. The government is the consolidated destiny of the nation."

How can we know this is true?

"Every experienced member of a legislature would know this from his own experience. A man with little experience, a new man standing to be elected as a member from his area, may have a great desire for accomplishment. 'If I become a legislator,' he might say, 'I will accomplish many things. Other men couldn't do it, but if I become a legislator, I will.' The same man, full of enthusiasm and ambitious for his community, when he comes to the legislature and sits there, he finds his whole thinking changes. And this is always the case. So many legislators are beautiful people—when you have them to your home for dinner they are so intelligent and full of good will—but when they sit in the legislature, what they do is so different. And this has always embarrassed the leaders of the communities in different parts of the world, that they are not able to think in the halls of government what they are able to think at home. And it's because their influence gets tossed about by the effects produced by all the people in a nation."

This would mean that the government would have to teach the Transcendental Meditation Program to people outside the government, too.

"This is the solution. Members of a government, when they find that their decisions are not bringing completely good results, they must run back to their people and get them to meditate. Teach people to use the Transcendental Meditation Technique and see that they start to function from that state of least excitation. Order is infinite at that level, and if the people begin to perform action from that level then their actions will be more orderly. And with the effect of that increased order in society, when the members come back to the legislature they will make more orderly decisions. Actions of the government will be full of reward."

Is orderliness all that is needed? Does an increase in orderliness necessarily produce greater progress?

"Every successful administrator knows if an action is orderly, the effects are going to be more successful than a disorderly action will ever produce. Success depends on orderliness of thinking and action. Everything in nature is orderly—everything is evolutionary because it has its basis in orderliness. And this is what we desire, that every nation, and every leader of a nation, should act perfectly in accordance with all the laws of nature."

So when we look at the whole—at the entire nation and its government—the way to improve it is by improving the parts, by improving the quality of life for the individual.

"Yes, and in the case of individual life, it is the holistic value—that pure level of consciousness that is unbounded, infinite, the field of all possibilities—that brings the orderly influence. So, from the side of the whole society, it is the individual that counts; from the side of the individual, it is wholeness that counts. It's a beautiful picture of complementarity governing the life of a society."

Do you think governments will act quickly to spread this knowledge?

"Many governments are already acting. In every government, the health department, the education department, the commerce department—all these departments are always ready to use any useful new technique. This is one purpose of inaugurating the Dawn of the Age of Enlightenment on all five continents, to let the leaders know that they must come out of failures and that now they can *enjoy* leading the people. And when nature supports the activity of the individuals, that will be the might, that will be the strength, of every nation. By improving the quality of life of every individual, all the aspirations of every government can be achieved."

Out to the West: Evolution in Progressive Societies

This is Bombay, our last stop in India. As if to gather momentum for our long jump back to the West, Maharishi is being driven rapidly around the city to give six lectures and a press conference in fifteen hours. Here, as everywhere we have been this week, high-level acceptance seems to be coming rapidly. Two of the most positive meetings of the day are with the Bombay Chamber of Commerce and the Indian Medical Association.

As we ride with Maharishi, the city sights start to reset our awareness for the West. More than anywhere we have been in India, the architecture in Bombay recalls India's once colonial status. Swelling Victorian buildings fill the main section of town, with baroque decorations dripping from roofs and window sills. A definite flavor of London is increased by several large traffic circles with centered statues. It's still India, no doubt of that—much of the heavy traffic is pushcarts and people balancing loads on their heads—but it's fitting that London is where we will stop next.

We arrived in Bombay late last night after the two-day series of conferences at the Ashoka Hotel in Delhi. Bombay is India's leading commercial city, and Maharishi felt it was worthwhile to squeeze in a day here. Lurching through these crowded streets is no easy endurance test, however. We are much further south now, and an oppressive wet heat hangs heavy in the air. The only one of us to take the day in stride is Maharishi—he seems as fresh at the last evening lecture as he was at the first one at nine this morning.

The setting for this last lecture is decidedly the best of the day—a penthouse garden twenty-five stories up into Bombay's evening breezes—and the soft grey-blue glow of the city's lights provides a backdrop to a lively interchange of ideas. The audience consists of more than a hundred businessmen and their wives, people invited by our host, V. K. Khandelwal, a Bombay industrialist. The questions that come have a personal touch.

> The setting for this last lecture is decidedly the best of the day—a penthouse garden twenty-five stories up into Bombay's evening breezes.

99

"Mistakes are of
the past, and
what is past is
past. Now we
have that formula
for uniting the
inner values of
life with the outer
values and so we
just go ahead."

"Maharishi," one lady asks, "you say we only need to do the Transcendental Meditation Technique and then go about our daily life. But is that really enough? Sometimes we feel that we have already done so much wrong in our life that there is no hope for us."

"It will be all right," Maharishi says. "There is no reason to feel desperate because great promise is ahead. Mistakes are of the past, and what is past is past. Now we have that formula for uniting the inner values of life with the outer values, and so we just go ahead. It is a waste of time to think about past actions, whether good or bad."

"You say the Dawn is coming," says someone else. "But isn't it also true that the night will follow the day?"

"What is coming now is the daylight. We don't mind if cycles are there, if darkness will come again. We are only glad to be able to enjoy the Dawn."

"When was the last Age of Enlightenment?" asks the same man.

"History does not record it. The history we have is all of suffering and struggle."

"But you said there are cycles in history."

"Then the last Age of Enlightenment must have been before the beginning of recorded history," Maharishi says. He stops and then smiles.

"It gives us the feeling that when the Age of Enlightenment comes, it will be with us for a long time."

The meeting concludes about eleven. When it does, we follow Maharishi's daylong momentum straight to the airport. As fast as we've been traveling on this trip up to now, the rest of it will be faster yet. In the next four days, Maharishi will be working on three different continents.

When we flew out to India, the trip had a hazy, dream-like quality, an evocation of time traveling. But the ride back is almost straight sleep consciousness, and that makes the transition this time seem quite sudden. Early morning brings a plane change in Rome and we receive breakfast from a crisp Swiss crew on the way over the Alps. When we arrive in Zurich, Maharishi and several members of the party take a small plane for Vittel, France, where Maharishi has twenty-four hours of work to accomplish at a teacher training course. The rest of us keep flying west, one more leg to London, and when we arrive we step out into an invigorating new atmosphere.

As we leave the plane, the sodden heat memories of Bombay are wiped away by a brief, chilling blitz of snow. Once inside the terminal we are braced again by a spontaneous display of that jolly good cheer I thought the British put only in movies. It's a refreshing change. The Indians we have known recently are gracious and warm, but with a certain dignity and formality. As we meet the everyday English, on the other hand—taxi drivers, hotel attendants, shop keepers—the exchanges are all off-hand and jovial, as though they feel good humor is a national product. Some of the buildings here may look like Bombay, but architecture and attitudes don't always go together.

The first scheduled event in London is a meeting with the local media. There is a press conference scheduled for the next afternoon at the Royal Festival Hall, a modernistic concrete outcropping on the banks of the majestic Thames river. The conference should give us a clear indication of how quickly Maharishi's announcement of the new age will actually be accepted in the West because the British press has usually given Maharishi a hard time in the past. Not that they have singled him out specially. Newspapers in England are known for their irreverence toward public figures, domestic and otherwise. From reports I've heard, the previous press conferences Maharishi has had here have been quite disorderly.

With this background in mind, preparations for today's conference have been thorough. Press kits have been prepared, including research booklets, newspaper coverage from other countries, and letters of recommendation from political, industrial and religious leaders. In addition, two psychiatrists and two physicists will share the podium with Maharishi to personify the modern validation of his traditional teaching. The conference is scheduled to start at three, and the plan is to have Maharishi and the experts talk until nearly four. Many of the reporters have said they must leave by then. The idea is to keep the presentation informative as long as possible, before opening up to the potentially frivolous questions from the audience.

The problem with this idea is that Maharishi doesn't know about it. In fact, Maharishi isn't even here. His work at the teacher training course has been accomplished, but the last we heard, weather was shutting down regularly scheduled flights from the Continent. He may have to take a small jet direct from Vittel to London.

It's already a few minutes past three. This large, low-ceilinged room off the main lobby was empty two hours ago, but now it has filled with teachers of the Transcendental Meditation Technique and more than forty representatives of the local media, including reporters from all of the major newspapers and the British Broadcasting Company. As the time goes by, the situation becomes slightly uncomfortable. With pencils tapping on pads and cameras looking blankly for subjects, one of the members of the World Plan Executive Council steps up to the microphone.

"Maharishi's flight has been held up by the weather," he begins, "and we are not sure when he will arrive."

There is a stir in the back of the room where many teachers are standing. An unmistakable voice comes from the door.

"I *am* here," the voice says.

People are shuffling back to form an aisle and Maharishi walks in with his arms full of flowers, smiling brightly at the small battery of cameras and movie lights. As if it were planned, a slight inconvenience has become a well-timed entry. Maharishi walks to the front of the room where a couch has been prepared for him.

"So," he says as he sits down, "it is a great joy to meet the press of this great nation and bring the news that a good time is coming for the world. We prefer to call it an Age of Enlightenment, a time when people will not be groping in the darkness to find the basis of success and fulfillment in life."

A quick check around the room shows that the reporters are writing down his words, at least. Maharishi goes on with a brief introductory speech.

"The Age of Enlightenment will be a time when people won't make mistakes," he says, "when individuals will not be a curse to the whole nation. I'm aware it sounds unorthodox to say that such an age is coming. But if the orthodox tradition has been ignorance and suffering, then an Age of Enlightenment must *be* unorthodox. We know we are surrounded by problems, but now we have the procedure whereby the trends of time can be reversed."

He goes on briskly for about twenty minutes, and then stops for a moment.

"I'm so full of joy at this beautiful time I could just keep talking," he says. "People should just interrupt me for questions."

There's another short pause. Maharishi has stopped much earlier than we expected. A reporter stands up in front, a large man in a dignified suit.

"Maharishi," he says, "let's assume the phenomenon of the Transcendental Meditation Technique is accepted. After all, the research is quite persuasive. My question is this: Is there any theory that accounts for the way this phenomenon operates?"

It's a direct, positive question. Maharishi looks over to the scientists sitting on his left.

"Perhaps Dr. Clements would like to answer that question," he says.

Dr. Geoffrey Clements is the physicist from Sussex University. In his beautifully modeled English accent, he answers the question with a quick condensation of the parallels between the state of least excitation in physics and the state of least excitation of consciousness. When he is done, he passes the microphone to Dr. Byron Rigby, the psychiatrist who works at Guy's Hospital in London. Dr. Rigby extends the point to discuss what the state of least excitation means for the physical nervous system.

"It's at a mechanical level," he says. "During the practice of the Transcendental Meditation Technique, the nervous system appears to de-excite itself, to generate less random activity than it does during waking or sleeping. And it is fascinating that subjectively the picture is similar. A person practicing the Transcendental Meditation Technique notices that the pressure of random thought diminishes—there are fewer self-interruptions in the thought process. This is reflected in the person's behavior which becomes more coherent and purposeful."

102

Another reporter, an older woman, is interested in the brief exposition Maharishi has made about the decline of crime in cities where one per cent of the population is meditating.

"Won't we have to emphasize the criminal segments of society?" she asks. "Won't these people have to start meditating?"

Dr. Rigby still has the microphone.

"It is not necessary," he says. "We don't imagine that in those cities where the one per cent phenomenon has appeared, it is the criminals who have started. All that is necessary is to have a reasonable number of people meditating in a reasonably fluid community. Then the orderly influence from the meditators propagates into their environment naturally."

The conference continues at the same level. The quality of the questioning is a satisfying surprise and the exchange runs forty-five minutes past the four o'clock deadline before anybody makes a move to leave. One sort of climax is provided by a reporter inexplicably versed in physics who asks a long question about the possibilities of quantum phenomena in the brain. It is fitting that the Nobel Laureate in physics, Dr. Brian Josephson, is there to take the question. With dark-rimmed glasses and slightly tousled hair, Dr. Josephson looks the part of the esoteric professor. I don't know how many people can follow his answer—I know I can't—but the concluding nod from his questioner strengthens the presentation for everybody.

The final question of the conference concerns the impact of the Age of Enlightenment on different political systems.

"Isn't the Transcendental Meditation Technique more suited to the type of governmental systems we have in the West?" asks a younger reporter.

"We have a World Plan," says Maharishi, "a plan for all mankind. If the people in a certain country believe in a certain system, what we want is for that system to be successful in that country. Our aim is not to change any systems. It's such a waste of energy that capitalism fights communism and all that. History records that no system is profound, no system has yet brought fulfillment either for individuals or the society. So we don't try to think which system is best. What we want is to improve the quality of life for the individual, and then every system will find fulfillment in its own right. When every individual rises to full potential, then every system will be successful and peace and harmony will prevail everywhere in the world."

A vision of world peace seems the correct way to end this optimistic meeting. During the properly English tea-and-biscuit conclusion to the conference, a casually-dressed man comes over to me at the serving table. He introduces himself as a reporter from a paper in a small town north of London. He's smiling as he pours some tea.

"It's so different from what I expected," he says. "Science and spirituality at one time—it will just melt the cynics."

There couldn't have been a more encouraging re-entry to the West.

Maharishi (lower left) presides at an Inauguration ceremony in Albert Hall in London.

Although acceptance in India has been gratifying, Maharishi still believes the Dawn will have to come first in the more advanced technological countries. It's good to know that news of an Age of Enlightenment seems to be news people want to hear.

After the press conference, there is only time for meditation and a quick meal back at the hotel before the evening ceremony which the London World Plan Center has scheduled to inaugurate the Dawn of the Age of Enlightenment for all of Europe. The schedule is tight because we leave tomorrow for Canada where there is another such presentation on the following day for North America. Tonight's meeting should be a relaxing time, however, more of a ratification than an inauguration. In contrast to the challenge presented by the forty anonymous media people this afternoon, the audience this evening will be forty-five hundred meditators coming to enjoy something of a family reunion.

The ceremony is to be held in Albert Hall, a nineteenth century London landmark sited a few blocks down the street from our hotel. It's a large, circular brick building built by Queen Victoria for her Prince Albert. The walk down from the hotel features the gracefully aging London landscape, brick and stone buildings that sit together well and seem to give a structural meaning to the word "civilization."

As lecture time approaches, the night turns cold and blustery, with touches of snow brightening the air beneath the street lamps. Heavily coated groups of people hurry down the street and through the outer door of the Hall. The lobby becomes a large meeting ground. People of all ages — children, parents, and grandparents—stop to enjoy the happy talk and smiling hugs common to old friends come in from the cold.

Inside, the hall is magnificent, a sweeping oval canyon decorated in maroon and gold gilt. Two-thirds of the floor is filled with chairs and at one end is a large stage decorated by the London World Plan Center with banners and posters declaring the Dawn. Static clouds of flowers sweep up from each side of the stage to the place where Maharishi will sit.

Then, as I approach the stage, I find Maharishi is already sitting there. He is silent, eyes closed, waiting while the last of the audience comes in and the other speakers find their places. Somehow the quiet pause is a powerful moment. We have seen Maharishi moving so quickly through so many unusual settings these last few days—in steel-cold airport waiting rooms and wilting traffic jams, in government hearings and university lecture halls. It feels right to see him sitting again in a dignified setting, ready to speak to people who are already enjoying the benefits of his teaching.

When the hall has settled down and the intercontinental hurry of the past two days has completely dispelled, Maharishi begins in a tone of voice that is soft and serene. This is an audience that needs no convincing, and his talk is more of a peaceful affirmation than a dynamic exposition. Even when a couple of the scientists take their turn, the evening keeps the serene feeling.

After the speeches are done, Maharishi asks for a moment that seems the perfect way to ratify his vision of the Dawn. There's a slight rustling in the auditorium as everyone gets comfortable, and then forty-five hundred people meditate together.

"It is so beautiful to see all the people come to inaugurate the Dawn," Maharishi says later. "All people of different ages enjoy the Transcendental Meditation Technique. It is important for all ages to enjoy these benefits. Otherwise what we find is a dangerous gap growing between the generations."

Concern about the "generation gap" has been growing for more than a decade.

"That concern is very natural. And given the present system of education, the gap is inevitable."

Why is that?

"What happens is that a man grows, he goes to school, and then at the age of twenty or twenty-five he is put out in a practical field. He plunges into the field of action and soon he is out of the habit of gaining knowledge. And the thing is, in a scientific age, new knowledge is coming all the time. Every

THE TM
TECHNIQUE AND
THE FAMILY

"The older
generation is
expected to be in
higher
consciousness. If
society has no
system to develop
such broader
comprehension,
then the value of
life begins to be
outdated very
soon."

ten years, every five years, the progress in engineering and technology in every field is so great that the world seems to be a completely different place. A man who is older, who no longer is gaining knowledge, is soon out of date. It's not that the youngsters don't want to respect their elders but that the elders fail to prove their utility."

The gap that is created is a very painful one for many families.

"Yes, it's such a pain to the heart of the parent that the children don't listen. The only desire of parents is to see their children grow up independent, successful and happy in their lives. And the parents think their guidance can really save the children from many pitfalls; but the children won't listen because there isn't any real substance there. There is no question of advice that is coming from higher consciousness, from a more evolved consciousness. And this is a pain for the children, also. Youngsters always want ideals, and if they have the ideal of living in their mother and in their father, then spontaneously their whole emotions and psychology are guided toward that ideal. The proper sprouting of a tree is so important. And if the parents are not able to uphold that ideal, then the children are sure to go astray. The only answer for it is the infusion of pure consciousness."

Meditation as a preparation for parenthood?

"This is the way to keep pace with the progress of modern civilization. This is the way that the older generation will never leave their youth. By practicing the Transcendental Meditation Technique, every day they will be losing their stress. Every day they will be gathering more and more of the value of pure consciousness, of the purity of life, of the effectiveness of life, of the support of nature. The elderly segment of society will only become more valuable to society with the passage of time."

The children will be meditating, too.

"But the children will never be able to catch up. They will always remain behind, not because anybody wishes them to but because there is a gap in time. They have not had as long a time to meditate, and so they have not yet had the time to develop as great a value of pure consciousness. And so every growing father and mother will be ideals to their children. In every expression of the parents, in every breath of the parents, the children will see something laudable, something they would like to imitate. They will see that the parents are happier every day, that their thinking is clear and profound. They may take a problem to their father and he will say, 'This is no problem. Just go this way.' And the result will be that the children will not have to face defeat or failure. They will not have to suffer because the older generation will have the ability to truly guide and protect them."

Then the practice of the Transcendental Meditation Technique helps people discharge their family and social obligations?

"This is looking at it from one angle. The older generation is *expected* to be in higher consciousness. When the society has no system to develop such broader comprehension, to develop greater purity of mind and heart, then the value of life begins to be outdated very soon—at the age of forty or fifty, perhaps—and this is a great loss to society. But now we have a procedure whereby, with the passing of the days and nights, very naturally a man rises to levels of more profound awareness, of broadened foresight and intuition."

If the older generation has developed greater wisdom, what will be the role of the younger generation?

"The youngsters will still study the new waves of knowledge in science and technology. The youngsters will run about and do the work, and the elders will guide all for the well-being and progress of society. This will be a complete society. There will be sound integration between head and hands. Otherwise, if the elderly generation becomes outdated, then the head of society is incompetent. And when the head is incompetent, how much can the hands accomplish?"

So meditation is the way the older generation can increase its usefulness.

"And not only will they fulfill their increased responsibility to the world as they grow in age, but also they will increase the fulfillment of their own life. Spontaneously they will be honored by the young. And when the children are loving to them and obey their guidance, then the older people will enjoy a life of always increasing joy."

Big cars and open country—we're back in North America again. After months living in the carefully planned crampedness of Switzerland and then the recent week in India's tiny cabs, the wide highways and large back seats of the American car culture seem like a revelation.

We're on a highspeed run from Montreal, where our plane arrived from England this afternoon, to Ottawa, where the inauguration ceremony for the North American continent will start tomorrow at nine in the morning. The constant travel is having its effect. One of our original group summed it up on the plane today.

"I slept through England," he said.

He has a chance to catch up on this ride, however. Yesterday's press conference received wide coverage all over England, and members of London's World Plan center passed us a collection of eight or nine clippings at the airport. The stories are uniformly positive—even those few reporters who could not manage to take the idea straight still wrote with humor that sounds gentle and affectionate. The research on the Transcendental Meditation Technique, and the support by responsible people, is simply too strong to be dismissed any more.

Our ride to Ottawa takes a couple of hours. When we arrive there is time for dinner and then most of us head for bed early. Maharishi, of course,

"You'll forgive
me for asking
this, Maharishi,"
the commentator
says, "but has
teaching the TM
Technique made
you a rich man?"

stays up late. Teachers have come to Ottawa from all over Eastern Canada to meet with him. He's also up early the next morning to make an eight o'clock appearance on a nationwide television show, "Canada A.M." This is one of Canada's most popular shows.

The television studio is a bizarre environment—a dim concrete room with thick rubber cables circling across the floor, and ladders, ash cans and disassembled stage settings waiting randomly in corners. Out of this dull grey confusion a bath of light from a tangle of overhead lights picks out one wall, and here the set stands garishly bright. The backdrops are propped up by sandbags, the carpet is laid on bare cement, but on the monitor the scene looks sharp and cheerful.

Maharishi steps into this electronic reality with easy grace. He sits in the center, with an interviewer on either side. The softness of his appearance, his comfortable posture and smoothly draped dhoti, contrast with the starkness of the set.

The show passes lightly, the questions produced in amiable order. And then, at the end of this relaxed give-and-take, one of the hosts looks down just a moment at the start of a question.

"You'll forgive me for asking this, Maharashi," he says looking up again, "but has teaching the Transcendental Meditation Technique made you a rich man?"

"Oh, yes," Maharishi says. There is a startled pause on the set. "The basis of being a rich man is fulfillment, and that I have. Being a monk, I have no pockets or possessions, but seeing the development of the scientific age into the Age of Enlightenment, that is my fulfillment."

It's a natural interest, the money question. So many unlikely organizations are operating in the world today, masking greed behind a wide variety of humanitarian images. For some people, the hardest thing to believe about the World Plan is that Maharishi has no money and no interest in money. The vows of his order allow him his dhotis, his sandals, and little else. In a sense he works like the members of the international staff, for room and board. When the show is over, our small group walks out to the car for the drive back to Maharishi's hotel, the Chateau Laurier. Another all-day inauguration like the one in Delhi is ready to begin.

The World Plan Executive Council in Canada is one of Maharishi's most effective organizations, and it has put together a program that is informative and inspiring. The five hundred seats are filled all day. More than seventy members of the Canadian national government sign the guest book at the door, and over a hundred other experts in the fields of business, education and health also attend. Those who stay the full twelve hours get to hear Maharishi several times and also listen to a long succession of specialists in various fields. Of these speeches, two of the best are given by older American men who have recently retired. The first of these men is Alfred Jenkins, who has just completed a thirty-year career with the United States Foreign Service. Dressed in soft grey, Mr. Jenkins seems the gracious embodiment of the diplomat. He was one of the State Department's ranking experts on the Far East, a member of the Senior Staff of the National Security Council and the director of the office concerned with the People's Republic of China. He worked closely with Secretary of State Henry Kissinger on the recent reopening of relations with China. Mr. Jenkins begins his speech with an exposition of the importance of the Transcendental Meditation Program in diplomatic life.

"The rate of change in the world today is so great," he says, "that we need a radically new approach to the question of living. I think there is none who feels this need more than one who has tried to act in the complex field of foreign affairs. What such a man needs is stability, and the TM Technique is a technique that gives you a fly wheel—it keeps you steady. And more than that, such a man needs steam and propulsion, and the Transcendental Meditation Technique is above all, that refueling process twice a day."

Then, toward the end of his speech, Mr. Jenkins turns to more personal thoughts.

"My wife and I have been meditating for five increasingly beautiful years," he says. "And you know, despite the fact I only just recently retired from diplomatic life, I almost want to sign up and begin my career all over again. What a joy it would be to work in foreign affairs in an Age of Enlightenment. Instead of the all too often frustrating, sterile and sometimes inamicable confrontations of today, negotiations then should be a love feast of human problem solving."

Mr. Jenkins is followed by William Murphy. A life-long politician, Mr. Murphy culminated a twenty-year career in the Illinois House of Representatives by serving as majority whip and then majority leader. Mr. Murphy was the first politician to sponsor legislation endorsing the Transcendental Meditation Technique and the Science of Creative Intelligence, a resolution the Illinois House passed in 1972. Since then hundreds of other national, regional and local governments have passed similar resolutions. Mr. Murphy speaks in an informal conversational style, and he begins by saying it was his children who first got him interested in the Transcendental Meditation Technique.

"Actually," he says, "I agreed to start as a sort of favor to my sons. After about a month, however, it commenced to occur to me that I was feeling somewhat better. I became very interested in reports of scientific studies being made on the subject and soon became convinced that the Transcendental Meditation Technique was just too good to be wasted only on the young."

After telling more about his personal experience, Mr. Murphy goes on to discuss his role in the resolution that passed the Illinois House.

"I think my action was quite a surprise to my colleagues," he says. "I was known as a rather rough and tumble leader of the House. But after the initial shock wore off, the resolution was debated on two separate days and then adopted. I think it was one of the best actions we could take. When Maharishi says it's the dawn of a new age, that harmony, brotherhood and tranquility will return to the world, I believe him. I ask you government officials present today, I ask all the friends of Canada, to join in this great mission of peace and love."

Similar endorsements, from leaders in both the United States and Canada, fill the twelve-hour presentation. It is an impressive program, but for those of us who have come along on the entire tour, the two most sparkling moments of the day actually occur outside the hall. The first of these comes just after lunch.

Maharishi and a small party are ushered away from the crowds, into a back elevator and down to the basement garage. From here, an automobile trip is taken all of about three hundred yards. Canada's national government is housed right next door, stretching away in one long park-like block in a series of grand old Tudor buildings. Maharishi has an appointment with the Canadian Prime Minister, Pierre Trudeau.

The meeting is a private one, just Maharishi and the Prime Minister. Five or six years ago, heads of state would have found little reason for a discussion with the teacher of the Transcendental Meditation Technique, but research has made its mark in the political field as well. Two years ago, on a swing through the United States, Maharishi conferred with the governors of several states and addressed two legislatures. Later on this inauguration tour, there are conferences scheduled with heads of state in Latin America and Africa. Governmental leaders need to solve problems, and they are beginning to realize that enduring solutions come from the level of consciousness.

As he usually does in a situation of this kind, Maharishi has asked us to keep this meeting quiet. It is only courteous to allow the Prime Minister to make the decision about publicity himself. For this reason, there are a few awkward moments when a tall, casually dressed man walks up to our group as we wait in the hall for the meeting to end. The man has two cameras around his neck.

"Is Maharishi Mahesh Yogi up here?" he asks of the group in general.

"Yes, he is," someone answers.

"Meeting with the Prime Minister, right?"

"Yes, he is."

"I thought so. I knew he was in town and I saw a car out front with some flowers left on the dash."

This is one of Canada's best-known news photographers. The capitol is his beat. He obviously knows how to do his job. He leans up against the wall opposite the door to the Prime Minister's office and settles in to wait for the meeting to break. The conference lasts nearly half an hour before the door

opens. As Maharishi and the Prime Minister emerge, the photographer steps up immediately. Instead of simply shooting, however, he catches the eye of the Prime Minister.

"You'd like some pictures?" the Prime Minister asks. "Fine, fine." He smiles and moves toward Maharishi. A flash bulb lights the darkened hall. The papers of Canada have a page one picture for tomorrow's editions.

We return to the cars and take the short trip back to the hotel. Before re-entering the hall, we are escorted up to one of the hotel's top floors. There is a radio studio here. Maharishi is going to be interviewed on one of Canada's most influential shows. The show is called, "As It Happens." The interviewer, Barbara Frum, has a nationwide reputation for sharp, intelligent interrogation—a magazine article that appeared recently called her a "tough inquisitor" and summarized her talents with slight hyperbole: "With Barbara Frum asking the questions," the story said, "even Superman—or Henry Kissinger—wouldn't know what hit them."

It's not an encouraging scouting report, but I can't say Maharishi looks concerned. The director of the show leads us into a small, spare room where there is a round wooden table with four microphones pointing out in four directions. Maharishi sits at one mike and the rest of us take open chairs. With everybody in place, it's suddenly obvious there is no room for Barbara Frum.

"You'll hear Barbara over these headphones," the director tells us. "She's in the main studio in Toronto."

"Maharishi," she
asks. "How can
you be so happy
all the time?"
"It's natural," he
says. "Life is
bliss."

Somehow headphones wouldn't seem right on Maharishi, and the director disassembles one pair and hands him an earphone to hold up with one hand.

"Can you hear her all right?" the director asks.

"Welcome to Canada, Maharishi," says Barbara Frum.

The show begins, and from the first question it's clear Ms. Frum is not only tough and intelligent. She also does her homework.

"I've been reading your book *The Science of Being and the Art of Living*," she says. "In there you make the statement several times that life is bliss. Now that's quite a flat statement and I'd have to say it contradicts my experience."

Boom. Scant pleasantries, no small talk about relaxation and release of tension. Barbara Frum is after the central issue immediately. Maharishi smiles and talks briefly about the inadequacies of education up until now.

"But Maharishi," responds Ms. Frum insistently, "life *isn't* bliss."

Maharishi laughs heartily, his head leaning over on the hand that holds his ear piece. He takes some time to describe the settled state of mind— the experience of bliss consciousness—but his description makes little headway.

"But isn't it true," asks Barbara Frum, "most of the trouble in life is simply because people can't face the truth—the truth that life is suffering and we are all going to die?"

And suddenly it becomes clear that Barbara Frum isn't hostile toward Maharishi. The sharpness of her comments seems to be an expression of her attitude toward life. And even though all we have of her is her voice, it feels as if she is not completely happy with the thoughts she is speaking. Maharishi laughs again, gently.

"Suffering is not natural to life," he says. "We suffer only when we don't know the technique to live life free from suffering. Darkness has no existence of itself—darkness is just the absence of light."

Ms. Frum waits a moment, then moves on to another area that has troubled her.

"Your books say that the Transcendental Meditation Technique helps a person to become more clear and dynamic," she says. "But couldn't the Transcendental Meditation Technique be used unscrupulously? Couldn't businessmen, for instance, use it to promote the mercantile values we should all be moving away from?"

"Business is a good thing," Maharishi says. "Business and industry are one basis of progress."

"But what I mean is, can't a bad person use the Transcendental Meditation Technique to gain control over others?"

"No, no," Maharishi says. "His control over *himself* becomes more orderly. The thing is, wrong doing is the result of discontent. And the

Transcendental Meditation Technique not only increases ability, but also leads to contentment very directly. And it is contentment that brings, builds and maintains character. The research is there to show that with the Transcendental Meditation Technique a man loses his stress, and becomes less hostile and more sociable. The Transcendental Meditation Technique brings more ability for achieving something through right means."

There's another pause, an empty space that sounds like thinking.

"Yes, I'm beginning to see," she says.

"And when evolution comes," Maharishi continues, "people naturally begin to enjoy more. Suffering naturally starts to disappear."

"Maharishi," says Barbara Frum, "it certainly seems to work for you."

Maharishi laughs again. The mood has changed and Barbara Frum's next question seems honestly puzzled.

"You are a monk, I understand, and there's something I really don't understand. How do you hold out? Why don't you succumb to the charms of the good life?"

"What I'm enjoying is better than any beautiful house or good climate or anything," he says. "After sixteen or seventeen years teaching the Transcendental Meditation Technique and the Science of Creative Intelligence, we can now see a new Age coming on. The feeling is incomparable."

Communication has been established. The show continues pleasantly. The basic questions about the nature and benefits of the Transcendental Meditation Technique—the ones that most interviews start with—now come as an explanation for the more theoretical points that have already been covered. And Barbara Frum's questions indicate that, even though she is hundreds of miles away, she seems more at ease with Maharishi by now than most reporters ever feel.

When the allotted time is almost gone, she starts to close the show.

"Maharishi Mahesh Yogi," she says, "I'd like to thank you very much for being on the show today."

"And thank you," he says, "and my greetings to all the people of Canada."

There is a pause and the show appears to be over. Then one last question seems almost to jump out of Barbara Frum, to surprise her as much as anyone else.

"Maharishi," she asks. "How can you be so *happy* all the time?"

"It's natural," he laughs. "Life is bliss."

She waits again for a moment.

"It certainly sounds like it," she says. "Thank you again. It was a pleasure speaking with you."

"It's beautiful."

"You're beautiful, Maharishi."

"It was a good interview," Maharishi says. "Many beautiful points were brought out."

One important question was asked about business. Apparently the interviewer was concerned that commercial values, economic values, are not proper in an ideal world.

"No, no. Affluence is needed. Affluence is the goal of economics, and there should be affluence in life on all levels."

But it seems that the interviewer was upset about materialism—she was concerned that money and material things might detract from the more important aspects of life.

"The consideration of wealth is a consideration of one part of life. It is important because it is necessary for progress. If one is not mindful of economics, one would fail immediately on the outer, surface values of life. But what is needed is to increase the range of economics so that it deals with the totality of life. Affluence is all right—a man can be a millionaire—but the purpose of being a millionaire, the purpose of affluence, is perpetual happiness. And this is missing. Economics has not been able to accomplish it's goal."

What should the nature of economics be?

"The purpose of economics is growth. It is there to help growth and evolution. It should help bring the flowering of life to its fullness. And the means of economics is integration. Economics should be the glue to bring the different aspects of society together. A simple example: if potatoes don't grow in Chicago then they should come from Idaho. Or we can think of people who work for other people, people who buy from other people, all the different activities and relationships in the market. All these different relationships are integrated on the ground of economics. But the problem is that economics has always been on such a superficial basis."

Why is that?

"Economics is, so to say, enclosed within the walls of the stock exchange. It is only concerned with the rise and fall of prices, with the rise and fall of currency rates. This can only be unfulfilling. Economics should not be restricted only to the integration of employer and employee, of buyer and seller. Economics is for life and life is too precious to be enclosed in the stock exchange. This partial, haphazard approach to economics should give way to an approach based on a more fundamental level, to an economics that integrates one field of life with another."

This is a new concept. What are the different "fields of life?"

"There are three fields of life: the field of action, the field of thought and the field of pure intelligence or pure consciousness. We know that action is based on thinking. One must think in order to act. And thought is based on consciousness, on intelligence. Action is based on thought and thought is

"The purpose of affluence is perpetual happiness. And this is missing. Economics has not been able to accomplish its goal."

Maharishi in rare close-up outside the government building in Ottawa.

based on consciousness. These are the three fields. And economics today concerns itself only with the most superficial field, the field of action. Economics is for integration, but so far economics has been for integration only for the field of action and for the physical, material values. The depth of life remains untouched."

This is why economics has not proved to be satisfying?

"Yes. The situation today is that the employer is not satisfied and the employee is not satisfied. Every employer feels he is the father of all those who are working for him, and he wants to see them happy and fulfilled. Every leader of a union is working day and night to see that all the members of the union have enough to live comfortably and in happiness. But because the field of economics is not based on awakening the abundance of life, the affluence of life, that is deep within everyone's awareness, these beautiful aspirations are not fulfilled."

Then the enjoyment of economic values depends on the integration of pure consciousness into daily activity?

"This is the thing. It's not the wealth that brings fulfillment to life. You could take the example of the ten wealthiest people in the world, and see that wealth in itself is not fulfilling. Those who take great responsibilities receive large salaries, but they do so at the cost of tension and stress. What is the value of riches if a man has insomnia? Even to *enjoy* the gift of wealth, a man has to grow. He must develop a bigger heart, a broader comprehension of the value of life. He must integrate all the fields of life in his own awareness, and then whatever he does he will be expressing that state of inner fulfillment in all outer phases of activity."

This is speaking only of the individual.

"Yes, and the field of economics as a whole will only be fulfilled when it is able to integrate all aspects of individual life with all aspects of social life, and then integrate both of these with all aspects of national life and all aspects of international life."

But isn't that paradoxical? How can all these competing aspects of life be reconciled?

"It's only a paradox for those who are not integrated in their awareness. When they focus outside, they are cut off from the inside. When they focus inside, they are cut off from the outside. But we have seen that diversity is based on unity. When economics is based on unity—on the integration of action, thought and consciousness—then it will bring that affluence which makes a man truly fulfilled, which makes a society truly fulfilled."

Economics will escape the walls of the stock exchange?

"And enjoy the infinite value of life. I don't want to surprise the world with the phrase, 'Infinite value of life.' But when it comes to that, life is something more than just action and objectivity. It is something more than

"Action is based on thought and thought is based on consciousness. So far economics has concerned itself only with the field of action."

Surrounded by flowers, Maharishi lectures in Montreal.

117

just materialism and physiology. Life has infinite value. And when this infinite value is experienced as a living reality in one's awareness, then this is a life of true affluence. Only on this basis can economics fulfill its highest goals of growth, integration and affluence for the individual and the society."

The engines fill the forward compartment with a shattering roar. We have to cover four cities in eighteen hours today, starting in Quebec and ending in New York, and the only way to do it was to charter a noisy turboprop. Today we are paying for speed with our ears.

The airborne commotion contrasts sharply with memories of last evening. If noise is the order now, silence was the situation then. We spent the night at the Forest Academy recently acquired by the Canadian World Plan Executive Council. Forest Academies are dedicated to peace and quiet—facilities situated in scenic spots where meditators can go for a quiet weekend and take a chance to see Maharishi on videotape. There are a number of them in operation now world wide.

This new one, a rustic wooden ski lodge in the resort area of Lac Beauport outside Quebec City, will serve the purpose well. The occasion of our visit last night was to allow Maharishi to conduct a dedication ceremony. The large living room area was packed with several hundred people spilling out the doorways and onto window sills and stairways. Maharishi gave a brief speech, but in today's memory at least, the informal occasion was nearly stolen by the delightful mayor of Lac Beauport. Mayor Pacquet is a big man with a dapper mustache, and he took to the microphone with an air of proprietary appreciation. His manner was totally winning, a genial combination of political gladhander and your favorite uncle.

He started out by congratulating Maharishi for two things: (1) the good taste of the World Plan Executive Council in choosing Lac Beauport, and (2) the spirit of enterprise that has brought this welcome addition to the commerce of the area. This last was an amusing thought—enlightenment can also appear as economic stimulation. He then read a long proclamation welcoming Maharishi and stooped down to sign it on the platform. He followed that with the presentation of a green and white, molded plastic plaque of Lac Beauport produced by the local chamber of commerce, and then he requested that Maharishi sign the community's guest book. All in all, it was a disarming performance. Then, when he turned to leave the microphone, another thought suddenly struck him.

"Psst, psst," he whispered to his wife in the front row. She reached down under her chair and handed him a small wrapped cylinder.

"When we first saw some of your literature," he said to Maharishi, "it was given to us by friends six months ago. My wife is something of a sculptor and she made this statuette to give to them. But if you want it, it's yours."

He removed the paper and produced a small, fired-clay likeness of Maharishi standing, flowers in hand. Maharishi took it with a smile.

"Today we receive wave after wave," he said.

Thinking back to that presentation last night still brings a smile. Prime Ministers and university presidents are all right, but in some ways that innocent gift by a small town mayor has made for my favorite moment on the tour so far.

Sitting here in this clattering turboprop, however, that exchange now seems to be quite far away. Maharishi is working in the seats up in front, his voice cutting through the racket. He is talking with Dr. Keith Wallace, the President of Maharishi International University. Dr. Wallace, a physiologist trained at UCLA, has just come up to join the tour from the new MIU campus in Fairfield, Iowa. He and Maharishi are discussing a presentation Dr. Wallace is going to make at an upcoming international conference on neurophysiology. The conference will be especially important because it is going to be held in Poland, and this will mark the first presentation made by a representative of the Transcendental Meditation Program behind the Iron Curtain.

Dr. Wallace is the man who did the first important research on the Transcendental Meditation Technique back in 1969, studies that first quantified the deep physical rest and more refined brain wave activity that occur during the meditation period. After conducting this research at UCLA and Harvard, Dr. Wallace began to work closely with Maharishi.

His invitation to Poland on behalf of the Transcendental Meditation Program resulted from a talk he made at a similar conference last year in India. The title of his presentation then was "The Neurophysiology of Enlightenment," and it is this title that he wants to discuss with Maharishi.

"Many of these people were very impressed with the research we presented last year," he says. He's almost yelling to make himself heard. "But several of them—especially the man who is organizing our appearance in Poland—says that at this conference we should just present research and stay away from the concept of 'enlightenment.'"

"Why is that?" Maharishi asks.

"What I found last year in India was that the East Europeans get upset at the very idea of enlightenment," Dr. Wallace says. "Just the word seems to incense them."

"It'll be all right," Maharishi says. "We must educate the people, uplift them. We can't allow them to live in ignorance."

"But the organizer wants to be very cautious."

"He *should* be cautious from his side," Maharishi says with a smile. "There is so much ignorance in the world. But from our side we must be very generous."

Maharishi is smiling and Dr. Wallace joins him.

"We land on the ground they have prepared for us," Maharishi says, "but we land in our own plane. They have to know the progress being made in the world. It won't be kind to let them stay behind."

Caution dissolves in laughter, and Maharishi moves on to another project. The chief designer for M.I.U., Lawrence Sheaf, has been working with Maharishi on the entire tour, and now the two of them begin a pamphlet design for the Forest Academy we visited last night. A tall Englishman who has worked with Maharishi for a number of years, Sheaf has cultivated the ability to work at all hours, in any circumstances. For the last several minutes we have been bucking through heavy air turbulence. The rest of my body is now as rattled as my ears, but Maharishi and Sheaf keep working while the plane bumps and slides down to the ground. We are an hour late into Montreal—held up this morning by snow in Quebec City—and as the plane taxis to a stop near the terminal, Maharishi stands up.

"Now we'll rush and run," he says.

That's the tempo for the rest of the day. An automobile convoy is waiting with motors running at the front door and we race off to a press conference and lecture. Our experience in Montreal is confined to the beautiful new Place des Artes, where feelings of luxury and understatement work together in elegant counterpoint. A press conference is followed by a lecture to three thousand meditators, and then we rush back to a late afternoon take-off. The turboprop thrashes to Boston, where another high-speed cavalcade whips us through night-time traffic. The lecture here is held in a huge, forty-five hundred seat motion picture palace, one of the grand old theaters featuring gilded angels and winged animals on every square inch of walls and roof. A packed house hears Maharishi for an hour and a half, and then it's cars again, and airport walkways, and one more time we're flying south, heading for the lights of New York City.

It's been ten fast hours, and the time is nearly midnight. Just sitting down feels very good. The seat leans back comfortably and I'm feeling tired, but my mind is moving too fast to sleep. Impressions of the day come up, sharply focused scenes that stand out in the blur of remembered activity. I hear again the sound of Maharishi's voice in Montreal, floating soft and full through a magnificent sound system, bringing thousands of people the feeling of his quiet, private conversation; I see again the frozen moment in Boston, Maharishi coming slowly out on stage with his palms together in greeting, sweeping in the audience with his eyes; I remember the brief image of Maharishi, late for this plane, stopping in the airport hall to pass out flowers to several children waiting for him.

"Now we'll rush and run," he had said, but something in him is timeless, something is there that never wavers, never changes in all the tumult. We have seen Maharishi in his biographical "home" in India—at the academy and with the Shankaracharya—but he seemed no more or less

Sometimes the only way for local Centers to get Maharishi to all appointments is to charter a small plane or helicopter.

121

comfortable there than he has in the hectic round of press conferences, interviews and lectures that have greeted him in the West. There is harmony at the basis of diversity, he says, and it seems to be with him wherever he goes.

By now my mind is starting to slow down. I could sleep, but when I glance out the window I see there's no time. The glittering energy of New York is pushing up to meet us.

"The world is made up of differences," Maharishi says. "Each place we visit is so different."

In terms of cultural values?

"Cultural differences are there, and then there are all the different values of economics, politics, religions, understandings. All these differences make up the world, and they lead to one important question: how to achieve a state of permanent peace in a world of differences."

Are the differences between various areas really that substantial?

"What we see is that the differences that are a barrier to world unity are the elements that are the very *life* of each country. They are the obvious and fundamental values of the culture of each country. And they cannot be eliminated. All men can't be made alike. All cultures in the world can't have the same values."

What is the purpose of these various cultures?

"The function of culture is in the name. It is to culture. It is to educate, to help evolution. Human life is cultured through traditional values which have filtered down through time. There are habits which children imbibe from their mothers, accents of speech, modes of thinking, values of right and wrong. This is the heritage of the country, and if a country is to be strong, these cultural values have to be secure. Otherwise, life will simply wither away."

But if the different types of cultures present a barrier to world unity and peace, shouldn't they be done away with?

"It's not possible. Cultures in different parts of the world cannot be made alike because climatic and geographic conditions are involved. The growth and values of a man in the desert are not those of a man on the banks of a great river. One can't behave the same way in both places and if one tries, nature will disallow it. This is why all those people who know the value of tradition and culture are frightened by the rapid communications and fast pace of progress in the modern world."

Why is that?

"Increasing tourism all over the world is a means for diluting the cultural basis of each country. The very friendship growing between countries means that the cultural values of each country are influencing the cultural values of many others. Moreover, science and technological progress also disrupt traditional culture in very fundamental ways. And what we find from all this is a disruption in the balance of nature. Basic values which hold true in an area are being ignored, and therefore man becomes frustrated and loses balance. Whole societies become imbalanced and are torn by riots and strikes."

Then perhaps some countries should try to wall themselves off, to protect themselves against outside influences.

"It's not possible today for any nation to remain aloof, to remain uninfluenced by the values of other nations. These influences are necessary for progress, and everyone wants progress. The nature of life is to progress and evolve. What is necessary is to eliminate those influences which serve as a dry rot to eat up the cultural values of a particular area. As it is now, each country seems to be a threat, a poison, to the cultural values of other countries. This atmosphere of doubt, fear and dissension must be neutralized, it must be dissolved. We have to find a practice which will enhance the individual dignity of a nation, while at the same time and through the same process, it makes that nation a fertilizer for the growth and evolution of every other nation."

How can this be done?

"The only way to make people more friendly is to raise their level of consciousness. The understanding of the people will always be on the level of their awareness, on the level of their consciousness. If a man is wearing green glasses he can only see green. If a man has stresses and strains his consciousness can only be restricted. All these conflicts that arise come only from the blinding narrowness of vision. A man can only see a small amount and so he focuses on himself too much. He gets blinded to all other areas of concern. This stubbornness, this rigidity, this arrogance is the cause of the eruptions of non-peace all over the world. Leaders in the world have to take so much action to level out eruptions of non-peace. Late night phone calls come to the Secretary of the United Nations, the Presidents of different countries fly to other countries. All this action is a constant feature of the world today, but it's not necessary. All that is necessary is to raise the consciousness of the people, to let them grow in the abilities of stability and adaptability, of purification and integration, and then the awareness of all the people will be able to reconcile between the local interest and the universal interest."

Adaptability and stability, purification and integration—why do these qualities seem important?

"With the practice of the Transcendental Meditation Technique, these qualities develop in the individual. And they grow at every level. Adaptability, for instance, grows at the level of physiology, at the level of psychology, at the level of sociology, at the level of ecology. And the increase in these qualities is the formula for world peace. Stability and adaptability

"If a man is wearing green glasses, he can see only green. If a man has stresses and strains his consciousness can only be restricted. Such a man can only see a small area."

123

increase at the same time. With increasing adaptability, a culture will be able to derive the maximum from other cultures, but at the same time, by increasing in stability, it will remain unshaken and established within its own glory. The growth of purification and integration means the outside influences will be sorted out—they will be purified—and then whatever is useful to a culture will be absorbed and integrated in a spontaneous manner. Whatever is not useful will die out naturally. In this way every culture can remain stable within itself and yet inherit those elements of progress from the outside that are suitable to the conditions in that region."

Can you explain this mechanism more fully?

"It's a very natural law. We can think of an analogy. When we inhale we take in oxygen and when we exhale we give out carbon dioxide. Our friend standing next to us knows we are giving out carbon dioxide, but nature takes care that he only uses oxygen for his metabolism. And what happens to the carbon dioxide we have produced? It goes to the plants. If something is not helpful in one area, it might prove helpful in some other area. This is what we call the process of purification in nature. Naturally one should only participate in things that are life-supporting. And it's only necessary to rid the system of stresses and strains to enliven this natural ability in the awareness of every individual and every society."

And this will reconcile the speed of progress and rapid communications with the need for cultural stability?

"Yes. This will preserve the cultural stability of a nation, and life can only be progressive on the basis of the maintenance of these cultural values. Then each nation will only be a fertilizer to every other nation. Then all these doubts and fears will be missing from the life of the world. One country will not be a poison to another, but each country will be necessary to all the others for their own growth and evolution. Only on this basis can permanent peace come to the world. This is why, if permanent peace is ever going to come, it is going to be through a technique whereby every individual can raise his level of consciousness in a simple, natural way. It is going to be through the Transcendental Meditation Program.

I am not really sure how I feel about a pink airplane, but Maharishi seems to like it.

"It's beautiful," he says. "The right color for the Dawn."

As long as we have to take so many planes, at least the variety is good. This one is not only pink, it's also tiny, with fourteen seats and two small engines. And even at that, the plane is too big for where we're going. The runway is so short in Fairfield, Iowa, that we can only take nine people on this trip out of Chicago. Eight of us are going with Maharishi on something of an occasion—his first visit to the university he has founded.

As a moment with a certain historical significance, this trip is the first episode that has stood out since we arrived in the United States. The last two days have all been rush and run—planes, taxis, lectures and hotel rooms—as the tour has hurried through New York City, Atlanta, Georgia, and on to Chicago.

Being in New York was a quick dip in compressed intensity—I've never been to a city where so many people were moving so fast in such a small space—but of Atlanta I'm afraid I have little impression at all. To paraphrase my friend, I slept through Atlanta. Maharishi has two more continents to cover, with major appearances in Buenos Aires, Argentina, for South America and in Abidjan, the Ivory Coast, for Africa. Right now, however, my plan to stop off in California with my family seems pretty sound.

At this moment, thirty-five hundred people are waiting for us out in heartland mid-America, in tiny Fairfield, Iowa. Our little plane is doing its best to rush us there, and it's bouncing us around considerably in the process. I don't feel so well, and Dr. Domash, the physicist, really appears to be suffering. He makes some comment to Maharishi, and gets a good-natured laugh in response.

"Riding in a pink plane," says Maharishi, "scientists may *feel* a little funny."

Maharishi is sitting in the back of the plane with a television commentator who is making the trip with us, giving him a brief summation of the tour so far. The news media haven't had much good news to report recently, and this man seems to be enjoying his opportunity to take part in a distinctly positive occasion.

The flight takes us out over another mid-continental plain like the one in India, agricultural land that is ruled off like pieces of tile. After an hour the plane begins to descend toward a tiny runway mowed out of a green field. Cross winds are gusting us sharply sideways. The pilot tips one wing up at a hard angle and skids us down the wind to the ground.

As we step out of the plane, we enter another new world. After weeks of cities and transportation machinery, we have suddenly been deposited in the midst of limitless, fertile farm land. It's mostly the smells that bring the beauty of the countryside, the smells of rich damp earth and green things growing. It's a good feeling, a healthy feeling.

But there's not much time for enjoying sensations. The pastoral mood is swallowed up by the big cars that have come to meet us. By an odd twist, this rural area is the first place on the tour where Maharishi has been met by shining luxury cars, large Chryslers donated for the day by a new meditator who owns a car dealership in Fairfield. The soft, comfortable ride is interrupted occasionally as the student drivers from M.I.U., more used to Volkswagens and Vegas, learn the delicacies of power braking. The drive takes about ten minutes and then we turn in through the university gates.

Maharishi International University has a classic campus setting, with gently rolling lawns, plenty of trees and an abundance of nineteenth century brick buildings. The school moved to this facility last September, taking over from Parsons College, a liberal arts school that succumbed to the financial pressures plaguing much of higher education. The move saved the large expense of building a campus and provided a traditional atmosphere.

As we step from the cars and look around, it's a surprise to remember what a short time it's been since M.I.U. was just an idea. It was less than two years ago, in the summer of 1973 in Seelisberg, that Maharishi was molding the catalogue, using that publication as a vehicle for thinking out the details of the university's organization. The school opened that fall, in a rented building in Santa Barbara, California, and this is its second year of operation.

The motto Maharishi has chosen for M.I.U. is an ancient phrase from the Vedas: "Knowledge is structured in consciousness." The limits of our consciousness are the limits of our knowledge—a small bucket can only hold a small amount of water. M.I.U. is the first university to focus on consciousness itself as well as on facts and theories studied by consciousness. Through the Transcendental Meditation Technique, M.I.U. provides each student with a practical method for expanding consciousness. Through the Science of Creative Intelligence, it provides a theoretical understanding for the mechanics of this expansion.

As freshmen, students study the Science of Creative Intelligence for one month and then take an intensive, one-week survey course in each of twenty-four disciplines—physics, literature, philosophy and other standard curriculum courses—studying each field in the light of the basic principles provided by the Science of Creative Intelligence. This interdisciplinary overview provides a clear awareness of the unifying principles common to all fields. In the second year, as in any other university, the students begin to specialize, and they choose a definite major by the third year.

The growth of the school has been rapid. More than five hundred students are already in attendance, and all of the requirements which will allow the school to be fully accredited have been met. All that is needed is for the first four year class to graduate, the final requisite for accreditation.

Some idea of the quality of the school can be gathered from the report of the independent accreditation committee, which visited the campus recently. Written by a professor and two deans from three respected midwestern institutions, this report advanced M.I.U. to candidacy for accreditation. The report points out that the educational program at M.I.U. "represents an attempt at a total and continuous educational experience which is remarkable in its scope and execution," and comments on "M.I.U.'s striking achievements in curricular reform, and in bending technology to the service of collegiate education." While recognizing that, as a new school, M.I.U. still has some growing pains, the report is clear about the reasons for recommending advancement to candidacy for accreditation. The conclusion points out:

"1. The faculty: singularly devoted to the University and its purposes, exceptionally well-trained, and young men and women of sensitivity and energy.

2. The students: active and involved in their learning, and enthusiastic in their participation in the work of the university.

3. The program of studies: a unique design for a curriculum but clearly substantive, and well conceived.

4. The climate: a pervasive sense of vitality and engagement, a pleasant and exciting place to be.

5. The physical plant: more than adequate for present or foreseeable needs in the sense of space and facilities."

As we walk through the grounds, it's a pleasure to watch Maharishi enjoy the way his ideas have been manifested into brick and green reality. It seems an apt example of the causal chain he talks about—consciousness is the basis of thought, action and achievement.

We walk across the campus and into the field house, the only one of the school's seventy-two buildings big enough to hold three thousand people. The audience is a mixture—five hundred students, many meditators and teachers who have driven in from all around the Midwest, and a large number

The motto Maharishi has chosen for M.I.U. is an ancient phrase from the Vedas: "Knowledge is structured in consciousness."

"As full potential
is developed,
problems fade
away. The man of
this scientific age
should be strong
enough to put an
end to the chaotic
history of the
past."

of Fairfield residents. This little town was somewhat apprehensive when the news first came that Parsons College was going to be filled with "meditators." By this time, however, twelve per cent of the population has joined that group.

When everyone is in a seat, the mayor of Fairfield, the honorable Robert Rasmussen, opens the proceedings with a brief speech welcoming Maharishi. At the conclusion, he presents Maharishi with a white pine tree which will be planted at the center of campus. The mayor reads a plaque that will be placed at the foot of the tree:

"To honor the first visit of Maharishi Mahesh Yogi to Maharishi International University. May this tree stand as a symbol of the growth, progress and beauty of this institution, and may its branches stretch to the limits of the universe."

The mayor is followed by Gordon Aistrap, a banker who represents the Fairfield Chamber of Commerce. Mr. Aistrap was selected as the outstanding citizen of Fairfield in 1974. He tells of personally starting to practice the Transcendental Meditation Technique after being involved in the negotiations to bring M.I.U. to Fairfield. He then goes on to talk of Maharishi's visit.

"For awhile we were thinking of presenting Maharishi with the key to the city," he says. "But I can assure you there will be no such presentation today. How could we be so presumptuous as to give the key to our city to the man who has brought us the key for fulfillment in life?"

After a round of applause, Mr. Aistrap continues.

"This key," he says, "or if you will, this common denominator, has been searched for throughout the ages by men of different creeds, religions and political beliefs. This is why I want to see Iowa rise to lead this nation in the number of meditators per capita. I want to be able to say to Maharishi on his next visit that the Age of Enlightenment is no longer in the sunrise stage in this state. I ask the citizens of Fairfield to join me in this task, for this is the greatest honor we could give ourselves, our city, our state, and all mankind."

Then it's time for Maharishi to speak. The name of the town provides an opportunity he doesn't refuse.

"It's such a joy to be in Fairfield today," he says. "What we see is the possibility for a 'fair field' for all people in the world. Every student at this university feels as his responsibility the enlightenment of all people in the world. Higher education is for higher consciousness. And what I wish is that the model of this university be taken by all universities. Then we will unfold the full potential of consciousness of all the students in the world. With that it should not take us long to create a 'fair field' everywhere."

Maharishi is enjoying himself, speaking in a light, informal tone that fits the mood of this younger audience. If the important appearances in Asia, Europe and North America have all been ceremonies, with appropriate levels of dignity, this meeting at M.I.U. is more of an informal celebration.

The rapid pace of the trip is still a reality, however. Maharishi is due back in Chicago for an evening lecture. Sooner than anyone wants the meeting comes to an end, and with the late afternoon sun lighting us warmly we walk back to the cars. People line the roadway and Maharishi's car carries him slowly through the smiles. "Jai Guru Dev," he says. "Jai Guru Dev."

The drive to the airport is quick and the pink plane is waiting. The afternoon provides one last bit of excitement—a takeoff that aborts halfway down the runway, when neither pilot can remember if the rear door is securely fastened. It is.

Another run jumps us up into the air. We are living with engine noise again, but most of the passengers settle back anyway and demonstrate one of the chief tenets of an introductory lecture: noise is no barrier to meditation.

"T he course of study at Maharishi International University is so beautiful," Maharishi says. "When every school makes the Science of Creative Intelligence available to its students, then progress will be very rapid. This will be the way to bring a solution to the age-old problems of government and economics, of education and religion, all the problems of disharmony, conflicts and war that have plagued mankind throughout recorded history. This will be the way to produce a fully developed nation and world, where problems will have no place."

THE SOLUTION TO PROBLEMS

This sounds as if the teaching of the Transcendental Meditation Technique is supposed to bring solutions to most of our problems.

"It will bring the solution to *all* problems. We have seen that problems arise from weakness. And what we know is that weakness can only continue as long as strength has not come. As the full potential of the individual is developed, problems fade away. The man of this scientific age should be strong and developed enough to put an end to all the chaotic history of the past."

But doesn't the solution to problems require effort and resources?

"The thing is, if there is a problem, we don't want to deal with the problem on its own level. We don't grapple with darkness—we bring light. We bring a second element. And if weakness has continued until now, it's time to bring the light of life through the experience of pure consciousness. And then what we find is that success does not come to a man on the basis of his effort or on the basis of some collection of means. Success is on the basis of orderliness and purity. If that level of purity is there, then the necessary means get collected spontaneously as a man moves innocently around in his environment."

Then the level of a man's evolution has an effect on the problems he faces?

"The knowledge
is available, and
now, in whatever
state of
consciousness
you want to live
your life, you are
welcome."

"Very naturally. We know the perception of a tense man is crude. His perception of everything will always be tied in knots—this is no good, that is no good. There is a knot inside and so the man sees knots outside. These two tie together and then the whole life is in knots. But a man with more refined perception will always be more favorably disposed to the environment. And naturally when we are more cordial to our environment, the environment becomes more cordial to us. It is a very old proverb: 'As you sow, so shall you reap.'"

So a man should deliberately try to think positively?

"No, no. There is no question of trying. This is not some mood we are making. This is on the very real basis of refined perception, of improved ability to appreciate our environment."

But then, at that level, to solve our problems we don't necessarily have to tackle each of them individually?

"This is the point. It is a waste of time, a waste of energy, a waste of this supreme knowledge about life, to dwell on individual problems. Our formula is to capture the fort. If we can capture a fort, all the territory around the fort will belong to us. And in our life, the 'fort' is that pure level of consciousness. If a man can permanently establish his awareness in contact with that pure field, then problems wither away. It's a very simple thing. When the light comes, then where is the darkness? And now we have in the Transcendental Meditation Technique that golden formula for creating fully developed individuals through whose expanded awareness the age-old problems of mankind will disappear. It's no longer necessary for any man to remain on a lower level of consciousness. The knowledge is there, and now, in whatever state of consciousness you want to spend your life, you are welcome. The physiology is capable of giving any state of development you want. And when the potential is there in the system, why shouldn't it be lived up to? If an architect has built a house with so many beautiful rooms—a living room, and a bedroom and a library and a meditation room, why should a man be stuck in the kitchen all the time? It's an abuse of the talent of the architect. Not to live our full potential is an abuse of life. And when our awareness is established in the infinite field of all possibilities, then anything is possible for us."

Anything?

"And anything means . . . anything."

My final two days on the tour will feature a commuter run up and down the California coast. Our flight from Chicago lands in Southern California in mid-afternoon and the first impression of Los Angeles comes on the freeway run north from the airport. The impression is that this must be the world's most horizontal city. It looks as if it has spilled down out of a semi-circle of surrounding mountains and spread out in all directions to the sea. Our freeway gives us a commanding view—it seems to be the tallest structure around—as we race toward Hollywood.

Our first destination is Merv Griffin's television studio, an edifice known, with forgivable show business hyperbole, as the "Hollywood Palace." Actually, it is a movie theater with a refurbished interior. We spend two hours here producing the first introductory lecture on the Transcendental Meditation Program designed to reach an audience of thirty million. The taping is as much fun as it looks on television, but there isn't much time to savor the feeling. As soon as the camera lights blink out everybody turns around and rushes back to the airport for an early flight to San Francisco. Since all the arrangements were made very late, the television show had to be squeezed in where it could, necessitating the shuttle operation up and down the coast.

In San Francisco the roller coaster city-scape presents a picture quite different from the horizontal expanse further south. Sudden hills are topped often by older buildings of impressive stature and charm. Local boosters have some justification for calling San Francisco "The City."

At the evening lecture, eight thousand people are in attendance. After listening to Maharishi's lecture, they catch a brief cameo from Merv Griffin, who has made the trip up from Los Angeles with us.

"I guess I was born in the Age of Enlightenment," Merv Griffin says. "I'm nine days old."

In a packed hall of meditators, that line has to work.

"I'd like to thank you for that rare appearance on our show," he says to Maharishi. "It was the most extraordinary show I've ever done."

For the teachers of the Transcendental Meditation Technique in the audience—and hundreds have come from all over the West—there is a bonus event at the close of the meeting. Maharishi announces a boat ride to commence at Pier 43. After a little searching down at the docks, everyone enjoys a refreshing triple-decked cruise around the twinkling darkness of San Francisco Bay.

Eight o'clock the next morning brings one more television show, and that is followed by a large press conference back at the hotel. At both events, the feeling is comfortable and positive. As in England, the edge is gone from most of the questions, melted away by the years of research and the fact that thirty thousand people meditate in the Bay Area. One reporter at the press conference is a holdout, however, and it is his questions that provide the most lively exchange of the session. A bulky man in a loose-fitting sports shirt stands up to put his questions.

"Maharishi," he asks, "do you consider yourself to be 'It'?"

Maharishi laughs.

"I'm not 'It'," he says. " 'It' is the neuter gender."

A certain amount of tittering in the room doesn't discourage the reporter.

"What I mean is do you consider anything to be above you?"

"Not *anything*," Maharishi says. "*Everything.* I don't proclaim that I'm a prophet or anything. That would be too superficial. What we are talking about remains on the level of man. Man as man is competent enough to take care of his problems. He is good enough to stand on his own feet and help himself."

By now the reporter seems puzzled.

"But if that's true," he asks, "what are your qualifications to run your organization?"

Maharishi lets a beat go by.

"I *started* it," he says.

The whole room goes up in laughter. Maharishi has a mannerism, a way when he's laughing sometimes of leaning forward a little and raising his eyebrows, as if to say, is that all right? He does it now, and the reporter nods and sits down again.

The conference ends soon after this exchange. There is time for lunch and a breezy walk on the city's hills, and then one more flight carries us down again to the evening lecture in Los Angeles. The meeting here is held in the cavernous new Convention Center downtown, one of the few places in Southern California large enough to hold all the people who want to come. Maharishi's talk seems to have a poignant feeling to it, perhaps because I know it will be the last one I will hear for awhile. His final thought has a special appeal.

"When I next see you," he says, "we'll not be talking much about the Dawn any more. We'll be talking about the bright sunshine. The Age of Enlightenment is coming. The sun will certainly come up. This is not a conditional thing. It is not that the Dawn is coming if we do this or if we do that. This is an age of science and it is through the window of science we have seen the Dawn of the Age of Enlightenment. It is now only a question of how fast the bright sunshine of the day will appear." He stops for a moment.

"It's like the train is going," he says. "It gives a whistle and it goes. You run and sit on it if you want to ride. It's only necessary for us to participate and enjoy."

After the meeting, Maharishi returns to the hotel and meets with local teachers. When he finally goes to his room to rest he is still scheduled to leave early the next morning—he has two more continents to cover on his tour. But a last minute change in plans leaves him with the day free to rest. Despite this sudden adjustment, by late morning his room is filled with teachers who have found him still here. It's the first break from travel and speaking he's had in nearly three weeks.

"It's been very constant," he says. "There has been no time to think."

Now that there is time it appears he intends to make use of it. He turns his attention in another surprising direction.

"What I'm thinking," he says, "is now that the Dawn is coming, the next thing is what to do to stabilize and perpetuate the Age of Enlightenment."

It's probably fair to say that not many of us have given that question much attention yet. Before we have a chance to start, he continues with his thought.

"One thing would be good," he says. "We should build a capitol for the Age of Enlightenment on each of the five major continents."

One more time he jumps way out in front. As long as I've known him—from the time of that overnight test in La Antilla—he has shown this same tendency to encroach on the improbable. Just when the Transcendental Meditation Technique was accepted as a means of rest and relaxation, he refocused attention on enlightenment. And now that we are getting comfortable with the Dawn, he is planning to perpetuate midday.

"We should start to work on this right away," he says. "The first thing will be to get some beautiful land to build on. And the physical buildings will be very important. They will last, and they will speak silently of the existence of a simple way to enlightenment. The spirit of the message will be in the evolved state of consciousness of the teachers and in the purity of the system of teaching. But the body of the message will be those buildings which will help preserve the spirit."

It makes sense, but as usual Maharishi is not too concerned with feasibility—or with most people's idea of feasibility, at least. It takes me a few minutes to get over my surprise. I'm just remembering how fast M.I.U. went from idea to reality, in fact, when the phone rings in the back of the hotel room. Someone picks it up and it's Merv Griffin. He knows of five hundred seaside acres between Los Angeles and San Francisco, if Maharishi has anything he would like to do with them. When the message is called across the room, everybody laughs and looks at Maharishi.

"Beautiful," he says. "We should see it."

Fictional timing, perhaps, but somehow it seems only logical as it happens. The fact is it would be hard to say just what is impossible for Maharishi any more. What he has done already can seem impossible—coming out of India alone, generating a world-wide organization with more than ten thousand teachers and more than a million meditators, establishing the effectiveness of his teaching in the research laboratories of the West. He has taken an ancient teaching and made it systematic in the Science of Creative Intelligence; he has founded one university and is founding another, Maharishi European Research University; he has established nearly fifteen hundred World Plan Centers to teach the Transcendental Meditation Technique, a growing network of Forest Academies that specialize in local teacher

"Dr. Salk
invented a
vaccine for polio
and in months
everyone was
innoculated. Polio
was missing from
American life.
When something
is found to work,
why delay?"

training courses (teacher training is now going on in more than thirty countries) and an efficient international organization to oversee all operations. Just this minute I'm having trouble keeping up with his imagination as he begins to plan for capitols for the Age of Enlightenment, and yet it is clear his work to this point has generated a momentum that should only go forward rapidly. And this is, obviously, still just the Dawn. In the last few years, more and more governments and large corporations have begun to support his work in a significant way. As the Transcendental Meditation Program begins to be taught on a wide scale in business, civil service and education, there seems to be no limit to the progress that can come.

Maharishi himself takes no credit for this rapidly growing success, of course. In his mind it is all a natural result of the effectiveness of the technique. If it weren't true about the ease of the Transcendental Meditation Technique, for instance, it's obvious that very few people would try it. If it weren't true about the immediate benefits, even fewer would stay with it. And if it weren't true about the cumulative nature of these benefits—the rapid progress that comes in all phases of life—it's hard to imagine why anyone would want to be trained as a teacher. Maharishi has many skills as a teacher and organizer, and he combines a far-reaching imagination with an endless dedication to detail. But none of these qualities could have come to much if it weren't for the effectiveness of the Transcendental Meditation Technique he is passing on.

Sitting with him in his hotel room on this last afternoon, it's natural to feel respect and gratitude toward him for the work he is doing. But when I get a chance to ask him for guidance in writing this book, I'm not surprised by the answer he gives.

"Don't waste the people's time with a lot of words about my life," he says. "The facts of a monk's biography are not important. They do not help the people. Just emphasize the teaching. Encourage the people to meditate. This is how we can help bring a better time for everyone in the world."

In the long history of mankind, it is this generation that has developed enough science and self-awareness to be receptive to the knowledge that is waiting. The time is right and as Maharishi sees it, his own contribution is very simple. He is teaching the world what he was taught by his master.

A CALL TO ACTION

"**I**t is such a joy to spread this knowledge," Maharishi says. "Working for the World Plan is such a joy. We are aware of the magnitude of the undertaking, but that for us is not a pressure but a delight. We know that the world has reached an extreme point and now the pendulum has started back. The Age of Enlightenment is not yet, but the trends of time are clear. When we have proof of the possibility that human beings can be better, then we feel bold to come out and shout it from the rooftops."

And the transformation can really come quickly?

"There is no reason why a new formula cannot be taken up quickly in this generation. Dr. Jonas Salk invented a vaccine for polio and in months everyone was innoculated. Polio was missing from American life. When it was found that something worked, why delay? Scientific research was behind it. Like that, the Science of Creative Intelligence has been found to eliminate the basis of problems, so why waste time? We have the methodology, the practical technique, and we have the theoretical understanding of the technique on the ground of modern science. We are not groping in the darkness for principles, we are not at a loss for the procedure. And it is a completely innocent knowledge. It does not touch anyone's economic beliefs or political beliefs or religious beliefs. There are no "do's and don't's." The only thing is that the responsible citizens in each society, the leaders, should take this up and make it available to all the people. As soon as we *can* do it, we *should* do it."

But aren't the teachers of the Transcendental Meditation Technique responsible for seeing to the spread of this knowledge?

"No. This is not something that only we are doing. This is not only *our* world. This is a universal effort to bring on something useful for all mankind. It is not like a formal dinner given by just a few people. This is like a picnic, and a picnic is prepared by everyone together for all to enjoy."

What should people do to help?

"The main thing is to practice the Transcendental Meditation Technique fifteen or twenty minutes morning and evening. Just fifteen or twenty minutes we let our minds settle down to that state of perfect order, and then we bring that influence of orderliness into our environment. Now we know that we no longer meditate only for our own benefit, but for the benefit of the whole society. A man has no right any longer to spread disorderliness into his environment. The practice of the Transcendental Meditation Technique is by now a social obligation."

And simply meditating is enough?

"When we know of the benefits of the Transcendental Meditation Technique, it is only natural to tell our friends. It is a chain reaction. We bring our friends to the teachers and help free our society of problems. But the main thing is that the leaders of society take it up. It is up to the wise people, the successful people, the influential people in every locality to bring this beautiful knowledge to the people. The educational systems are already there, governmental training programs are already there, industrial training programs are already there. All that is needed is to use these established channels. Now it only depends on the leaders when we begin to eliminate problems. What we need are highly qualified people to be the teachers of the Science of Creative Intelligence, and the facilities to give the training. The

"Those who are
not for the TM
Program today
will be for it
tomorrow. We
just get ready and
go ahead."

procedures we have already."

Will enough people be interested?

"They must be. It's the need of the time. It's not enough to read the newspaper and talk about all the problems and suffering. That is no good. We can't be a witness to this derangement without doing something about it. And helping our neighbors is very natural to life. Already so many people join together to help people. They join this organization or that, and contribute their time to doing good in some area. But if we can spend time on something which will really glorify *all* aspects of life, why waste time in attending to different aspects? If we can glorify the leaf and the flower and the branch and the stem all with one operation of watering the root, why waste time attending to every petal? Let every well-meaning head of state, every well-meaning community, religious, educational and medical leader champion the knowledge of the Transcendental Meditation Technique, distribute it to the people and free themselves and the world of the burden of all these problems."

Not everyone knows about this yet. Not everyone is ready to act.

"It doesn't matter. Those who are not for it today will be for it tomorrow. We just get ready and go ahead. And when the World Plan is complete, and there is one teacher available for every one thousand people, then on that basis we will feel so fulfilled, so highly honored. Our children will grow and live in a time of greater and greater harmony and peace. And eventually world peace will be a permanent reality. The Transcendental Meditation Program is ushering in a new age for a new humanity, a humanity fully developed in all the values of life—physical and mental, material and spiritual. Accomplishments will be great in the family, the society, the nation and the world. Suffering will be missing. Problems will be missing. And man will live naturally, in peace and fulfillment, generation after generation."

The work continues;
Maharishi leaves for
the Southern
Hemisphere and the
rest of the tour.

"Our movement belongs to those who move."
—Maharishi

Science Looks at Enlightenment: An ABC of Personal Evolution

The aim of the first three chapters in this section is to take the most fundamental concepts presented by Maharishi in Part One and examine them in the light of scientific research. The fourth chapter stands by itself as a discussion of the mechanics of the Transcendental Meditation Technique—with special attention given to the question of the "mantra."

The Transcendental Meditation Technique is helping to bring about a union of the best from both the East and West, and laboratory investigation is providing the objective, unarguable "glue" for the synthesis. Ideas about "pure consciousness" and "evolution" might seem surprising when they are first heard, but in fact scientific investigation has gone a long way toward defining them already. Research on the Transcendental Meditation Technique has shown that the body, the nervous system and the brain are capable of a rapid process of self-correction or "normalization," a process of evolution basically unsuspected even five years ago. Through research, the TM Technique is providing new insights into the nature of man, a new paradigm for human psychophysiological functioning.

Each of the first three chapters in this section has a specific aim. Chapter One examines Maharishi's contention that the TM Technique produces a fourth state of consciousness, and that the experience of this fourth state of consciousness is the basis of evolution toward enlightenment. Chapter Two compares Maharishi's definition of stress with those current in medical science, and analyzes research showing that the Transcendental Meditation Technique reverses the damages of the "stress syndrome." Chapter Three compares Maharishi's definition of evolution in personal life with (1) research on the TM Technique and (2) the needs of modern man as detailed in Alvin Toffler's book *Future Shock*.

Through research, the TM Technique is providing new insights into the nature of man, a new paridigm for human functioning.

Chapter One
The Breakthrough: Discovering the Fourth State of Consciousness

The Transcendental Meditation Program has become a part of mainstream American life. In the midst of a practical technological culture, the TM Technique has gained wide acceptance—even in the most unimpeachably "establishment" circles.

• More than seventy businesses have instituted Transcendental Meditation Programs, including the General Foods Corporation, and Blue Cross.

• The Transcendental Meditation Program has been taken up by many professional athletic teams, and athletes practicing the TM Technique include such well known names as Arthur Ashe in tennis, Joe Namath in football and Willie Stargell in baseball.

• The Transcendental Meditation Program is being used in many other areas, including secondary schools, universities and military academies, hospitals, rehabilitation and retraining programs, prisons and retirement homes.

• Increasing media acceptance of the Transcendental Meditation Program reached some sort of popular highpoint in the fall of 1975 when TIME magazine put Maharishi on its cover. The accompanying article, far from calling the TM Technique exotic and unusual, labeled it "refreshingly dull and commonplace." The Transcendental Meditation Program has become an accepted part of modern life.

There is a reasonably simple explanation that can be given to account for this widespread acceptance of the Transcendental Meditation Program. Summed up in a few phrases, this explanation is admirably logical: The Transcendental Meditation Technique refreshes the body and mind with profound levels of rest and relaxation; this deep rest dissolves the stress and fatigue that block the system from full and free activity; with these blocks removed, it is natural for the experience of life to improve—worries are less, energy is greater, activity seems to flow with less effort.

This explanation has several virtues. In the first place, it is easy to understand. It lends itself to simple analogies ("When the gas line of a car is cleaned of dirt and sludge, naturally the car performs better; when the body and nervous system are cleared of backed-up stress and fatigue, naturally life

Rest and relaxation normally lead toward sleep, but the TM Technique leads to an experience often referred to as "restful alertness." It is this experience that needs explanation.

becomes easier and more enjoyable"). And it speaks to an issue that concerns many people—stress might be the most common "perceived problem" in modern society. The effectiveness of the Transcendental Meditation Technique as an antidote to stress deserves careful attention, in fact, and the next chapter focuses solely on this issue.

As a fundamental explanation for the mechanics of the Transcendental Meditation Technique, however, no theory based solely on rest and relaxation can ever be satisfactory. The reason for this is clear from the nature of the practice. During the practice of the Transcendental Meditation Technique, a person not only experiences profound levels of rest and relaxation, but also a pleasant, refreshing quality of "inner wakefulness." Rest and relaxation normally lead toward sleep, but the TM Technique leads to an experience often referred to as "restful alertness" or "refined awareness."

It is this experience of rest plus alertness that needs explanation. And it is this experience that Maharishi has defined in the first part of this book. He covers his thesis in great detail, but again, the core of his teach-

ing can be condensed into a few thoughts: The rest and relaxation brought about by the Transcendental Meditation Technique is actually a result of the mind settling down to a "state of least excitation," a "fourth state of consciousness;" it is the experience of this basic level of consciousness that enlivens both the body and mind, leading to rapid "evolution," physically, mentally and emotionally; this process of evolution leads to the enjoyment of full potential in all areas of life, a state Maharishi terms "enlightenment."

Now the question about this explanation—as opposed to the one that confines itself to rest and relaxation—is that the whole vocabulary of concepts is something new for most of us. Stress and tension may be common complaints, but the topic of "consciousness" is hardly a conversational staple in most American homes. It is pretty well accepted that the Transcendental Meditation Technique relieves stress and tension, but it is not at all clear to most people that it leads to such experiences as "pure consciousness," "evolution" and "enlightenment." And the difference between these two ways of looking at the Transcendental Meditation Pro

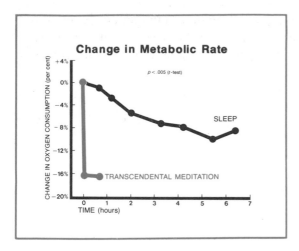

Change in Metabolic Rate

$p < .005$ (*t*-test)

SLEEP

TRANSCENDENTAL MEDITATION

CHANGE IN OXYGEN CONSUMPTION (per cent)

+4%
0%
−4%
−8%
−12%
−16%
−20%

TIME (hours)
0 1 2 3 4 5 6 7

Physical Rest

Finding: Metabolic rate is determined by measuring how much oxygen the body is using. This first study on the Transcendental Meditation Technique showed that oxygen usage decreased 16 per cent on the average within a few minutes of the start of the meditation period. The study showed the decrease to be quicker and deeper than sleep.

Interpretation: The decrease in oxygen usage during the TM Technique indicates a state of extremely deep physical rest. This deep level of rest is the basis for increased energy and vitality.

Reference: Robert Keith Wallace and Herbert Benson, "The Physiology of Meditation", *Scientific American*, vol. 226, no. 2, 1972: pg. 84–90.

gram is vital. If the TM Technique is nothing more than a relaxation technique—a "non-medicinal tranquilizer"—it will be able to bring great relief to many tension-ridden people, and that will be the end of it. But if Maharishi is right, if the Transcendental Meditation Technique is a rapid means all people can use to unfold their full conscious potential, then a new possibility for human life has appeared and is already becoming an integral part of modern society.

The goal of this chapter is to define Maharishi's terms through the objective results of scientific research. It is certainly true that up until recently, few people have been thinking in terms of consciousness and personal evolution. But there is nothing hard about these ideas, and much that is already verified. Scientific studies have given substance to an ancient teaching about the nature of life.

The first concept that needs to be discussed is the contention that the TM Technique leads to the experience of a "fourth state of consciousness." To get a start on this point, we need to be comfortable with the basic idea of "consciousness." That should be easy, because starting from consciousness is like starting from home. We all know we *are* conscious—we have to be conscious before we can function. The only problem is that we usually don't pay much attention to how well we do at *being* conscious. We don't much notice the quality of our consciousness.

The reason for this neglect is something like the reason we neglect the movie screen when watching a movie. In a movie theater, our attention is on the action, not the screen that underlies the action. In much the same way, during our day-to-day life our attention is on the things that happen, rather than on the consciousness that *experiences* those happenings. A movie plays on the screen. Life "plays" on our consciousness. Even if we don't much notice it, therefore, our consciousness is the continuous, basic background condition for all our experiences. And this is the important point: the quality of our consciousness determines the quality of our life. To continue with the movie analogy, if the screen is dull and dirty,

Consciousness goes through several states. Every normal human being is familiar with three of these: the state of being awake, the state of sleep and the state of dreaming.

the picture is not bright and clear. If our consciousness is dull and "smudged" with stress, life does not seem bright and enjoyable. Consciousness, as Maharishi says, is the basis of thought, action and achievement.

Despite this clear connection between the quality of consciousness and the quality of life, until recently there has been little talk about the topic of consciousness in the technological cultures of the West. Consciousness can seem to be a vague, fuzzy subject, and most people today feel more comfortable with ideas that can be pinned down in the laboratory. Analogies about movie screens are all right, as far as they go, but they hardly produce anything precise and measurable. Consciousness has been hard to measure and a scientific age wants to look at those hard numbers.

In recent years, fortunately, technology has advanced enough to begin to make a contribution in this field. Biomedical measurements have increased in both range and refinement. These advances have helped to move the topic of consciousness from the realm of vague abstractions and place it squarely in the field of scientific fact. Not that researchers have been able to measure consciousness directly, of course—you can't lay a ruler next to a non-material entity. But two basic facts about the nature of the human system have opened consciousness to systematic study. Both these facts are obvious enough—Maharishi also discusses them in the first part of this book—and between them they allow for the "quantification of consciousness."

To begin with, consciousness may be non-material, but it is not cut off from a physiological basis. The mind and body are very closely interconnected. If the body is tired, the mind is dull. If the body is fresh and rested, the mind is sharp and clear. The functioning of the body, and especially the nervous system and brain, correlates to the quality of the mind's consciousness. In addition, it is a simple observation that consciousness is not always in the same "state." During every day, in fact, consciousness goes through several different, clearly defined states. Every normal human being is familiar with three of these: the state of being awake, the state of being asleep and the state of dreaming.

145

The discovery of a fourth state of consciousness is a completely new and extremely fundamental finding about the nature of the human system—as if we just now determined that oxygen is basic to human life.

We all know we are sometimes awake, sometimes asleep and sometimes dreaming. And the important fact is that a medical scientist can tell which of these "states of consciousness" our mind is experiencing by measuring various aspects of our body's activity. In other words, if a scientist measures the electrical activity of the brain, the amount of oxygen the body is burning, and so forth, he can tell if a person is awake, asleep or dreaming. Even if a subject tries to fool him by lying down and closing his eyes, the researcher can tell if he is awake or not by the brain wave patterns, the metabolic rate, and so on. States of consciousness can be measured physiologically. These measurements are so accurate, in fact, that scientists have been able to identify many different "sub-states" of, for instance, the sleeping state.

It is this capability that has opened the Transcendental Meditation Technique to scientific investigation and definition. The mind and body are intimately connected; measuring changes in the body's activity can define changes in the mind's state of consciousness; and it is by using this knowledge that modern science has been able to validate the ancient wisdom about the human mind embodied in the TM Technique.

When a person practices the Transcendental Meditation Technique, there are many clear changes in the body's activity. Both the metabolic rate and the brain wave patterns change dramatically. And looked at scientifically, these and other alterations in physical activity add up to a vital new research discovery. The mind *is* capable of experiencing a fourth major state of consciousness.

The discovery of a fourth natural state of consciousness is obviously one of the most important discoveries in recent history. It is a completely new and extremely fundamental finding about the nature of the human system—as if we just now determined that oxygen is basic to human life. Yet the importance of this discovery is only now beginning to be appreciated, seven or eight years after the first studies began to appear. It is not hard to understand this lag.

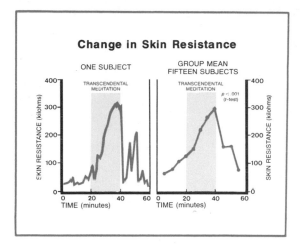

Change in Skin Resistance

ONE SUBJECT

GROUP MEAN
FIFTEEN SUBJECTS

Physical Relaxation

Finding: When a person relaxes, his skin resistance will go up. During the TM Technique, skin resistance goes up consistently and markedly, indicating profound physical relaxation.

Interpretation: The relaxation brought about by the TM Technique is the basis for decreased stress, tension and anxiety. It is important to note that during the TM Technique, relaxation comes naturally and automatically, with no deliberate attempt to relax.

Reference: Robert Keith Wallace and Herbert Benson, "The Physiology of Meditation", *Scientific American*, vol. 226, no.2, 1972: pg. 84-90.

The breakthrough came in a field of science that was still fairly new, answering a question most researchers weren't even asking yet.

About the basic facts, however, there is no doubt. The body's activity during the practice of the Transcendental Meditation Technique is totally different from its activity in any of the other three states. And the "new" state is more than merely different. It has all the signs of being just what Maharishi has called it—a basic state, a fundamental state, a state of "least excitation."

The first definition of this fourth state of consciousness was proposed by Dr. R. K. Wallace in a pioneering article on the Transcendental Meditation Technique that appeared in the journal *Science*. The definition has since been refined by many other experiments. Two of the physical manifestations are most important.

In the first place, during this fourth state of consciousness, the body gains a deep, concentrated level of rest and relaxation. The metabolic rate declines much more rapidly than it does in sleep, and at many points during the meditation period this level of rest is much deeper than the deepest point in sleep. At the same time, the heart rate and rate of breathing also slow down markedly. In the second place—and this is a point researchers have just begun to evaluate in detail—the brain wave patterns become highly coherent. During the usual waking state of consciousness, brain wave patterns are quite disorderly. Different parts of the brain are doing different things, and the pattern from any one part of the brain is changing constantly. In the sleep state, the phase coherence between any two points in the brain drops even more markedly. When a person begins the TM Technique, on the other hand, there is an immediate tendency for all the different parts of the brain to synchronize their activity. Phase coherence begins to develop between the front and the back of the brain, and between the left side and the right. In addition, the patterns coming out tend to stabilize around one or a few frequencies. Researchers have defined several "sub-states" of this fourth state of consciousness, and at the "deepest" point—apparently the point that Maharishi refers to as "pure" consciousness—the entire brain

Biochemical Changes

Finding: During the Transcendental Meditation Technique the concentration of blood lactate markedly decreases and remains low for some time after meditation.

Interpretation: Some scientific studies indicate that high blood lactate is associated with anxiety; some studies have not found this correlation. Since the TM Technique reduces both blood lactate *and* anxiety, this tends to support the idea that blood lactate and anxiety do correlate. This is one indication of the ways the TM Technique has become a research tool for examining the relationship between physiology and psychology.

Reference: Robert Keith Wallace, Herbert Benson and Archie F. Wilson, "A Wakeful Hypometabolic Physiologic State", *American Journal of Physiology*, vol. 221, no.3, 1971: pg. 795–799.

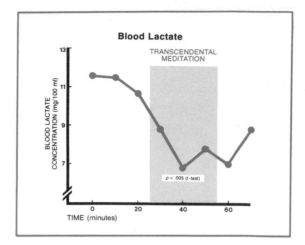

tends to produce a stable, integrated pattern. The usual pattern of random, chaotic activity changes to coherent, orderly activity.

It is easy to see how these findings—replicated by now in several research institutions and published in various professional journals—have defined a state of consciousness that can logically be called a "state of least excitation." The body reaches its lowest level of activity, and the brain stabilizes into integrated, orderly patterns. Moreover, these findings give substance to the subjective reports of people who practice the Transcendental Meditation Technique. These people often describe their experience during the period of meditation by using the phrases "restful alertness," or "refined awareness." Five years ago there was a question if they were talking about anything real or tangible. Research has answered that question now.

Scientific descriptions of a fundamental state of rest and orderliness would, of course, only be frustrating without some way to enjoy that state. Fortunately, the same research that indicates the *existence* of the fourth state of consciousness, has also identified a simple technique anyone can use to

experience it. And it is important to understand that the total pattern of measurable changes occurring during the Transcendental Meditation Technique is unique to this specific practice. Of the various types of "relaxation techniques"—including those that are claimed to work "just like the Transcendental Meditation Technique"—some do indeed produce relaxation, of course. However, none of them has been shown by independent research to produce relaxation as rapid and profound as the TM Technique. And more important, none of them has been shown to produce the changes in brain wave activity typical of the fourth state of consciousness. Nor does hypnosis produce any alteration of brain wave patterns in the direction of the fourth state—hypnosis patterns are usually indistinguishable from waking, sleeping or dreaming patterns. In fact, the only published studies that show brain wave changes similar to those occurring in the Transcendental Meditation Technique are studies involving Zen and Yogic masters, men who have persevered at austere life styles for fifteen or twenty years. With the Transcendental Meditation Technique these

It is easy to see how these findings—replicated by now in
several research institutions and published in various
professional journals—have defined a state of consciousness
that can logically be called a "state of least excitation."

changes have been shown to occur from a person's first meditation.

There is an important question to ask about any new discovery, of course. It is slightly rude but totally relevant. The question is this: So what?

There may be a fourth state of consciousness, but what difference does it make? Why should anyone want to experience it? Sitting quietly with the eyes closed could only have a certain charm, even if a person does enjoy a pleasant state of relaxed inner wakefulness. And the fact is, nobody practices the Transcendental Meditation Technique simply to experience a fourth state of consciousness. People do it for another reason altogether. They like the benefits they begin to enjoy in all aspects of their life. The Transcendental Meditation Technique is a preparation for active living.

This is the point Maharishi sums up in the word "evolution." Regular practice of the Transcendental Meditation Technique enriches all levels of life. The experience of the fourth state of consciousness brings rapid progress to life—progress enjoyed physically, mentally and emotionally. Here again, scientific research has been able to objectively verify the reports of people who practice the technique. So much research has appeared showing the benefits of the TM Technique that the problem is no longer to tell whether the technique works. The problem is to tell how so many benefits can come from such a simple procedure. Most people have only heard of the research linking the TM Technique with relaxation. But even if we limit our attention solely to the twenty-two studies already published in established research journals, we are actually faced with an extremely wide-ranging list of benefits (see box on next page). And these published reports are duplicated and supplemented by a backlog of numerous other studies not yet published, studies showing everything from keener intelligence to decreased insomnia. Virtually every measurable aspect of life seems to improve with the practice of the Transcendental Meditation Technique.

The TM Technique does not produce isolated, fragmented results. It does not treat the human being in small pieces. The practice 149

Published Research on the TM Technique:
A Partial Listing

Physical Benefits

Deeper rest and relaxation than at even the deepest point in sleep
Wallace, R.K., and H. Benson, "The Physiology of Meditation," *Scientific American*, vol. 226, no. 2, 1972: pp. 84–90.

Reduced blood pressure
Wallace, R.K., and H. Benson, "Decreased Blood Pressure in Hypertensive Subjects Who Practice Meditation," Supplement II to *Circulation*, vol. 45 and 46, 1972.

Improved balance of blood chemistry (reductions in lactate acid and cortisol)
First reference: Wallace, R.K., *et al.*, "A Wakeful Hypometabolic Physiologic State,"*American Journal of Physiology*, vol. 22, no. 3, 1971: pp. 795–799.

Second reference: Jevning, R., *et al.*, "Plasma Prolactin and Cortisol During Transcendental Meditation," *The Proceedings of the Endocrine Society*, 1975.

Increased stability of the nervous system
Orme-Johnson, D.W., "Autonomic Stability and Transcendental Meditation," *Psychosomatic Medicine*, vol. 36, no. 4, 1973: pp. 341–349.

Improved adaptability of the nervous system under stressful stimulation.
Orme-Johnson, *op. cit.*

Reduction of asthma
Honsberger, R., and Wilson, A., "Transcendental Meditation in Treating Asthma," *Respiratory Therapy: The Journal of Inhalation Technology*, vol. 3, no. 6, 1973: pp. 79–81.

Reduction of drug abuse
Shafii, M., *et al.*, "Meditation and Marijuana," *American Journal of Psychiatry*, vol. 131, no. 1, 1974, pp. 60–3.

Reduction of use of alcohol
Shafii, M., "Meditation and Prevention of Alcohol Abuse," *American Journal of Psychiatry*, vol. 131, no. 9, 1975, pp. 942–945.

Psychological Benefits

Increased orderliness of functioning of the brain
Banquet, J-P.,"Spectral Analysis of the EEG in Meditation," *Electroencephalography and Clinical Neurophysiology*, vol. 35, 1973: pp. 143–151.

Improved ability to focus attention while maintaining broad awareness
Pelletier, K., "Influence of Transcendental Meditation upon Autokinetic Perception," *Perceptual and Motor Skills*, vol. 39, 1974, pp. 1031–1034.

Decreased anxiety
Hjelle,L.,"Transcendental Meditation and Psychological Health," *Perceptual and Motor Skills*, vol. 39, pp. 623–628.

Reduced depression and neuroticism
Ferguson, P., and Gowan, J., "Psychological Findings on Transcendental Meditation," *Journal of Humanistic Psychology* (in press).

Therapeutic aid for psychiatric patients
Glueck, B., and C. Stroebel, "Bio-Feedback and Meditation in the Treatment of Psychiatric Illnesses," *Comprehensive Psychiatry*, vol. 16, no. 4, 1975: pp. 303–21.

Improved self-regard, self-acceptance, inner directedness, spontaneity and flexibility
Seeman, W., Nedick, S., and Bantam, T., "Influence of Transcendental Meditation on a Measure of Self-Actualization," *Journal of Counseling Psychology*, vol. 19, no. 3, 1972: pp. 184–187.

Increased inner control
Hjelle, *op. cit.*

Increased self-actualization
First reference: Seeman, *op. cit.*
Second reference: Ferguson, *op. cit.*

Improved performance in a job setting.
Frew, D., "Transcendental Meditation and Productivity," *Academy of Management Journal*, vol. 17, no. 2, 1974: pp. 362–368.

A natural momentum of progressive improvement is set up. Mental refinement allows physical refinement which then produces even greater mental refinement.

of the TM Technique produces a natural, integrated response that affects the functioning of the system at many levels at once. The wide range of benefits, in other words, is not haphazard or accidental. It is a reflection of the growth occurring at the most basic levels of the human system.

Five years ago there was no research to indicate the human system had such an in-built mechanism for rapid personal "evolution." Even if the discovery is relatively new, however, it is already quite clear how the process works. The Transcendental Meditation Technique allows the body and mind to work together in an interchange that could be labeled "mutual purification." At the beginning of meditation, the mind begins to settle down toward more "refined" levels of awareness, levels marked by more coherent functioning of the brain and nervous system. (See Chapter Four for a detailed description of this mental experience during the Transcendental Meditation Technique.) Because the mind and body are closely integrated, as the mind settles down, the body also settles down to a deep state of rest. This profound level of rest and relaxation allows the body to

refine its *own* functioning by throwing off fatigue and stress. As the functioning of the body improves—especially the nervous system and brain—this in turn allows the mind to become even more subtle in its awareness. A natural momentum of progressive improvement is set up. Mental refinement allows physical refinement which then produces even greater mental refinement. The experience of the fourth state of consciousness brings rapid "normalization" for both the body and mind.

This progress, which begins as refinement in a person's state of consciousness, carries over into all aspects of life. Physical health is improved by the refreshing effects of deep rest and relaxation. The mind is, almost literally, "tuned up" by the experience of greater integration and orderliness in the nervous system. With tension and anxiety reduced, life is more enjoyable. As a person begins to feel greater strength and energy, brought about by the increased efficiency of his system, it's also natural to feel increased self-confidence and psychological stability. With all of these benefits making life more rewarding at the individual level, 151

The basic state has been missing. Almost all people have been "deprived," left out of touch with the fundamental state of rest and revitalization that is part of their nature.

then this good feeling automatically begins to be shared with others. Improved interpersonal relations are a spontaneous result. This scientifically verified picture of personal evolution has been summed up quickly by Maharishi.

"With the experience of the fourth state of consciousness," Maharishi says, "waking, sleeping and dreaming states of consciousness gain more richness. The waking state becomes brighter, the sleep state brings better rest, the dreaming state more efficiently carries out its function of release of stress and strains. When the pure state of consciousness is located and experienced and this experience is repeated, then the enrichment of life in all states rises quickly."

These ideas have now been backed up by research. And what the studies show, when taken all together, is that something vital is missing when a person only experiences waking, sleeping and dreaming. Mankind has been limping along on three states of consciousness, like a four-cylinder car hitting on only three. And it is the basic state that has been missing, the state that both stabilizes and enlivens the others. If the sorry condition

of the world today is a testimony to man's weakness and imbalance, science has now defined a major reason why. Almost all people have been "deprived," left out of touch with the fundamental state of rest and revitalization that is part of their nature.

This is why the Transcendental Meditation Technique can have such profound effects, even though it is an easy, natural process. It works from the basic level of human consciousness. As Maharishi says, allowing the mind and body to experience the fourth state of consciousness is like watering the root of a tree.

The central point is summed up in a quote that has come down to us from philosophical debates in classical Greece two thousand years ago. It is short and to the point: "As a man's mind is, that is how he is."

Consciousness is the basis of thought and action. And when a man's consciousness evolves, all of him evolves along with it.

It's a spate of neglected ideas all at once—that consciousness is important, that there exists a largely un-

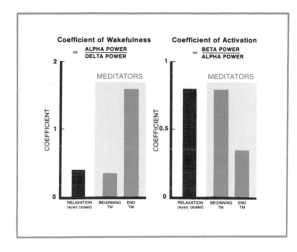

Liveliness During Rest

Finding: Electroencephalographic (EEG) studies of brain wave activity show a shift in the distribution of electrical power among the different types of brain waves during the TM Technique. These changes show increased wakefulness and decreased activation.

Interpretation: This study validates the reports of meditators that they experience full consciousness together with increased inner quietness. Simple relaxation, on the other hand, produces a *decreased* coefficient of wakefulness. This is one of the findings that establishes the experience during the TM Technique as a major fourth state of consciousness.

Reference: Jean-Paul Banquet and M. Saillan, "Analyse E.E.G. d'etats de conscience induits et spontanes", *Revue d'Electroencephalographie et Neurophysiologie*, vol. 4, 1974: pg. 445–453.

suspected fourth state of consciousness, that alternation of this fourth state with the other three results in rapid, measurable evolution for the system as a whole. But as Maharishi has said, if an Age of Enlightenment is to come, it must be on the basis of thinking and procedures that appear to be new—"only a new seed will yield a new crop." Science and technology had already discovered a great deal about the outer, material world. It was time for the "discovery" of consciousness and a technology for its rapid growth.

And once it is established that the human being has such a natural mechanism for measurable "evolution," the next question is whether this process has a cumulative goal. Maharishi, of course, says it does. This is the state he terms "enlightenment." In his definition, a definition handed down by an ancient tradition of teachers, enlightenment is the normal state for human life. It results automatically when all stress has been eliminated, and when the progressive refinement of the body and nervous system has reached full value. At that point, the quality of life assumes a totally positive character. As pointed out earlier in this book, the state of

serenity and peace, first noticed only during the practice of the TM Technique, becomes a living reality in daily life. The body and nervous system evolve to the point where they can produce the state of least excitation of consciousness—pure consciousness—simultaneously with states of greater excitation. The fourth state, the basic state, is always there. A person is "at home" in any situation.

"Experience of pure consciousness on a permanent basis," says Maharishi, "means we will never be lost to ourselves. It permits one to live life in its full stature and significance. It eliminates fear, tension and suffering on both the individual and social levels, bringing peace to life. And through the permanent experience of pure consciousness, man is able to use his full potential. It is then possible to live life in freedom while accomplishing the maximum in our daily life."

Maharishi describes many beautiful qualities that come when life is lived at this level of full potential—qualities such as a greatly enhanced awareness and appreciation of life, a permanent sense of inner happi-

Brain Wave Synchrony

Finding: During the practice of the Transcendental Meditation Technique, alpha brain waves (8–12 cycles per second) spread spontaneously (without any attempt at specific training) from the back to the front of the brain. Other findings indicate that these alpha waves are coherent ("in step"); that coherence can involve theta waves and beta waves as well; and that coherence develops between the left and right hemispheres, as well as between the front and the back of the brain.

Interpretation: The increased integration and coherence of the brain over wide distances is a striking feature of the fourth state of consciousness. This type of long-distance coherence goes down in sleep.

Reference: Jean-Paul Banquet, "EEG and Meditation", *Electroencephalography and Clinical Neurophysiology,* vol. 33, 1972: Pg. 454.

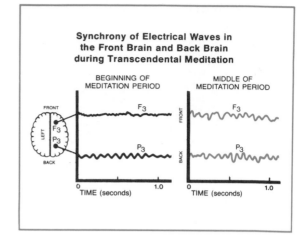

Synchrony of Electrical Waves in the Front Brain and Back Brain during Transcendental Meditation

ness, and unshakable stability combined with the ability to act spontaneously and correctly in any situation. From the standpoint of an age of science, however, the first important issue is more technical. It must be established that "enlightenment" is not just an imaginary mood a person experiences. Enlightenment must have some tangible basis in the operation of the body and nervous system. If there *is* a state of enlightenment, in other words, it should be measurable physiologically.

Producing such measurements should not be difficult. Maharishi defines enlightenment as the ability to experience "pure" consciousness at the same time as the waking state of consciousness—or at the same time as the sleep state, or the dream state. This sort of "dual" awareness—two states of consciousness at once—should produce an easily identifiable pattern of brain waves.

At this stage, unfortunately, no research on long-term meditators has been published. It has taken some time just for researchers to show that the Transcendental Meditation Technique works for the simplest

problems such as high blood pressure and insomnia.

In one of the studies that has appeared, however, there is at least an indication of the type of finding that could establish the definite physiological "fingerprints" of enlightenment. This finding was part of a pioneering study on the electroencephalographic readings during the Transcendental Meditation Technique. The study was done by Dr. Jean-Paul Banquet at the French National Institute for Medical Research, and published in the world's most respected journal of electroencephalography. This particular finding occurred at first accidentally during Dr. Banquet's research. Although most of his subjects had practiced the Transcendental Meditation Technique a relatively short period of time, he did have several people who had been meditating between three and five years. During the experimental period, one of these long-term meditators fell asleep.

Brain wave patterns produced during that time were similar to the "dual" theta-alpha patterns Dr. Banquet saw during normal meditation periods (see box on facing

EEG Research
on the TM Technique

The Transcendental Meditation Technique, viewed scientifically, is now much more than a phenomenon in need of verification. It has become a stimulus for new and increasingly subtle investigation into the workings of the human system.

Much of this research has centered on the brain. The important research tool is the electroencephalograph, the machine that measures electrical "brain waves." The "EEG" equipment is quite remarkable, but it has limitations. It records different types of brain waves by drawing oscillating lines on paper; the more oscillations per inch, the "faster" the brain wave measured. This method of recording electrical information from the brain is extremely rough, and the inexact nature of this "paper record" was the cause of some confusion in the early research on the Transcendental Meditation Technique.

The very first study on the TM Technique showed that during meditation there tends to be a spreading of alpha waves (alpha waves generally correlate to an experience of relaxed awareness) from the back of the brain up to the front. This was unusual, but not unheard of, and seemed to correlate with meditators' reports that they felt restful and alert at the same time.

Soon other reports came, however, that seemed confusing. Not only did alpha appear during the TM Technique, but so did theta waves (theta waves usually indicate dreaming). This was significant because an alternation of alpha and theta usually means the subject is drowsy and drifting back and forth from waking to sleep.

This finding was difficult to understand because it didn't agree with the reports of mediators. Although people sometimes do fall asleep in meditation, they usually feel wide awake.

The first breakthrough in this impasse was made by Dr. Jean-Paul Banquet. He showed that alpha-theta patterns of meditation are not the same as drowsiness. He did this first in a very simple way. He made sudden noises while his subjects were meditating. A drowsy person would, of course, wake up at a noise, and his brain wave patterns would change. The alpha-theta patterns of meditators did not change, however, indicating something new was happening.

Dr. Banquet's second proof was more elegant. He fed his data into a computer set up to perform a "Fourier Transform" on the numbers. By using this sophisticated new technique he was able to show that the theta and alpha of meditation do not alternate back and forth. They are simultaneous and continuous, a type of pattern that was previously unknown. Improved technology had helped establish a clear indication of the fourth state of consciousness.

Even more subtle computer programs have produced further information. Scientists at Maharishi International University under the direction of Dr. Paul Levine have borrowed programming methods from radar technology that filter out most random signals and interference. This produces a much more "pure" picture of brain wave activity. Using this new methodology, Dr. Levine and his co-workers have been able to quantify exactly what many researchers had seemed to see in the more obscure paper records. During the TM Technique, the entire surface of the brain begins to produce wave patterns that are coherent (exactly "in step"). This "long-distance" coherence is very low in sleep, somewhat higher during waking, and highest during meditation. The fourth state of consciousness is the state of maximum integration and orderliness.

Evolution of the body and mind through the experience of the fourth state of consciousness is a natural phenomenon, and it goes on regardless of why a given person decides to meditate.

page). But there was an important difference. Instead of theta, these patterns combined *delta* waves with alpha waves. While theta waves are ambiguous—they can appear while a person is either awake or asleep—delta waves are usually a clear sign of sleep. Since alpha waves are usually a clear sign of (relaxed) wakefulness, a delta-alpha pattern that is stable and continuous seems to be an indication that the subject is experiencing two states of consciousness at once. After noting this unusual pattern, Dr. Banquet deliberately measured some of his subjects while they were sleeping. In several cases the same delta-alpha pattern appeared again.

Such fragmentary findings prove nothing definite, of course, and Dr. Banquet drew no conclusions from them. But some such evidence should certainly be forthcoming if the state of enlightenment is truly a living reality. Maharishi is now encouraging scientists everywhere not only to do research on meditators of six weeks or six months experience—which is the usual case—but to examine carefully people who have been meditating for a number of years. In addition, Maharishi has set up new, intensive, six-month residence courses for people who have been practicing the Transcendental Meditation Technique for a number of years. The goal of these courses is to speed up the evolutionary process even more, and the participants are being closely monitored by a team of bio-medical specialists. It could easily be a matter of but two or three years before a clear physiological definition of the state of enlightenment is available.

Even when enlightenment becomes as verifiable as deep rest, however, most people will continue to practice the Transcendental Meditation Technique for much more basic reasons. Even with no thought to the "evolution of consciousness," athletes will use the Transcendental Meditation Technique in order to compete more effectively, businessmen to handle the pressures of the job more easily, students to do better in school.

And it is this very practical basis to the Transcendental Meditation Technique that makes an "Age of Enlightenment" seem to be a viable possibility. The Transcenden-

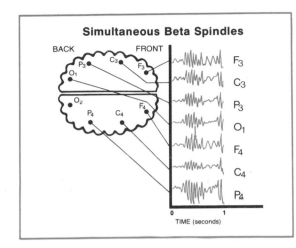

Simultaneous Beta Spindles

BACK   FRONT

TIME (seconds)

Increased Orderliness of Brain Functioning

Finding: Subjects practicing the Transcendental Meditation Technique were asked to push a button after noticing the experience described as "pure awareness" or "pure consciousness". The EEG recordings showed that just before this signal, synchronized beta wave "spindles" (coherent bursts of activity at 22 cycles per second) appeared at all points on the scalp.

Interpretation: Synchronous beta wave spindles seem not to have been reported in any other EEG study. The phenomenon appears to be specific to the TM Technique, and indicates the most profound sub-state of the fourth state of consciousness.

Reference: Jean-Paul Banquet, "EEG and Meditation", *Electroencephalography and Clinical Neurophysiology*, vol. 33, 1972: pg. 454.

tal Meditation Program is not just another pie-in-the-sky proposal that could be a nice thing if only people would get involved. The TM Technique is practical not only because people *should* do it, but because they *do* do it, they *like* to do it. This is why the technique became a part of the mainstream in American life even before most people knew of its true value. "Enlightenment" might sound interesting, but most people simply want to be able to sleep better at night, or cope better during the day. Under many circumstances, a thousand dollars right now can sound more appealing than a million in five years.

Fortunately, it appears we don't have to make any such choice. The benefits people notice from the Transcendental Meditation Technique are not limited by their own preconceptions. A person may start the practice only to gain relaxation, for instance, or to enjoy more energy. But evolution of the body and mind through the experience of the fourth state of consciousness is a natural phenomenon, and it goes on regardless of why a given person decides to meditate. This is why a man who begins the TM Technique in order to help himself stop smoking may suddenly find himself enjoying his family life more and being more creative at his work. Evolution at the level of consciousness is holistic in nature—it involves all aspects of life at once. The benefits people notice as they begin the Transcendental Meditation Technique are just an introduction to the cumulative progress that scientific research is now defining.

Chapter Two Dissolving Stress: The End of the Age of Anxiety

Nobody wants to suffer from stress. There is no doubt that up until recently most people who have begun the Transcendental Meditation Technique have done so simply because of its proved ability to "dissolve" anxiety, tension, fatigue and other negative effects caused by the stress syndrome.

Still, the whole topic of stress can seem quite mundane. Compared to the avowed purpose of the Transcendental Meditation Technique—the achievement of enlightenment through the evolution of consciousness—talking about the release of stress sounds somewhat watered down. It makes it seem as if the major goal of meditation is simply relaxation. The ability to relax, of course, is all to the good. But aiming for relaxation when the goal is enlightenment is like digging out a runway when the goal is flying. It may be necessary but it doesn't seem too interesting.

It would be a major error, however, to underestimate the problem of stress. Everybody knows that stress isn't a good thing, but non-medical people frequently don't know how bad it is, or even precisely what it means. Stress is far more than a surface case of tension or "nerves." Stress tears at physical health, at psychological stability, and at interpersonal relationships. The period of time since World War II has frequently been called an "Age of Anxiety" and in that time the stress of modern life has become one of the major problems we face, both as individuals and as a society.

It is important, therefore, to have a clear understanding of the destructiveness of stress, to understand the problem as it is seen by medical science; then we can appreciate the fundamental benefits produced by the Transcendental Meditation Technique. Enlightenment may be the goal but, as Maharishi points out, dissolving stress is necessary to attain that goal. Basic and little understood facts about the human psychophysiological system are hidden in such simple statements as, "The Transcendental Meditation Technique dissolves stress."

Stress is a relatively new concept in the medical literature. Dr. Hans Selye, the world's most eminent authority on

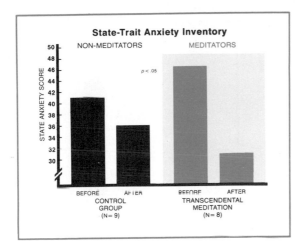

State-Trait Anxiety Inventory

NON-MEDITATORS   MEDITATORS

STATE ANXIETY SCORE

p < .05

BEFORE   AFTER
CONTROL
GROUP
(N = 9)

BEFORE   AFTER
TRANSCENDENTAL
MEDITATION
(N = 8)

Decreased Anxiety

Finding: This study is one of many showing that the TM Technique markedly reduces anxiety. As is often the case in these studies, the subjects who began the TM Technique were more anxious than the control group before beginning the technique, and then less anxious than the control group after six weeks of meditation.

Interpretation: Reduction in anxiety frees a person in thought, feeling and action. This and other studies have shown that the TM Technique brings a much greater reduction in anxiety than relaxing with the eyes closed or practicing a muscle relaxation technique.

Reference: Sanford Nidich, et. al., "Influence of the Transcendental Meditation Program on State Anxiety", *Journal of Consulting and Clinical Psychology* (in press).

the topic, published the first paper on it in the 1930s. Since then it has quickly become one of the most important areas of research in modern medicine. Thousands of papers on the topic now appear every year.

Stress has been recognized as a contributing cause to so many problems—from heart disease and ulcers to neurosis and depression—that many medical authorities now think of it as *the* basic ailment. In a modern industrial society the main problem is not the specific diseases people catch. The main problem is the general level of stress that weakens them in the first place. Stress has become the definitive "dis-ease" of the twentieth century.

For a definitive concept, however, stress has a disconcerting number of meanings. It's not immediately obvious what different people are talking about when they use the word. When most laymen say they are suffering from stress, for instance, they mean they are afflicted by something outside themselves. They are "under" stress. Circumstances are too much for them.

Dr. Aaron T. Beck, of the University of Pennsylvania, a noted expert on the prob-

lem of anxiety and depression, sums up this definition in technological terms. "The word 'stress' was borrowed from physics and engineering," he says. "In those fields it has a very precise meaning: a force sufficient to distort or deform when applied to a system." If we are "under" enough stress, we "bend" or "break."

Although this common sense notion of stress obviously has truth to it—circumstances *can* affect people—many medical experts feel it is more useful to define stress as something that goes on inside of a person, rather than outside of him. Stress is not in the environment, but in our *reaction* to the environment.

The most popular theory along these lines is that the human biochemical apparatus was set up to handle problems very different from the ones we face in modern urban life. The system was built to deal with the short-run emergencies of pre-historic times—the hungry bears and flash floods our ancestors had to face. The current reality, however, is usually slow-burn aggravations—the traffic jams and irate bosses that disarrange day-to-day existence.

Increased Inner Control, Decreased Anxiety

Finding: Compared with a control group of non-meditators, subjects practicing the Transcendental Meditation Technique were shown to be significantly more internally controlled and significantly less anxious.

Interpretation: In modern psychology high 'internal locus of control' is considered a reliable index of overall personality adjustment and ability to learn from and deal effectively with complex situations. This study shows that the TM Technique not only reduces anxiety, but positively increases a person's psychological strength and stability.

Reference: Larry A. Hjelle, "Transcendental Meditation and Psychological Health", *Perceptual and Motor Skills*, vol. 39, 1974: pg. 623–628.

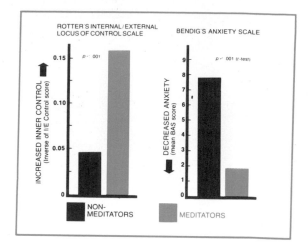

The result of this inappropriate match-up is neurochemical overkill. A loud horn or disapproving memo can trigger the system into a full-fledged "fight-or-flight" response. The adrenal and pituitary glands flood the system with hormones and the sympathetic branch of the autonomic nervous system mobilizes the body for defensive action. Together, these neuro-chemical signals tense the skeletal muscles, restrict digestion, constrict surface skin vessels, and increase the breathing and the heart rate. The system goes into its most excited state, ready for a fight to the death or a full-speed escape.

The problem is that usually there is no outlet for all this arousal. In the modern world there is rarely anything for the excited system to attack—except itself.

"The fight-or-flight response had obvious survival value when we were living in the jungle," says Dr. Harold Bloomfield, the Director of Psychiatry at the Institute for Psychophysiological Medicine in San Diego, California. "But it has become a maladaptive response in civilized society. It's not very often that we really have to fight or flee, and so we wind up suffering from the chemical consequences of overexcitation."

Under modern conditions, the tendency is for the system to become hyperaroused and then stay that way for long periods of time with no effective way to discharge the energy. Trapped in this excited state, the body not only strains its cardiovascular system and damages its digestive apparatus, it also wears down its supply of the vital arousal chemicals. The result is vulnerability to real dangers and diseases.

Dr. Selye, working at the University of Montreal, has done much of his most important research on the chemical occurrences during the stress syndrome (of which the fight-or-flight response is the first stage). By now his research has led him to define stress in a very broad way.

"Stress is the non-specific response of the body to *any* demand made upon it," Dr. Selye says. "Even breathing involves some stress."

The closest everyday expression to this definition of stress is "wear-and-tear." It doesn't matter if an automobile is driven in forward or reverse, there will still be wear-and-tear on the engine. Similarly, it doesn't

Stress is not a problem only for people who feel excessively
nervous. Stress is a part of the process of living,
and the effects are there even if they aren't clearly felt.

matter if we have to escape from a bear or we want to compose a symphony, at a basic level in the biological system, there is always stress involved. This definition emphasizes the fact that stress affects everybody. It's not a problem only of people who feel excessively "nervous." Stress is a part of the process of living, and the effects are there even if they aren't clearly felt. All people need some way to minimize what Dr. Selye has called in one of his book titles, *The Stress of Life*.

The definition Maharishi uses for stress is slightly different than any of those already covered. Rather than focusing on the stress that is in the environment, or on the process of stress as it occurs in the body, Maharishi is concerned with the physical *results* left behind in the body by any experience.

"Stress," Maharishi says, "is a physiological abnormality caused by an overload of experience." This definition shifts the focus from the "stressful" experience to the "stressed" body and nervous system. The point is that any abnormality in the system restricts healthy living. Again, with this definition, stress is obviously of concern to everyone. And the important question does not concern the way any particular "stress" happened to an individual. The question is how to get rid of it. "Dissolving" stress should lead toward normal, healthy life.

Despite these different abstract definitions of stress, the concrete problem is quite obvious. The reason why stress is such an important medical concept—the reason why the Transcendental Meditation Technique is so important for its anti-stress effects—is that stress causes such wide-ranging damage.

Doctors have long been aware of the relationship between stress and such physical maladies as hypertension, ulcers, asthma, skin allergies and headaches. And the connection between stress and heart disease is a recent discovery. Previously, heart disease had been linked with diet, smoking or lack of exercise. However, research conducted on more than 3500 subjects by Dr. Meyer Friedman and Dr. Ray H. Rosenman at the Harold Brunn Institute of Mount Zion Hospital in San Francisco, has shown that the most im-

**Studies have shown that people in management positions—
people responsible for other people—suffer the most stress.
And the result is a reduced quality of leadership.**

portant factor in heart disease is actually a person's personality. If a person is type "A"— aggressive, hard-working, time-conscious— he is much more likely to have a heart attack than the more relaxed and spontaneous (though not necessarily less efficient) type "B". A "stressed" personality engenders heart attacks.

And the physical effects of stress aren't confined to any specific disease. Stress can weaken the system in a general way and make it susceptible to nearly any form of physical ailment. In an informative article on stress that ran in *Fortune Magazine* in 1972, Walter McQuade calls attention to Claude Bernard, the most respected nineteenth century French physician. According to Bernard, the problem of health is not embodied in the germs that float around like seeds in the wind. The problem is the "terrain" in the human body. If the "terrain" has been "plowed" (by stress, to use the modern term), then the ever-present germs can flourish. The twentieth century has provided proof of this. A period of mental depression, for example, has been shown to alter nasal mucus membranes, making the area more susceptible to

infection. Stress leads toward illness in obvious, physiological ways.

The relationship between stress and problems of psychology is just as clear. Tension and anxiety are the most common complaints brought to psychiatrists. Although other symptoms may vary from case to case, anxiety is a common feature in almost all psychological and emotional disturbances. In cases where the anxiety is prolonged, especially if the patient sees no way to help himself, the state of mind may eventually give way to a downward spiral of depression.

"Thoreau said that most people live lives of 'quiet desperation,'" says Dr. Byron Rigby, psychiatrist at Guy's Hospital in London. "Now we know there is a style of physiological functioning that accounts for this. The system is in a state of hyperarousal, of excessive readiness for action. It becomes fixed in a state of high excitation and the result is chronic mental disorganization and anxiety."

This state of excess excitation not only affects a person's state of mind. It also interferes with his relations with other people. Tension and worry can result in the

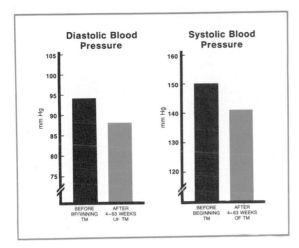

Diastolic Blood Pressure

mm Hg

105
100
95
90
85
80
75

BEFORE BEGINNING TM — AFTER 4–63 WEEKS OF TM

Systolic Blood Pressure

mm Hg

160
150
140
130
120

BEFORE BEGINNING TM — AFTER 4–63 WEEKS OF TM

Reduction of High Blood Pressure

Finding: Two different studies of hypertensive patients have shown that the Transcendental Meditation Technique is effective in reducing high blood pressure.

Interpretation: In the U.S.A. alone, hypertension (high blood pressure) affects over 23 million citizens, including one out of three adult males. Hypertension increases the risk of death and disease due to heart attack, stroke, and damage to vital organs. The Transcendental Meditation Technique is apparently an important method for the treatment of hypertension and, by extension, for the prevention of cardiovascular disease.

Reference: Barry Blackwell et. al., "Effects of the Transcendental Meditation Technique on Blood Pressure: A Controlled Pilot Experiment", *Journal of Psychosomatic Medicine*, (in press).

slammed doors and black glances that poison communications. And when we put stress out into our environment, we increase the amount of stress that comes back to us. A heated departure in the morning is one way to get a cold dinner that night.

These social repercussions of stress extend to entire communities and nations. The "social cost" of stress is extremely high. The most important resource of any society is the people in that society. The use of all other resources is dependent on how much creativity, intelligence and good will the individual members of a society are capable of using. In the fast pace of modern life where most of the individuals are victims of stress that debilitates them physically and psychologically, the society is being robbed of its most vital resources.

The problem is worst where the stress is greatest, on the people who are the leaders of society. Studies have shown that people in management positions—people responsible for other people—suffer the most stress. And the result is a reduced quality of leadership. As stress inhibits the abilities of the leaders, they make mistakes that increase the stress

on themselves and on the people for whom they are responsible. An individual problem becomes a social problem, which then increases the individual problems.

Until the recent emergence of the Transcendental Meditation Technique as a means of breaking in on this self-renewing cycle, the major tool for combating stress has been drugs. Statistics here paint a staggering picture of the problem. An estimated five billion doses of tranquilizers are produced every year, as well as another five billion doses of barbiturates. Stress has turned America into a drug-oriented culture.

Doctors prescribe these drugs in order to force a patient's over-excited system into a state of greater rest. The drugs do have that effect, but few medical experts are really happy with using them. Drugs often have physical side-effects. Many people become addicted to them, as well. Even more basically, many drugs decrease the excitation in the system at the cost of lowering the alertness of the mind. Mental abilities are impaired, including learning and memory. A

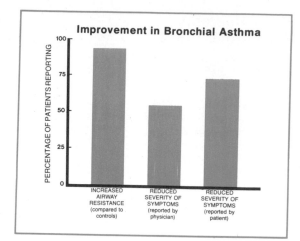

Improvement in Bronchial Asthma

PERCENTAGE OF PATIENTS REPORTING

INCREASED AIRWAY RESISTANCE (compared to controls)

REDUCED SEVERITY OF SYMPTOMS (reported by physician)

REDUCED SEVERITY OF SYMPTOMS (reported by patient)

Beneficial Effects on Bronchial Asthma

Finding: After beginning the practice of the TM Technique, 94 per cent of a group of asthmatic patients showed improvement as determined by the physiological measurement of airway resistance. Fifty-one per cent of the asthmatic patients showed improvement as reported by their personal physicians, and 74 per cent showed improvement as reported by the patients.

Interpretation: Bronchial asthma has been consistently correlated with the level of psychological stress of the individual. By relieving stress, the TM Technique appears to be an effective therapy for psychosomatic diseases.

Reference: Ron Honsberger and Archie F. Wilson, "Transcendental Meditation in Treating Asthma", *Respiratory Therapy: The Journal of Inhalation Technology*, vol. 3, no. 6, 1973: pg. 79–81.

person who was making mistakes because of stress before using drugs often makes mistakes because of dullness while using drugs.

There is also a rebound effect from this sort of medication. The chemicals do artificially suppress overexcitement, but after awhile the tendency of the body to arouse itself begins to fight through the drug. More and more sedatives and tranquilizers may be needed, and when the medication is finally discontinued, the anxiety frequently returns.

Besides the use of drugs, there is another common "technique" used to fight stress, a method that also brings its own problems. This is not a method doctors prescribe. People simply find themselves doing it without knowing precisely why. The tactic is to escape from the discomfort of a high level of excitation by moving up to a level of excitation that is even higher. Some people escape the tension, crowding and noise of city life, for instance, by immersing themselves in the even greater tension, crowding and noise of a football stadium. Other people accomplish the same thing by going to a rock concert, by speeding on a highway, by riding

on water skis, or going to a horror movie. This sort of behavior is a variation of banging one's head against a wall: after a period of "super" excitation, the normally excited state of arousal seems more restful by comparison.

Dr. Ivor Mills, a Professor of Medicine at Cambridge University in England, has been studying this tendency to fight excitation *with* excitation for a number of years. He makes an interesting point. Not only do many people get relief from high states of arousal by going even higher, but more than that, if a person goes down toward lower, more normal levels of excitation, this can sometimes cause depression. Just as people can become addicted to the artificial excitement of amphetamines, they can also become habituated to the excess excitation of stress. For these people, loss of stress seems like loss of vitality and alertness.

Talking about stress isn't too enjoyable, but at least the problem defines its own ideal solution. Stress overloads the physical system and overexcites the mind. A perfect prescription would allow the body and nervous system to quiet down to states of lesser excitation while at the same time it would allow the mind to experience levels of greater peace and satisfaction.

Simple physical relaxation would not be enough. Relaxation alone leads to lethargy and mental dullness. As Dr. Mills points out, this can produce a sense of depression and loss. Relaxation by itself is simply a halfway house on the way to the total loss of alertness and life experience that comes with sleep. This is one of the important reasons why techniques aimed simply at relaxation are never very satisfactory. There is nothing attractive or enlivening about feeling slow and dull.

What is needed is the combination of relaxation and alertness, a state of "restful alertness." This is, of course, precisely the experience during the practice of the Transcendental Meditation Technique. The body attains a deep level of rest and relaxation while, at the same time, the brain's activity becomes more coherent and integrated than normal. The experience is pleasant and satisfying—deep relaxation combined with an at-

tractive and enlivening increase in the quality of mental alertness. The system loses stress *and* gains in awareness. Not only are the negative problems of tension, anxiety and fatigue done away with, but they are replaced by a more subtle and rewarding ability to experience life.

Dr. Bloomfield, who has prescribed the Transcendental Meditation Program as an adjunct to the standard medical and psychiatric treatment of hundreds of patients at the Institute of Psycho-Physiological Medicine, has written two books about his experiences.

"Transcendental Meditation quiets down the hyperarousal characteristic of so many psychiatric patients," says Dr. Bloomfield. "The state of restful alertness elicited by the Transcendental Meditation Technique maximizes the abilities of the mind and body to heal themselves naturally. The practical result for a patient is that, regardless of the particular symptoms he is experiencing, as his system becomes more stable, his symptoms tend to diminish. We know what the effects of stress are—disorder, disease and dissatisfaction. Now we can see what hap- 165

The TM Technique tends to reduce high blood pressure. The heart does not work as hard. The circulatory system seems to become more relaxed and more efficient at the same time.

pens when we have a chance to experience the opposite of stress on a regular basis—increasing order, ease and satisfaction."

Dr. Rigby has also been working with the Transcendental Meditation Program at Guy's Hospital in London. He is concerned with individual health, of course, but also with the problems that individual stress can bring to groups and organizations.

"When stress is severe," Dr. Rigby says, "a person becomes locked in a state of hyperarousal. He loses adaptability. His attention tends to narrow down. This is why it is dangerous for a person in a management position to be in an excited state when he is planning. A leader has to be so *calm* that he takes everything into account, and at the same time he has to be so *alert* that he takes everything into account."

This is why Dr. Rigby has become interested in the Transcendental Meditation Program.

"The Transcendental Meditation Technique reduces arousal and increases alertness," Dr. Rigby says. "This keeps the physiology from being locked into a state of hyperarousal. If we look at what it means for a culture to have access to this state of mind, the benefits are enormous. We know that in any organization, stress is a major component in mistakes, in illness and absenteeism, in accident rates and in interpersonal friction. The Transcendental Meditation Technique reduces all these problems. The savings will be great just in terms of money, not to speak of the levels of satisfaction and fulfillment for the people involved."

A great deal of research has already appeared to back up the clinical experiences of Dr. Bloomfield and Dr. Rigby. The deep state of rest produced by the Transcendental Meditation Technique, along with the more orderly style of functioning in the nervous system, seems to serve as a "balancing" element for the entire physical system. The studies indicate that every aspect of the problem of stress is positively affected.

The Transcendental Meditation Technique reverses the tendency to excess excitation and chemical imbalance. The basic studies, of course, have shown that the Transcendental Meditation Technique reduces metabolic rate rapidly to an extremely low level. The body attains a deep level of

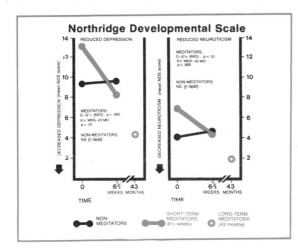

Northridge Developmental Scale

Decreased Depression and Neuroticism

Finding: Research using the Northridge Developmental Scale showed that practice of the Transcendental Meditation Technique significantly reduced the level of depression and neuroticism in subjects. The level was significantly lower for long-term meditators.

Interpretation: Psychological health increases with length of time in the Transcendental Meditation Program. This study shows that with the Transcendental Meditation Technique the standard of the "normal" personality is raised from the mere absence of disease toward the expression of full potential.

Reference: Philip C. Ferguson and John C. Gowan, "Psychological Findings on Transcendental Meditation", *Journal of Humanistic Psychology*, (in press).

rest. Other tests have measured the "jumpiness" of the nervous system, using equipment similar to that of a lie detector. These tests show that the nervous system itself quiets down markedly during the practice of the TM Technique, and that, even outside the period of meditation, this tendency for very low levels of excitation continues. In addition, biochemical tests have shown that the Transcendental Meditation Technique produces a reduction in lactate acid (produced mostly when the system is overworked) and a reduction in cortisol (one of the chemicals that is part of the stress syndrome). Statistically it is clear that the Transcendental Meditation Technique is reversing hyperarousal at fundamental physical levels.

The Transcendental Meditation Technique has positive effects on high blood pressure and the heart. Tests at Harvard University have shown that the deep relaxation of the Transcendental Meditation Technique tends to reduce blood pressure if it is too high. In addition, during the meditation period the heart does not work as hard—it does not beat as often per minute—and this tendency for reduced work load on the heart

continues after meditation (even though people notice they have more energy and research has proved they have greater endurance). The entire circulatory system seems to become more relaxed and more efficient at the same time. Although a complete study on heart disease would take at least a decade, it is obvious that these positive changes should produce greater health for the heart.

The Transcendental Meditation Technique has positive effects on allergies and infectious illness. The TM Technique has been shown to alleviate asthmatic conditions. It also tends to increase the strength of the body's immune system—the defense line against sickness—giving substance to personal reports of reduced tendency to illness.

The Transcendental Meditation Technique reduces anxiety and increases positive psychological attitudes. Studies have shown such a quick and dramatic reduction of anxiety that the TM Program is being used in psychiatric hospitals, where the problem of anxiety is often unbearably severe. More than a dozen separate studies have documented this rapid and cumulative

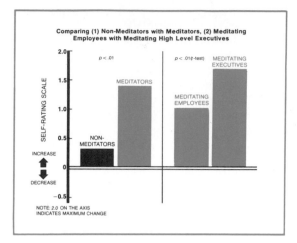

Comparing (1) Non-Meditators with Meditators, (2) Meditating Employees with Meditating High Level Executives

Improved Relations with Co-Workers

Finding: This study showed that working relationships with co-workers were significantly improved through the practice of the Transcendental Meditation Technique. This improvement was seen at both employee and executive levels.

Interpretation: As stress is reduced in any interpersonal situation, it is natural to expect improved relationships. The TM Technique is an established means for developing harmonious interaction among individuals working together in any organization.

Reference: David R. Frew, "Transcendental Meditation and Productivity", *Academy of Management Journal*, vol. 17, no. 2, 1974: pg. 362–368.

release from anxiety. A number of other studies have shown marked reductions in many other stress-related personality traits—irritability, hostility, nervousness, inhibition and depression have all been shown to decrease in a cumulative manner. The research shows, in other words, that psychological symptoms of stress decrease rapidly at the same time as the purely physical manifestations such as high blood pressure and nervous system instability.

The Transcendental Meditation Technique replaces the artificial mental excitation produced by stress with new, more refined levels of awareness. The tendency to increased mental orderliness apparently has the effect of "fine tuning" the mind, and studies show that memory, learning ability and measurable intelligence all increase with the regular practice of the Transcendental Meditation Technique. More important, the personal experience of increased mental clarity means that a person feels more alert and aware, even though he is more relaxed. It is no longer necessary to substitute stress for a natural state of enlivened awareness.

The Transcendental Meditation

Technique improves performance and enjoyment in social and organizational settings. In a school situation, research indicates that the Transcendental Meditation Technique allows students to improve their grade point average while also helping them relate to their peers in more open and constructive ways. A large study in a business setting, conducted by David S. Frew and published in the *Academy of Management Journal,* shows similar results. People improve in their job performance and their personal job satisfaction while also enjoying better relations with their co-workers. And it is the people in leadership positions who notice these effects the most.

It is a remarkable picture. At every level in the human system—from the subtle levels of neural functioning to more obvious manifestations such as physical health, mental alertness and social cohesiveness—the effects of stress seem to diminish with the practice of the Transcendental Meditation Technique. Clearly, this is not simply a question of relaxation. The research docu-

Stress produces imbalance and disorder in the body, the
nervous system and the mind. The TM Technique allows
the experience of balance and order in a natural manner.

ments a thoroughgoing revitalization of the entire system.

Even if the topic is stress, in other words, it is not possible to understand the effects of the Transcendental Meditation Technique simply in terms of physical rest and relaxation. The fundamental and wide-ranging benefits can only be understood with reference to the concept of the fourth state of consciousness. As the mind settles down to experience this fourth state—a state of "least excitation"—this brings an integrated response throughout the body and nervous system that is balanced and orderly. And this integrated response is, in every measurable aspect, the reverse of the stress syndrome.

Perhaps the most important fact about this whole process is that it is completely natural. The effects of stress are unnatural—imbalance and disorder in the normal functioning of the body, the nervous system and the mind. The Transcendental Meditation Technique allows the system to experience a situation of balance and order in a natural manner. A person practicing the Transcendental Meditation Technique does not try to reduce the amount of cortisol in his blood stream, obviously, or try to increase the orderliness of his brain waves. These and all of the other benefits of the practice come as a natural, integrated response when the mind settles down to the fourth state of consciousness.

The Transcendental Meditation Technique appears to be an extremely effective way to dissolve stress and "unlock" the potentials available in every individual. Finally, then, the importance of the problem of stress in modern society is that we have had to search for a way to get rid of it. It can perhaps be said it was necessary for society to become very "stressful," and for science to identify and define the internal nature of the "stress syndrome," before a cure for stress could even be appreciated. And when stress *was* discovered, and when it was found to be an unnatural state of imbalance and disorder, then only a natural method to allow the system to evolve toward greater balance and order would suffice.

In the search to escape stress—in the desire to end the "Age of Anxiety"—the modern world has rediscovered a natural procedure for rapid evolution.

169

Chapter Three   Past Future Shock: The Fundamentals of Progress

The Transcendental Meditation Technique is easy. It is natural. Anyone can do it immediately and benefits begin to appear right from the first session.

And often, precisely because the technique *is* so easy and natural, people have a difficult time understanding how profound it is as well. The benefits that come are welcome, but they appear in a gradual, progressive way, masking the fundamental nature of the progress that is occurring. There is less tension, the mind seems clearer, health improves—but it is not obvious there is an overall pattern to this growth, let alone that it leads to a state of enlightenment.

The previous chapter has hopefully made some contributions in this area. By thinking in terms of stress, and dissolving stress, we can get some overall understanding of the process. Stress is something everybody wants to get away from. But the trouble with this understanding is that it is only negative. Getting away from stress is fine, but what are we going toward? What does evolution mean in a positive sense?

Presumably, the large amount of scientific research should help with these

questions, as it does in defining a reversal of the stress syndrome. In a sense, however, the problem is precisely that there *is* such a large amount of research. A simple listing of proven benefits can seem random and disconnected, and the importance of a reduction of lactate acid, for instance, or an increase in the ability of "field independence" can easily escape us.

What is needed is a frame of reference. We need some way to organize our approach to the research. One logical way to do this is, again, to look at the challenges posed by the fast pace of modern life. What qualities are needed to survive and progress in our rapidly changing world? If we know what qualities we need, we can know what to look for in the studies.

Fortunately, a thorough analysis of the needs of modern man has already become an enormously popular part of the "public conversation." Alvin Toffler's book *Future Shock* supplies a vivid, insightful description of our turbulent times. Based on his observations, Toffler comes to some conclusions about the qualities necessary for man to successfully confront the challenges of the future. His analysis rings true enough to have made his book a mass market phenomenon, and it provides a stimulating angle for viewing the research on the Transcendental Meditation Technique. By comparing the research against Toffler's requirements, we can gain some appreciation of the positive impact of the Transcendental Meditation Technique. And the conclusions that emerge apply to one of the central issues of American life. The "evolution of consciousness" brings a new definition to the concept of freedom.

The main theme of *Future Shock* is a powerful one: the future is rushing at us as an 'avalanche of change and free choice. Society is evolving rapidly to a "super-industrial" state, Toffler says, where a bewildering variety of constantly changing things, places, people, institutions and ideas invade each person's life. The stability that once came from reasonably permanent homes, jobs, friends and family relationships is being dissolved by this rapid pace of change. People are left to flounder in an ever-varying flux of unfamiliar stimuli.

"Future shock," Toffler says, "is the dizzying disorientation brought on by the premature arrival of the future. . . . (U)nless intelligent steps are taken to combat it, millions of human beings will find themselves increasingly disoriented, progressively incompetent to deal rationally with their environments."

With lively powers of observation, Toffler sketches in the causes of this new malady. He identifies three as most important: diversity (myriads of objects, places and life-styles that produce the problems of "overchoice" and "decision stress"), transcience (rapid turnover of people, places, things and ideas in our environment), and novelty (change in unknown directions).

"When diversity . . . converges with transcience and novelty," Toffler says, "we rocket the society towards an historical crisis of adaption. We create an environment so ephemeral, unfamiliar and complex as to threaten millions with adaptive breakdown. This breakdown is future shock."

This concern with "adaptive breakdown," the inability of the human being to keep changing rapidly and continuously, is

Toffler mentions the need for stability and integration, but his main concern is the crisis of adaptability. The need to continuously adapt is a threat to physical and psychological well-being.

the core of Toffler's book. As he builds his argument, however, he does touch on other problems. One of these is the need for new sources of stability in a changing world. "Man must search out totally new ways to anchor himself," he says, "for all the old roots—religion, nation, community, family, or profession—are now shaking under the hurricane impact of the accelerative thrust." The need for integration, at both the social and personal levels, is also given prominent mention. "A society fast fragmenting at the level of values and life styles challenges all the old integrative mechanisms and cries out for a totally new basis for reconstitution . . . [And] if we shall face disturbing problems of social integration, we shall confront even more agonizing problems of individual integration. For the multiplication of life styles challenges our ability to hold the very self together."

But if Toffler mentions the need for stability and integration, his main concern is the crisis of adaptability. We are being inundated by change, and the need to continuously adapt to this state of flux is a threat to physical and psychological well-being.

"Rapid change in the environment makes repeated calls on the energy supply of the body," he says. ". . . [We] adapt: we live. Yet there are finite boundaries; we are not infinitely resilient . . . [Each] adaptive reaction exacts a price, wearing down the body's machinery bit by minute bit . . ."

In addition to these physical difficulties, rapid change brings difficult psychological challenges as well. Excess information and incessant need for decisions overload the thinking process. "It is no accident that so many ordinary people refer to the world as a 'madhouse' . . . ," Toffler says. "The assertion that the world has 'gone crazy' . . . the snowballing belief that reason has failed man, reflects the everyday experience of masses of ordinary people who find they can no longer cope rationally with change."

The world is moving too fast and man seems to be coming to his limits, both physically and psychologically. "[We] must be able to operate at a level of adaptability never before asked of human beings," Toffler says at one point. The demands of change "cry out for a new breed of man," he says at another. Yet he realizes that, at least as he

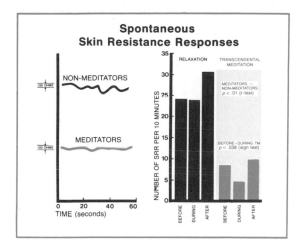

**Spontaneous
Skin Resistance Responses**

Increased Autonomic Stability

Finding: Subjects practicing the Transcendental Meditation Technique were found to have fewer spontaneous skin resistance responses than non-meditating control subjects, indicating greater stability in the autonomic nervous system.

Interpretation: The Transcendental Meditation Technique reduces the "noise level" of the nervous system. Psychophysiologists have shown generally that a condition of fewer skin resistance responses is highly correlated with greater resistance to environmental stress, psychosomatic disease, and behavioral instability.

Reference: David W. Orme-Johnson, "Autonomic Stability and Transcendental Meditation", *Psychosomatic Medicine*, vol. 35, no. 4, 1973: pg. 341–349.

wrote his book in the late 1960s, education and science had discovered no way to bring about any increase in man's usable capabilities. "I gradually came to be appalled by how little is actually known about adaptivity," he says. "Earnest intellectuals talk bravely about 'educating for change' or 'preparing people for the future.' But we know virtually nothing about how to do it." A compelling problem with no fundamental solution—Toffler's book is a brilliant analysis leading to a bleak conclusion. Man needs to increase his adaptability—as well as his stability and integration—but no technique to bring about these beneficial effects has been scientifically verified. Or at least none had been as *Future Shock* was published in 1970.

Just as this discouraging "state of the world" message went out, however, the first information was appearing that promised a solution. Dr. Robert K. Wallace's pioneering article on the Transcendental Meditation Technique in *Science* also appeared in 1970. It was the first research study to indicate there is an easy way for man to experience the rejuvenating fourth state of consciousness. Suddenly the limits of man's capabilities became an open question.

The new state of consciousness was quickly described in the scientific literature as the reverse of the stress syndrome. But the more interesting question was whether this new state could produce any *positive* results. Could it do more than undo previous damage?

Sparked by Wallace's original paper, and by the wide availability of people practicing the Transcendental Meditation Technique, scientists all over the world began to investigate the possible benefits. Hundreds of studies appeared in the next five years— science had not only identified a fourth state of consciousness, but it was now measuring the growth, the evolution, that came with it.

After several years of this research, Maharishi and a group of scientists working with him at the international headquarters of the TM Program in Switzerland began to analyze the flood of data that had appeared. They were looking for threads, for common concepts in the wealth of material. The Transcendental Meditation Technique clearly al-

Increased Autonomic Adaptability

Finding: In this study induced changes in skin resistance response to a stressful stimulus were measured. Subjects practicing the Transcendental Meditation Technique were found to adapt more rapidly to a series of auditory stresses (loud noises) than non-meditators.

Interpretation: Those practicing the TM Technique recover from stress more quickly than non-meditators. This adaptability is known from other psychophysiological studies to be correlated with a more mature style of functioning of the nervous system and a more stable and expressive personality.

Reference: David W. Orme-Johnson, "Autonomic Stability and Transcendental Meditation", *Psychosomatic Medicine*, vol. 35, no. 4, 1973: pg. 341–349.

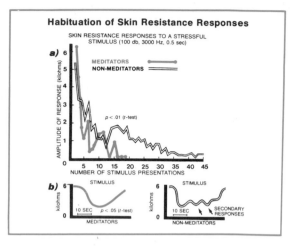

Habituation of Skin Resistance Responses

lowed people to grow in a rapid way. But what were the main lines of this growth? What were the broad outlines that gave structure to the process? Their work distilled into five "fundamentals of progress," five parameters that measure man's evolution.

The first three of these fundamentals would bring hope to Alvin Toffler and all those concerned with man's ability to deal effectively with his rapidly changing society. The Transcendental Meditation Technique apparently produced rapid and cumulative improvements in a person's adaptability, stability and integration.

The full five "fundamentals of progress" extracted from the research by Maharishi and the scientists were adaptability, stability, integration, purification and growth. All five are shown by the research to progressively increase in people who practice the Transcendental Meditation Technique. They begin as physical improvements in the functioning of the body and carry through to mental abilities, emotional attitudes and interpersonal relationships.

Speaking of Toffler's basic concern, adaptability, the research shows that the Transcendental Meditation Technique produces increased adaptability at every important level in the human system. The basis for this improved adaptability is found in improved physical efficiency. The Transcendental Meditation Technique improves reaction time, for instance, allowing the body to adapt more quickly to outside demands. It also allows the body to recover more quickly from heavy exertion (as measured by how fast the body temperature and heart rate return to normal). People who practice the TM Technique also recover from the loss of a night's sleep more quickly.

And the most important single study on the body's improved adaptability shows that the operation of the nervous system itself becomes more flexible and efficient. This is one aspect of the study using "lie detector" machinery (machinery that measures "skin resistance response," the electrical conductivity of the skin). The study was originally performed by Dr. David Orme-Johnson at the University of Texas and published in the journal, *Psychosomatic Medi-*

With the TM Technique, improvement in adaptability, stability, integration, purification and growth begins as physical improvements in the functioning of the body.

cine. Dr. Orme-Johnson jarred the nervous system of his subjects by clanging a loud bell over their heads at irregular intervals, and measured the changes in skin resistance response. The results showed that people practicing the Transcendental Meditation Technique quickly adapted to the bell's ringing. This adaptation was three times quicker, on the average, than for people not practicing the Transcendental Meditation Technique. The conclusion was that meditators adapt to stressful situations much more quickly than non-meditators.

"Studies on the Transcendental Meditation Program are the only ones that indicate a technique which will improve the adaptability of autonomic functioning," says Dr. Orme-Johnson. "No one had thought to investigate how to improve autonomic functioning since no one knew there was a technique that would have such an effect. But the Transcendental Meditation Technique has proved to be such a procedure. Now other researchers have found that its use also produces all the behavioral benefits already known to be correlated with healthy autonomic functioning, including decreased blood pressure in hypertensive patients, improved attention, greater ability to recover from stress, and a stronger ego."

Improved physical adaptability leads to improvement in other aspects of life. As the body becomes healthier, it is natural for the mind and the emotions to improve, too. Many studies have demonstrated an increase in psychological adaptability, for instance. The repeated finding is that the Transcendental Meditation Technique reduces psychological barriers to adaptability such as inhibition and rigidity while it simultaneously increases efficiency, flexibility and spontaneity. Other tests have shown improvement in such mental traits as learning ability, intelligence and creativity, which are the basis of rapid and successful adaption to a changing environment. The Transcendental Meditation Technique produces a thoroughgoing increase in psychological adaptability.

Based on these improvements in physical and psychological adaptability, there is also a natural improvement in adaptability at the level of interpersonal relations. Again, research shows that the Transcenden-

175

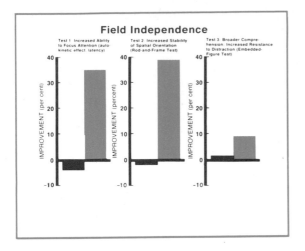

Field Independence

Test 1. Increased Ability to Focus Attention (auto-kinetic effect: latency)

Test 2. Increased Stability of Spatial Orientation (Rod-and-Frame Test)

Test 3. Broader Comprehension: Increased Resistance to Distraction (Embedded-Figure Test)

Broader Comprehension and Improved Focusing of Attention

Finding: In this study three tests were administered that directly measured field independence, the ability to focus attention on specific objects without being distracted by the environment of the objects. Meditators changed significantly in the direction of increased field independence compared with non-meditating controls.

Interpretation: Increased field independence is known by psychologists to be associated with increased mental health, reduced anxiety, and increased stability of the autonomic nervous system. It was previously believed these abilities do not improve beyond early adulthood.

Reference: Kenneth R. Pelletier, "Influence of Transcendental Meditation upon Autokinetic Perception", *Perceptual and Motor Skills*, vol. 39, 1974, pp. 1031–1034.

tal Meditation Technique decreases such personal traits as "social introversion" and "tendency to dominate," and increases such traits as "tolerance," "sociability," and "acceptance of others." Meditators become more adaptable in social situations—they relate to the people around them in more comfortable, positive ways.

Examined overall, then, the research shows that the Transcendental Meditation Technique brings an increase in adaptability at every important level of a person's life. Toffler had said we are headed for a "crisis of adaption," that we are near "the limits of adaptability." Against this urgent analysis of the plight of modern man we can understand the historic importance of the discovery that man *can* increase his adaptability naturally and progressively. It turns out that the "limits of adaptability" are elastic—the nervous system *can* become more resilient, mental capabilities *can* increase, personal relationships *can* become more responsive. And the research so far shows that the longer a person meditates, the greater this adaptability becomes. The end of the process has not been seen. Maharishi maintains it is endless.

"Evolution is natural to life," he says. "There is always more."

The same type of analysis used for adaptability also applies to Toffler's concern with the basic traits of stability and integration. The scientific research is just as complete. The Transcendental Meditation Technique increases physiological stability (reduced blood pressure and heart rate, increased stability of the autonomic nervous system, and increased coherence of brain waves) leading to increased psychological stability (increased ego-strength, self-acceptance and inner control) and increased sociological stability (reduced irritability, increased capacity for meaningful contact, increased job satisfaction). Similarly, the Transcendental Meditation Technique improves physiological integration (perceptual-motor coordination, neuromuscular integration, coordination of left and right hemispheres of the brain), psychological integration (improved self-regard at the same time as improved respect for others, increased self-actualization, improved aca-

The challenge of "Future Shock" apparently does have an answer—there is a way to stimulate rapid growth in adaptability, stability and integration. The TM Technique produces objectively measured evolution.

demic and job performance) and sociological integration (decreased distrust, improved on-the-job relations between co-workers and between workers and supervisors, improved tolerance among high school students).

The challenge of *Future Shock* apparently does have an answer—there *is* a way to stimulate rapid growth in adaptability, stability and integration. But what accounts for this rapid growth? What is there about the practice of the Transcendental Meditation Technique that produces this objectively measured evolution? The answer is summed up in the final two "fundamentals of progress": purification and growth.

The category of purification is the one concerned with dissolving stress. As the previous chapter has shown, purification leads to progress in a natural way. Physically, this purification shows up in blood chemistry, and in the tendency of brain waves to "purify" into a few constant frequencies rather than continuing in the normal disorganized activity. Psychologically, purification is marked by the reduction in such negative traits as anxiety, depression, irritability, inhibition, schizophrenic tendencies and para-

noia. Sociologically, behavior is purified by the clear reductions in such traits as hostility and aggression, as well as by a reduction in the abuse of drugs and alcohol. Again, purification begins in the physical body and carries through into attitudes and interactions.

The final fundamental is growth. In a way, this seems to be the *basic* idea—progress must include growth. And much of the growth that comes with the Transcendental Meditation Technique comes in areas that were previously thought to be relatively invariant. Intelligence, for instance, was widely supposed to stop growing after maturity. So were the abilities of "field independence" (the ability to orient oneself against a distracting background) and perceptual discrimination. All of these abilities have been shown to increase with the practice of the Transcendental Meditation Technique.

Despite the importance of such growth, however, there is good reason for leaving this fundamental for last in a discussion. Unchecked growth can be imbalanced and excessive, a curse instead of a blessing. This is why it is important to know that the

The qualities of adaptability, stability, integration, purification and growth are fundamental to life because they lie at the basis of the process of natural, biological evolution.

growth enjoyed because of the Transcendental Meditation Technique is associated with all the other fundamentals. Since there is growth in both adaptability and stability at the same time, and since the growth comes throughout the system in an integrated way, there is less and less chance for excess or imbalance. And because growth is associated with the parallel process of purification, it cannot become the instrument of negative influences. Purification keeps growth channeled in a positive direction.

What emerges from this recitation of scientific findings is a bright and heartening vision—a vision of man evolving rapidly toward a higher quality of life. Toffler had asked for "a new breed of man." At the time he sounded almost wistful—he knew that philosophers in every age have been discouraged by the seemingly fixed level of human nature. But now a technology has been discovered that allows every man to "re-new"himself progressively.The storms of change no longer need to batter against a static target. Mankind is capable of rapid progress.

It is not excessively dramatic to say that this discovery comes just in time. Toffler quotes sociologist Lawrence Suhm of the University of Wisconsin with the pertinent thought. "We are going through a period as traumatic as the evolution of man's predecessors from sea creatures to land creatures . . . ," Suhm says. "Those who can adapt will; those who can't either go on surviving somehow at a lower level of development or will perish— washed up on the shores."

It's a question of rapid evolution. We must progress quickly at the level of our actual physical, mental and emotional make- up—we need a "new breed of man"—if we are to stay on top of the changes forced on us by our own technology. And if a few years ago no one knew there was a way to do this, science has made the discovery now.

According to Maharishi, moreover, the benefits science has validated so far only begin to describe the cumulative progress that is possible.

"The experience of pure conscious- ness influences the life of the individual to such a degree," he says, "that with time the whole value of life is transformed almost

178

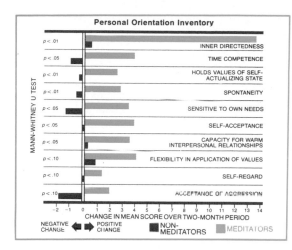

Personal Orientation Inventory

MANN-WHITNEY U TEST

p < .01	INNER DIRECTEDNESS
p < .05	TIME COMPETENCE
p < .01	HOLDS VALUES OF SELF-ACTUALIZING STATE
p < .01	SPONTANEITY
p < .05	SENSITIVE TO OWN NEEDS
p < .05	SELF-ACCEPTANCE
p < .05	CAPACITY FOR WARM INTERPERSONAL RELATIONSHIPS
p < .10	FLEXIBILITY IN APPLICATION OF VALUES
p < .10	SELF-REGARD
p < .10	ACCEPTANCE OF AGGRESSION

-2 -1 0 1 2 3 4 5 6 7 8 9 10 11 12 13 14
CHANGE IN MEAN SCORE OVER TWO-MONTH PERIOD

NEGATIVE CHANGE ◄ ► POSITIVE CHANGE   ■ NON-MEDITATORS   ■ MEDITATORS

Development of Personality

Finding: Subjects practicing the Transcendental Meditation Technique showed significant positive improvement in the following traits when compared with a matched control group of non-meditators: inner-directedness, time competence, self-actualization, spontaneity, sensitivity to one's needs, self-acceptance, and capacity for warm interpersonal relationships. Two independent studies also confirmed these results.

Interpretation: All the personality changes brought about by the Transcendental Meditation Technique are in the direction of what is generally recognized as the development of a healthy, self-actualized personality.

Reference: William Seeman, Sanford Nidich, and Thomas Banta, "Influences of Transcendental Meditation on a Measure of Self-Actualization", *Journal of Counseling Psychology*, vol. 19, no. 3, 1972: pg. 184–187.

beyond imagination. What was thought and felt to be impossible really is not impossible. Conscious capacity increases and therefore when one engages in experience and action, the experience of life becomes deeper, fuller and more substantial. One engages in activity with greater energy, more intelligence and improved efficiency. With increased strength and broadened awareness, everything becomes possible."

Use of the word "evolution" to describe growth in this direction is both emphatic and accurate. That's why it was no coincidence that the qualities called for by Toffler were echoed in the research of the Transcendental Meditation Technique. The qualities of adaptability, stability, integration, purification and growth are fundamental to life because they lie at the basis of the process of natural, biological evolution. Even a cursory glance at the history of biological evolution shows this to be true. The five "fundamentals of progress" shows up at every stage.

Life has always tended to become more adaptable, for instance—from single-celled organisms that can live only in the correct medium, to man, who can live on deserts, ice caps and in outer space. In the same way, life has always tended to become more stable—the stability of warm blood is the breakthrough that gave mammals and birds the advantage over reptiles, who depend on the sun to keep their variable temperature high enough. Again, life has always tended to become more integrated—the development of more complex nervous systems for coordination and control is a hallmark of higher forms of life. Also, life has always tended to purification—the ability to resist and eliminate impurities, poisons and waste is vital to all organisms. And finally, life has always tended to growth—if mere survival were the goal, evolution might have stopped with the cockroach, which has survived in its present state longer than any other land creature.

It is also important to realize that the process of evolution is not only biological. Progressive change starts long before the appearance of life—involving the evolution of elements within stars, for instance, or the geologic evolution of planets. And the pace of progress escalates rapidly with the emer-

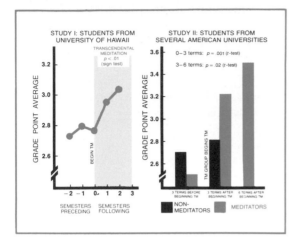

STUDY I: STUDENTS FROM
UNIVERSITY OF HAWAII

STUDY II: STUDENTS FROM
SEVERAL AMERICAN UNIVERSITIES

TRANSCENDENTAL
MEDITATION
$p < .01$
(sign test)

GRADE POINT AVERAGE

3.2
3.0
2.8
2.6

BEGIN TM

-2 -1 0 1 2 3

SEMESTERS
PRECEDING

SEMESTERS
FOLLOWING

GRADE POINT AVERAGE

3.6
3.4
3.2
3.0
2.8
2.6

0-3 terms: $p = .001$ (t-test)
3-6 terms: $p = .02$ (t-test)

TM GROUP BEGINS TM

3 TERMS BEFORE
BEGINNING TM

3 TERMS AFTER
BEGINNING TM

6 TERMS AFTER
BEGINNING TM

NON-
MEDITATORS

MEDITATORS

Improved Academic Performance

Finding: In two studies academic performance, as measured by grade point average, was shown to improve sharply after students began the TM Technique.

Interpretation: The generalized improvement in neurophysiological and psychological functioning caused by the Transcendental Meditation Technique brings about improvement in a holistic measure of mental effectiveness, the ability to succeed in academic studies.

First Reference: Study I: Roy W. Collier, "The Effects of Transcendental Meditation upon University Academic Attainment" (Paper presented at the Pacific Northwest Conference on Foreign Languages, Seattle, Washington, U.S.A.)
Second Reference: Study II: Dennis P. Heaton and David W. Orme-Johnson, The Transcendental Meditation Program and Academic Achievement", *Scientific Research on the Transcendental Meditation Program: Collected Papers*, vol. 1, 1975.

gence of intelligent life, involving far more than basic changes in gene structure or physical organization.

This idea of the "escalation of evolution" is already well known. Toffler touches on it briefly, pointing out that evolution speeded up tremendously when it transcended the biological level and began to include the level of human social organization. He quotes biologist Julian Huxley saying, "The tempo of human evolution during recorded history is at least 100,000 times as rapid as that of pre-human history." This evolutionary speed-up accelerated greatly after the Renaissance, due to the rapid accumulation and printing of factual knowledge, and incredibly since 1900, because of the eruption of technology.

And now the focus of evolution has moved on, one more crucial step, to consciousness. With that step, progress is so quick that the scientific research on the Transcendental Meditation Technique is virtually redefining what it means to be a human being. The breakthrough is that human nature need not be seen as fixed and immutable. With mankind, the natural process of evolu-

tion has developed the ability to be conscious of itself. All man has to do is put his attention on the process—directly experience the evolutionary processes of consciousness that produce thoughts—and this innocent experience speeds up his own evolution enormously in ways that can be measured exactly in scientific laboratories. The fact that the five "fundamentals of progress" develop rapidly in people who practice the Transcendental Meditation Technique is just the definition of evolution when it reaches the level of man's consciousness.

As mentioned in the previous chapter, the discovery of this natural path to rapid evolution has come because of the need of the time. The stress of modern life that Toffler sums up as "future shock" has forced us to search for an answer. And what we have found is not so much an antidote as it is a culmination. The problem of "future shock" is essentially a problem of freedom— we have too many choices to make too fast. And now we find that the answer is not in retreat, but in going forward; we need to improve not only the *quantity* of freedom, but also the *quality* of freedom. We have overloaded ourselves with freedom in order to find out what freedom really means.

Toffler touched briefly on this connection between "future shock" and freedom. "The people of the future," he said at one point, "face not choice but overchoice. For them there comes an explosive extension of freedom." A little later he pointed out, "It is precisely the super-industrial society, the most advanced technological society ever, that extends the range of freedom. The people of the future enjoy greater opportunities for self-realization than any previous group in history."

Increasing freedom is the basis of "future shock," but it also brings increasing opportunity for "self-realization." Freedom is both a problem and an opportunity. At this point, Toffler's exposition converges with the brilliant analysis laid out more than thirty years ago by the eminent psychiatrist and philosopher, Erich Fromm. One of Fromm's many books, *Escape From Freedom*, has become a staple of modern education. Writing in 1941, he was concerned with the problems of alienation and isolation, rather than rapid change, but his thought gives a clear definition to the challenge of freedom and the possibilities of "self-realization."

"Freedom," Fromm said, "though it has brought [man] independence and rationality, has made him isolated and thereby, anxious and powerless. This . . . [problem] is unbearable and the alternatives he is confronted with are either to escape from the burden of this freedom with new dependencies and submission, or to advance to the full realization of positive freedom which is based upon the uniqueness and individuality of man."

Fromm wants to move on from "negative" to "positive" freedom.

"This freedom man can attain by the realization of his self, by being himself," Fromm said. "What is the realization of his self? . . . It is the realization of man's total personality by the active expression of his emotional and intellectual potentials. These potentials are present in everybody; they become real only to the extent to which they are expressed. In other words, *positive freedom consists in the spontaneous activity of* 181

The TM Technique frees the latent potentials within every individual. And surely this is the final rationale for freedom— that human life should grow to the dignity of its full potential.

the total, integrated personality."

Freedom no longer means simply "negative" freedom from external restraints—from poverty, or governments, or parents. That sort of freedom by itself leads, in Toffler's words, to "overchoice" and "future shock." To Fromm, real freedom means "positive" freedom, "the full realization of the individual's potentials. . . ."

Talking about the development of this "positive freedom," Fromm makes two points. First, he says, "Life has an inherent tendency to grow, to expand, to express potentialities." Then he points out the area where modern man faces the blocks to this natural tendency. ". . . [A]lthough man has rid himself of the old enemies of freedom, new enemies of a different nature have arisen; enemies which are not essentially external restraints, but internal factors blocking the full realization of the freedom of the personality."

Freedom has brought the need for more (and better) freedom, and the problem now is internal blocks, not external restraints. Like Toffler, Fromm offered no technique to resolve the problem, no method to

purify the system of these internal blocks. But the discovery has been made now. Maharishi talks with much the same vocabulary as Fromm, and his hopeful analysis is backed up by the research.

"With the practice of the Transcendental Meditation Technique," Maharishi says, "the nervous system purifies itself by itself. Stresses that block the normal functioning of the nervous system are thrown off. If the practice is continued every day, a day will come when life is lived free from all prejudices, inhibitions, boundaries, stresses and restrictions. The conscious mind is free to live its full potential. The state of enlightenment is a state of realization—realization of the self, of truth, of reality—so that one may live life to the full extent it is possible to live it."

Toffler and Fromm used the phrase "self-realization." Another term is "liberation:" freedom from all internal stress and hindrance, the free play of all potentials. And another term is enlightenment: the qualities of adaptability, stability, integration, purification and growth all developed to their maximum extent—the human being living the

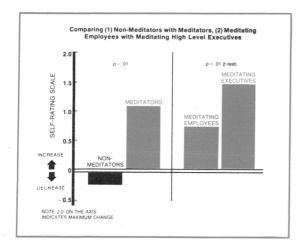

Comparing (1) Non-Meditators with Meditators, (2) Meditating Employees with Meditating High Level Executives

Improved Job Performance

Finding: Meditators at all levels of organization showed a significant increase in job performance compared with non-meditating controls. Meditating executives at higher levels of responsibility showed a comparatively greater increase in performance than those who worked at less responsible levels.

Interpretation: Individuals at all levels of organization benefit from the development of creative intelligence through the practice of the Transcendental Meditation Technique. Meditating executives at higher levels of responsibility, where greater creativity is demanded, find an even greater application of their increasing creative intelligence.

Reference: David R. Frew, "Transcendental Meditation and Productivity", *Academy of Management Journal*, vol. 17, no. 2, 1974: pg. 362–368.

full potential of the evolutionary process. This is what Maharishi means by enlightenment.

In this sense, the Transcendental Meditation Program has not only become an accepted fact of modern American life—it is also the fulfillment of much of the best in this country's heritage. Two hundred years ago, America became the world pioneer in "negative" freedom—freedom from despotic governments and exclusive religions. Over the course of the past two hundred years, this thrust toward freedom has grown to include many more aspects of life. Technology has brought freedom to travel, and freedom from the demands of work ("free time"). Many factors have combined to increase social freedom—the unfettered right of each individual to find his own ethics and life style.

And now, perhaps, we can begin to see what the point to all this freedom has really been. The search for freedom on every level has moved on to include the level of internal, "positive" freedom. The Transcendental Meditation Technique is a systematic procedure that frees the latent potentials within every individual. And surely this is

the final rationale for freedom—that human life should grow to the dignity of its full potential.

The fact that the answer to "future shock" is a technique thousands of years old is just a gentle irony. Just as we had to discover stress in order to try to find an antidote to it, so also we had to reach an extreme of material and technological progress—"external freedom"—before we could appreciate the need for this ancient knowledge about subjective and personal progress—"internal freedom." And probably, without the technical ability to prove it works—without the scientific research showing that the Transcendental Meditation Technique does indeed enliven the "fundamentals of progress" in the individual—we never would have accepted it at all.

It is true that the full range of the benefits coming from the practice of the TM Technique are beyond the reach of scientific investigation. Personal experiences of these benefits are much more fulfilling than verbal or statistical descriptions of them. But in an

At this stage, all people with influence are virtually obliged to study the research, to listen to those who have already made use of the TM Technique, and then to use their influence to help spread this information.

age of science and objective validation, it is good to know the main lines of growth can be verified by analysis and experiment.

This is why Maharishi is speaking so strongly now, inspiring the leaders of the world to come out and help to spread the benefits of this technique. Until recently, responsible people have been correct to maintain a "wait-and-see" attitude. So many odd ideas have been floating around in the environment, strange concepts with no practical basis. But by now research has isolated out the Transcendental Meditation Technique as a viable procedure anyone can use for rapid self-improvement. At this stage, all people with influence are virtually obliged to study the original research articles, to listen to those who have already made use of the technique, and then to use their influence to help spread this information. With the whole world suffering from "future shock," mankind is in too precarious a position for us to wait any longer.

So far, the financial burden of supporting this work has been carried by those people who come to learn the technique. But that must change. Everyone should have free

access to rapid evolution. The leaders in government, business, education and other institutions should now be responsible for taking up the Transcendental Meditation Program and making it available to all the people.

"There is no longer any question whether the Age of Enlightenment is coming," Maharishi says. "The sun will certainly come up. It is now only a question of how fast the bright sunshine will come. We must all take our part and *drag* the sun up to midday."

The Transcendental Meditation Technique: Mantras and Mechanics

We live in a society that prizes convenience. Instant food, wrinkle-free clothes and "home entertainment centers" all characterize a generation that wants more and more enjoyment from less and less effort. In this age of rapid gratification, the effortless nature of the Transcendental Meditation Technique can seem to be just another convenience. "You'll like it," people can tell their friends. "It's easy." And it is quite obvious that nearly a million Americans would never have begun the practice if it *weren't* easy.

But the ease of the Transcendental Meditation Technique means far more than mere convenience. It implies the single most important fact about the technique—the reason for its universal effectiveness. *The Transcendental Meditation Technique is easy because it is a completely natural process for the mind and nervous system, an automatic response that occurs with no effort.*

It's natural. This is why a person can meditate even from his first session with a teacher. We don't have to learn how to *do* the Transcendental Meditation Technique. All we have to do is learn how to let the process start, and then it goes by itself. Once the mind begins to settle down to states of lesser excitation, naturally it continues until it reaches the state of least excitation, the state of "pure" consciousness. The whole process is a natural, in-born ability of the mind and nervous system.

Ironically, the effortlessness of the TM Technique was at one point a barrier to its rapid acceptance. Something that is so easy goes counter to many of our preconceptions. Everybody "knows" that life is hard, that discipline, sacrifice and toil are necessary to gain anything worthwhile. Such an attitude makes it difficult to accept the fact that something with as many benefits as the Transcendental Meditation Technique actually takes no effort at all. This is one reason Maharishi chose to come out of India and bring the Transcendental Meditation Technique to scientific nations. It was necessary to get objective validation for this surprising teaching.

"The experience of pure consciousness is completely natural and without difficulty," he says, "and all the misery of the world is due to missing just this one point.

185

"For centuries past, the message has been broadcast that meditation is difficult, that it is for some chosen few in life. But the reason for that has just been lack of proper guidance."

Now it belongs to the scientific age to bring clarity to this field, to expose the mistakes and confusion of past generations that have been passed on to us. From the mystical ages we have stepped on to the age of science and that is why this is the atmosphere that is bringing out the truth about the nature of life."

Science has certainly shown that the Transcendental Meditation Technique does work (while indirectly indicating how easy it is, too—people can do the TM Technique with the oddest assortment of scientific apparatus strapped onto all parts of the body). And science has provided more than objective validation of the technique's effectiveness. It has also provided theoretical understandings of the nature of objective reality, understandings that run parallel with the theoretical concepts about the nature of consciousness put forward by Maharishi. Modern physics, for instance, has demonstrated that our "common sense" notions about the need for effort and discipline are contradicted by the mechanics of natural processes. The fact is that at the most basic levels, nature always works with the least possible effort. In the microscopic world of atoms, for instance, every atom has a natural tendency to settle down from states of greater excitation to its own state of least excitation (called the "ground state" by physicists). In the telescopic world of the galaxies, moreover, all the stars, planets, comets and other inertial travelers in space move naturally along their own paths of least resistance. Scientists sum up this tendency toward effortlessness in nature as the "law of least action." All motion and interactions take place with the least possible expenditure of energy. It is what Bertrand Russell once called "the cosmic law of laziness." Actually, of course, it is a natural tendency toward efficiency—nature always wants to do less and accomplish more. And this provides the background for the true significance of the effortlessness of the Transcendental Meditation Technique.

"The Transcendental Meditation Technique is easy because it is natural," Maharishi says. "Evolution is natural to life. It is the natural tendency of the mind to settle down to more refined levels. This is why we know that if a technique is hard, it is unnatural. If it is hard, it is against the natural tendency of life. For centuries past, the message has been broadcast that meditation is difficult, that it is for some chosen few in life. But the reason for that has just been lack of guidance, lack of proper guidance."

To begin the practice of the Transcendental Meditation Technique, it is only necessary to sit with a trained teacher for a few minutes. The presence of a teacher is necessary because the experience of the fourth state of consciousness is highly personal. Different people have different experiences as they begin to meditate. A teacher is able to provide the student with the necessary guidance for his particular experiences, and in this way everyone can have a correct meditation even in the first session.

Although it is not possible to write down a set of instructions that will work, it *is* possible to give some idea of the mechanics of the Transcendental Meditation Technique. Word pictures are possible, analogies that give some concept of the nature of the process.

It is important to understand that this procedure involves no concentration or control, because the use of concentration has been a common mistake in this field. There have always been people who have known it would be a great thing to quiet the mind. The goal of inner peace—the desire to enjoy a "state of least excitation"—has been a common understanding among people seeking a better quality of life. Unfortunately, most people who have sought this inner peace have considered the nature of the mind to be their adversary in this quest. Their mistake has been understandable. The mind does not seem to *want* to be quiet. It naturally wanders around from thought to thought and resists any effort to make it hold still. People who have had no procedure for allowing this mental activity to settle down in a natural way have been left to try to do it by main force. At the cost of great effort and discipline, these people have tried to concentrate the mind on some one point to force it to stop moving about. Such a struggle is one-sided and the mind usually wins easily.

The way out of this confrontation with the mind is almost childishly simple. Only one basic point has been missed. All

187

The way the TM Technique looks to scientists is that the brain becomes much more coherent and orderly than usual. The way the experience feels to a meditator is pleasant and comfortable.

that is needed is to understand the reason for the mind's ceaseless activity. It is true the mind is always wandering around, but this activity is not random or purposeless. It has a definite goal. The mind wanders around because it is always looking for an experience that will bring greater happiness. It is always looking for more satisfaction, more fulfillment.

"If a radio is playing," Maharishi says, "and then a better, more melodious song comes on another radio, instantaneously the mind goes to it. Every mind has a natural inclination, a natural instinct, to go to a field of greater happiness. And just this tendency is quite sufficient to lead the mind from the outer glories of life toward the bliss of pure consciousness."

There is no need to force the mind to settle down. Once the mind starts to experience states of lesser excitation, it begins to enjoy greater happiness and peace. Each more subtle level within the mind is more attractive and satisfying and the mind settles down toward the state of least excitation gradually and naturally.

"Outside in the world the mind is not

found steady on any one point," Maharishi says. "No point is able to fascinate the mind to such a great extent as to satisfy the thirst for happiness of the mind. That is why the mind is being tossed about from point to point. But once the mind turns within, spontaneously and automatically it will get on to pure consciousness, to that field of pure creative intelligence, which is like an ocean of happiness inside. The inward march of the mind is very spontaneous. Only the direction of experience has to be turned inside, that's all. We are experiencing the outside, the grosser levels. Just take a turn of 180 degrees. One full turn taken and one step gone that way, and then it pulls. The inner, subtle levels are more charming to the mind."

The way this looks to scientists when they take brain wave measurements of a person doing the Transcendental Meditation Technique is that the brain loses its tendency to random excitation and becomes much more orderly and coherent than usual. The way the experience feels to a meditator is pleasant and comfortable. The mind becomes more and more wakeful at more and more subtle levels.

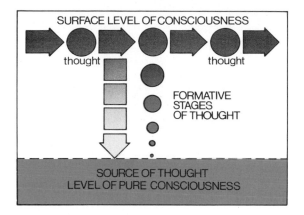

SURFACE LEVEL OF CONSCIOUSNESS

thought   thought

FORMATIVE
STAGES
OF THOUGHT

SOURCE OF THOUGHT
LEVEL OF PURE CONSCIOUSNESS

The Mechanics of the TM Technique

This is a diagram of a simple analogy to help explain the TM Technique. Normally the mind moves from thought to thought on the conscious thinking level (indicated by the arrows moving from dot to dot). During the practice of the TM Technique, the mind begins with one specially chosen thought (the "mantra") and then experiences that one thought vertically, as it were, in its earlier, formative stages. By following the thought "inward," the mind arrives at the "source of thought," the level of pure consciousness.

"It's a very simple system of drawing the attention toward the inner glory of life," Maharishi says. "It's a method whereby our mind can explore the inner avenues of consciousness and fathom the depths of the real, lasting values of pure consciousness."

Although most other meditative techniques have always been based on concentration—on forcing the mind to do something it doesn't want to do—with the Transcendental Meditation Technique the mind is set free to move in the direction it wants to go. All that is necessary is to set up the initial conditions that allow the mind to begin to slip beneath its normal surface level of consciousness. It is like diving into a swimming pool. Once we jump off the side, we are sure to get wet.

The whole process is a natural automatic response once the start is correct.

Even though we want an effortless experience, it is obviously necessary to have a very specific procedure to follow. Otherwise we will be trapped in contradictions. We can't try not to try, for instance—that would simply be an efficient path to frustration. Nor can we slip into the tautological absurdity of "doing nothing." If we do nothing, we go nowhere—a recipe for dullness and lethargy. The goal is a specific procedure that will allow the mind to settle down naturally.

To understand how this can happen, we need a simplified picture of the operation of the mind. And the most important point for us to realize is that, normally, we are aware of thoughts only after they have already reached the surface of our minds. We are like a swimmer moving about on the surface of a lake. If a bubble started rising from the very bottom of the lake, the swimmer wouldn't see the bubble until it reached the surface. In a similar way, the mind isn't aware of a thought until it has already appeared at the surface thinking level of the mind. But thoughts come from somewhere within the mind. They don't simply jump into existence full blown by spontaneous generation. They go through a process of formation that brings them finally to the surface level of the mind. And the point is that the mind is capable of experiencing a thought in its ear-

"When the finer faculties of experience are not used, then
life becomes dry and dull. The TM Technique is a way of oiling
the machinery and making the unused parts come into use."

lier, formative states. Just as a swimmer could dive beneath the surface of the lake and follow a certain trail of bubbles back to its source at the bottom of the lake, so the mind can take one thought and experience it "backward," or "inward," following it through the finer, more subtle stages of its development.

The mind dives beneath the conscious thinking level in other words, and begins to experience its own inner nature. When the mind experiences a thought in its earlier, less concrete stages, it is experiencing the process that *creates* finished thoughts, instead of experiencing the finished thoughts themselves. And, to change to a botanical analogy, just as the first green shoot is much more delicate than the full-grown plant, so each earlier stage of a forming thought is more delicate and refined than the last. As the mind travels "inward" in this way, experiencing its own processes in more and more refined stages, the consciousness itself becomes more and more subtle—a state indicated by the increasingly coherent brain wave patterns.

Finally, even the faintest, earliest

"shoot" of the one thought the mind has been following disappears entirely. The mind is left by itself. It is aware, awake within itself, at a state of the greatest possible refinement. It is conscious, but conscious of "no-thing" in particular, not even the earliest, most delicate aspect of the thought it was following. This is "pure" consciousness, consciousness uncluttered by any specific object of thinking.

"The Transcendental Meditation Technique starts from the conscious thinking level of the mind," Maharishi says. "We take a thought and allow that thought to reduce below the conscious thinking level. One step and then the thought keeps on reducing by degrees until it is reduced to just a point-thought. Then we transcend that thought and get to the 'source of thought.' This is the state of least excitation of consciousness, pure consciousness. And just as the physicists know that the state of least excitation—the 'vacuum state'—is the source of all change, the field of all possibilities, so we know that the state of pure consciousness is the home of all creativity and intelligence."

And the whole process goes all by

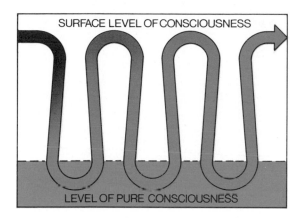

SURFACE LEVEL OF CONSCIOUSNESS

LEVEL OF PURE CONSCIOUSNESS

Evolution Through Meditation and Activity

During meditation the mind dips inward to experience pure consciousness. When the mind returns out to normal activity on the surface level of consciousness the value of purity fades away, but it doesn't fade away completely. By alternating meditation and activity, the mind is gradually purified of stress until it can maintain the full value of pure consciousness even during daily activity. This is the state of enlightenment.

itself once the start is right. Each level of greater refinement, each step toward pure consciousness, feels better to the mind.

"This is the way to increase our capacity to experience," Maharishi says. "As it is, our senses may be capable only of the gross, outer experiences of daily life. And if we experience the gross levels for a long time, the capacity for subtle experience is rusted because the machinery is not used. When the finer faculties of experience are not used, then life becomes dry and dull, brittle and tense. The Transcendental Meditation Technique is just a way of oiling the machinery and making the unused parts come into use. It refines the faculty of experience and enriches all aspects of life."

This is the point to the Transcendental Meditation Technique. The experience of subtler values enlivens the mind, and when we come out of the meditation period we notice that the mind is clear and therefore life goes more smoothly.

To begin this experience, a person needs to know two things. First it is necessary to have a thought to use, and then it is necessary to have a procedure for using that thought correctly. Both aspects of the learning are important, and one of them has even become something of a *cause celebre* in discussions about the Transcendental Meditation Technique. This is the "mantra," the specially chosen thought used during the practice.

To begin meditation, we have to start with a thought on the conscious thinking level of the mind, since that is where we are to begin with. And the thought we use must be carefully chosen. It has to allow the mind to settle naturally beneath the conscious thinking level, and it has to have positive effects for the mind and nervous system at the very subtle and delicate levels reached during the process of meditation.

The name given to this type of thought is "mantra." A mantra is a thought we take only for the value of its *sound*. It's not really a word—though people often refer to it that way—because a word has meaning. A mantra is only a sound.

There is not a different mantra for every person, but different groups of people

These possibilities for confusion can only make us glad that the TM Technique is not an experimental procedure invented by someone in the recent past. It is a traditional knowledge thousands of years old.

do receive different mantras. And it is imperative each person receive a mantra correct for him, a sound suitable for his nervous system. Even at the level of common sense, we know different sounds have different effects on our sensibilities. The sound of a bubbling brook feels good to the nervous system, for instance; fingernails on a blackboard can have a very bad effect. During the experience of meditation, when the mind has settled down to very delicate and subtle levels, these effects of sound are greatly magnified. If the sound is correctly chosen, it will allow the mind to settle down easily and naturally to the state of least excitation. If it is incorrect, however, the effects can be extremely disruptive on the functioning of the nervous system.

This is why, as the Transcendental Meditation Technique gains wide popularity for its proved benefits, people must be careful to receive instruction from teachers trained by Maharishi Mahesh Yogi in the ancient tradition of knowledge on this subject. This is important because imitators are naturally beginning to appear. Since these imitators do not have this knowledge of the effects of sound on human consciousness, they usually tell a person to simply choose any sound he wants. This is like a doctor telling his patient to choose any pill he wants—the results of the use of just any sound is that a person will get just any effect. This type of mistake is usually made by people who only think of the Transcendental Meditation Technique as a means for superficial relaxation. They have not bothered to study the detailed research on the brain and the nervous system, they have no concept of consciousness as the basis of the process, and in their ignorance they spread misinformation that is at best of little use and at worst extremely harmful.

The situation is awkward for a teacher of the Transcendental Meditation Technique when he tries to make these points. It can sound like biased judgement. But a research project carried out at the Institute for Living, a highly respected psychiatric hospital in Hartford, Connecticut, has made the point in scientific terms. A project under the direction of Dr. Bernard Glueck has tested many techniques, including progressive relaxation techniques, alpha-wave biofeedback, and the best-known of the techniques which claims to work "just like the Transcendental Meditation Technique" but which uses randomly chosen sounds for mantras. This study, which has covered several years and involved hundreds of patients, is one of the most exhaustive so far conducted on the Transcendental Meditation Technique. Writing in the journal *Comprehensive Psychiatry*, with his co-worker, Dr. Charles Stroebel, Dr. Glueck has summed up his comparative research quite clearly.

"To date," the two researchers say, "as observed in our laboratory, the TM-type meditation would seem to produce a maximum effect more rapidly than any of the other techniques. Maharishi and his followers insist that the mantra is the critical factor in the technique and we tend to agree with this. . . . [The] mantra seems to be the key factor in achieving the kinds of psychophysiological changes observed. . . ." (Vol. 16, No. 4, pg. 314)

The most important research finding involves brain wave patterns. When random sounds are substituted for mantras, the electroencephalographic changes characteristic of the Transcendental Meditation Technique—changes that indicate the mind is settling down to the fourth state of consciousness—do *not* appear. Apparently the mind is not going through the natural process of refining its level of awareness. What *is* going on is anybody's guess.

These possibilities for confusion and error can only make us glad that a long tradition of masters in this field has passed this knowledge down to us. The Transcendental Meditation Technique is not an experimental procedure invented by someone in the recent past. It is knowledge thousands of years old. It has been preserved by an unbroken tradition of teachers who have taken as their primary field of interest the effects of sound on consciousness. As the most recent of the teachers in this long tradition, Maharishi designates the mantras to be given to each group of people, and teachers of the Transcendental Meditation Technique simply follow his instructions. This is why it is not necessary to take chances with the mind, to simply try any sound and see what the effects will be. A systematic knowledge is available on the subject, an ancient wisdom

Keeping mantras private provides security that no untrained person will attempt to teach the technique. It is insurance of the purity of the teaching procedures.

that has been "discovered" and verified by modern science. All we need to do is take advantage of it.

There is one more aspect to the procedure of teaching mantras. When a person learns the mantra that is correct for him, he is asked not to divulge it to anyone. Some people think this request mysterious, but in fact it has a very practical basis. It is a protection against inaccurate teaching. If we tell our mantra to someone else, the odds are, in the first place, that it is the wrong mantra for that person. And just as important, *a person who has not been trained as a teacher of the Transcendental Meditation Technique does not know how to teach the procedure of using the mantra correctly.* Each student who comes to learn the TM Technique hears only those instructions that relate to the personal experiences he or she is having with the meditation. This does not give a person the expertise for teaching other people, even if all the particular instructions could be remembered on one hearing. Nor does it give any basis for dealing with the questions that

can come up a week, a month, or a year after a person starts to meditate.

Teachers of the Transcendental Meditation Technique, on the other hand, receive detailed instructions in all phases of the teaching. Their course of instruction is six months long. Viewed this way, we can see that keeping mantras private provides security that no untrained person will attempt to teach the technique. It is insurance of the purity of the teaching procedures, and the purity of the teaching is Maharishi's main concern.

"We have been hearing for centuries past that there is a tremendous potentiality hidden in man," says Maharishi. "It is not a new message that a great storehouse of peace and happiness and creativity and wisdom lies at the heart of everyone. And now an age of science has verified that there is a simple, natural procedure to unfold this full potential, to maintain a connection of the outer life with the inner values of pure consciousness. This is why we put such emphasis on the purity of the teaching. It is this knowledge that is bringing forth an Age of Enlightenment."

A Symposium:
Experts Assess the TM Program

PART THREE

Most people begin the Transcendental Meditation Technique because they hear about it from someone they know. Abstract theories can be interesting and scientific studies are reassuring, but personal experience of the TM Technique is the most lively evidence of its benefits.

In this section of the book, experts in seven different fields discuss the impact of the Transcendental Meditation Program in their own vocabulary. The subjects for these interviews have deliberately been chosen from walks of life that are very unlike each other—from the arts, business, education, government, health, sports and science—in order to present as wide a range of opinion as possible. The aim of these interviews is to give some indication of the rich diversity that develops as individuals begin to unfold their full potential.

The TM Technique is a practical procedure that brings immediate and tangible benefits. The growth of the value of pure consciousness is, in Maharishi's phrase, a living reality. It can easily be noticed in day-to-day activity. "Spontaneous right action" can be seen in a painter's working methods. "Improved ability to focus attention" can be seen in a baseball player's experience up at the plate. "The integration of life" can be seen in relationships on the job between co-workers.

Discussions with people from many walks of life clearly show that the TM Technique is not limited in its application only to certain types of people or certain areas of expertise. The conversations also make it obvious that the experience of the fourth state of consciousness does not lead all people in the same direction. When life begins to evolve, it evolves naturally along its own lines of strength, and each person begins to develop whatever potentials inhere in his or her makeup. Evolution is enjoyed by all people in their own terms.

When life begins to evolve, it evolves naturally along its own lines of strength. Evolution is enjoyed by all people in their own terms.

Athletics

Larry Bowa, Joe Namath,
Willie Stargell, Del Unser

Professional athletes are under extreme pressure to perform at their full potential. In a world where success and failure is often measured in fractions of inches and hundredths of seconds, athletes have to deliver their best in situations of extreme tension. For these reasons, it is not surprising that the TM Program is spreading very rapidly in professional sports. Many sports organizations have operated TM Programs, including in baseball, the Pittsburgh Pirates and the Philadelphia Phillies, and in hockey, the Buffalo Sabres and New York Islanders. More than twenty of the top professional tennis players have begun the practice, including Arthur Ashe, Roscoe Tanner and Bob Lutz. Many other individuals have started, including the surprise silver medal winner in the 1976 Winter Olympics, Bill Koch.

From the standpoint of athletics, the TM Program provides a "training technique" that improves an athlete in every important area—in physical ability, in mental alertness and in the elusive quality of "character"—the ability to play well in pressure situations. In terms of physical abilities, research studies have shown that the TM Technique improves an athlete's reaction time, agility, endurance and running speed. In terms of mental alertness, the key study has shown that a person practicing the TM Technique can focus his attention more easily while also maintaining awareness of the surrounding situation. And in terms of character the effectiveness of the TM Technique in combatting stress and tension is well known.

Four of the better athletes in America are included in this conversation. They enjoy the TM Technique and they enjoy talking about it. They are Larry Bowa, all-star shortstop of the Philadelphia Phillies; Joe Namath quarterback of the New York Jets; Willie Stargell, many times an all-star as the right-fielder for the Pittsburgh Pirates; and Del Unser, centerfielder for the New York Mets. Stargell begins the discussion.

"I like TM," he says, "because I'm refreshed where before I wasn't. We started the TM Program a couple of years ago in training camp and right away I noticed I was feeling stronger. It used to be I'd come home from practice with nothing but a tired body to carry me through the evening. And I think a lot of people are this way. The average gentleman might come home from work, pick up a paper, turn on the TV, and that's about it. But I find that with TM, once I do it in the evening when I come home, I'm more into my family and my kids. TM has come in to make the day more rounded."

Namath: "I've noticed the same type of thing. I just don't get as tired as I used to. Many times in the past, after a practice I'd really be dragging. I'd go home and lie down to get some rest, but I still wouldn't have any steam. Practicing TM, I find that this doesn't happen. I feel rested and energetic. I just feel good. I don't feel like sitting around. After I meditate I'm ready to go and get things accomplished."

Is this the major benefit you have noticed in your athletics, also, more energy and endurance?

Namath: "That, and also the mental part. The mental aspect of any sport is so important. When you're playing football, most of the time you are in a very chaotic situation. A lot of things are happening at once—your receivers are running their patterns, the defensive backs are doing their thing, and the front four is bearing down on you. And with all that going on, you have to be able to totally concentrate on what your objective is."

Bowa: "It's the same in baseball. Concentration is the whole thing. You have to be able to go up and concentrate every single at bat. I know before I started TM I might be able to concentrate one or two times at the plate in each game. Then maybe I'd get a hit or two, and I'd let up—'I've got my hits now.' Or else I'd find my mind wandering off to something off the field, worrying about getting the car fixed or something. It's hard

enough to play this game without having a lot of other things to think about. And since I started TM, I can really feel the concentration more. My mind is sharp nearly every time up. I don't have any other worries on my

> "The mental aspect of any sport is so important. A lot of things are happening at once, and with all that going on, you have to be able to concentrate totally on your objective."

mind. To play the game I think you have to be relaxed, and I think through TM, I'm a much more relaxed ball player."

Why is relaxation important? Don't you have to be keyed up to play well?

Namath: "You have to be ready, yes. But you can be keyed up and emotional and still have yourself together. What you have to watch out for, when you get revved up and that adrenalin starts to flow, is reacting too quickly. You can get rolling too fast, and then it's easy to make a mistake. But if your mind is functioning smoothly, if you are relaxed, then the adrenalin can flow and you can react quickly, but the concentration is still there. And the more one does TM, it seems, the easier the concentration comes."

Unser: "The kind of thing that used to happen to me sometimes is that I'd go up to the plate with a pretty good idea of what I wanted to do. Maybe I needed to hit behind the runner to move him over. I'd go up thinking that, but then if the pitcher would fool me with the first pitch—give me a big curve where I was looking for a fastball, say—I might lose my concentration, forget what I wanted to do. Now I find I go up there, and maybe a pitcher still fools me sometimes but I just step out of the box and hit my cleats a couple of times and then I'm ready to go again. The concentration is there."

Concentration is important, but what about competitiveness? Can an athlete be aggressive enough if he is feeling relaxed? Some players might worry that the TM Technique will make them too mellow.

Namath: "I think that's a fallacy. I don't think I've lost a bit of competetiveness through TM."

"To me, TM makes the day seem unbelievably super. I like TM because it's made me the person I've dreamed I always wanted to be, but never could live up to."

Bowa: "The fact is, I think I'm *more* aggressive since I started TM. I think that's a big part of why I'm stealing bases better. But I think I'm being aggressive in a more relaxed manner. In a situation where things are tight, the bases are loaded, an infielder might not want the ball hit to him because he might make a big error. But in times like that now, I feel I *want* the ball hit to me. I'm relaxed, I'm confident. I know I can make the play, so I go at the situation with an aggressive attitude."

What about activities off the field? Has the TM Technique brought benefits there as well?

Unser: Off the field to me is where TM did its best. It's brought me a little of something you might call inner peace, and maybe a little more awareness about who I am and where I'm going. It gave me some energy as far as trying to find out what I want to do with myself when I get out of baseball. That's always been a problem with me. After I'd been in TM awhile I just said to heck with it, I'll get into a real estate class if I like it. I was surprised. I got through the course very clear mindedly. I enjoyed it."

Namath: "I started Transcendental Meditation because I felt like I wasn't doing enough for myself. I wasn't really growing. And so I started meditating because of the effects it has on your body and your mind. And it's done a great deal for me. It's the start to improvement. With TM, I feel like going out and learning things. I feel like being active. I'm always interested in what's going on."

Stargell: "I like TM because it has enabled me to do a lot of things I have never done before, on a massive level. It helps with your work, it helps with your family, it helps with your outside activities. I think anybody who is the type of person who has a lot to do with a lot of things, anybody who is interested in keeping his head screwed on properly, and being able to maintain sanity, anybody who wants to be able to relax and unwind and enjoy—then I think it's worth whatever it takes to check TM out."

Bowa: "I'll tell you the truth. To me, TM makes the day seem unbelievably super. I wake up some mornings feeling really bad, and I meditate for twenty minutes and I see a whole new side of life. I like TM because it's made me the person I've dreamed I always wanted to be, but never could live up to."

Stargell: "I have nothing but pluses to say for it. It might just be the key to everything. We need something to bring this country back together."

You really think it can help people?

Namath: "I don't *think* it can help. I *know* it can help."

Government

Arlen Gregorio
State Senator, California

Arlen Gregorio is serving his second four-year term in the California Senate. He was originally elected in 1970 in his first try for elective office. Senator Gregorio graduated from Stanford University and Stanford Law School, and was active in the law before becoming a legislator. One of the hardest workers in Sacramento, Senator Gregorio has earned recognition for major legislation in the areas of alcoholism, the arts, consumer protection, education, election and legislative reform, the environment, foster care, housing and judicial reform. He is chairman of both the Senate Health and Welfare Committee and the Joint Committee on the Arts.

"I first learned about Transcendental Meditation from reading an article in the Wall Street Journal several years ago," says Senator Gregorio. "It sounded like it might be helpful. Then a neighbor gave me more information, particularly the Benson and Wallace study about metabolic activity. I was quite impressed and took instruction soon after that."

You think it's helped you?

"Oh, yes, I think it's helped significantly. There's a lot of stress on a full-time legislator representing half a million people."

What are some of the difficulties of the life of a legislator?

"Days are long, in the first place. Three nights a week I'm in my office until midnight. Beyond that, a legislator is paid to make some extremely important decisions affecting people, their lives and their property. The stakes are high."

Which means there is a lot of pressure on you.

"That's right. Any politician who carries a good deal of controversial legislation—and I do—has to spend a lot of time dealing with people who are quite upset. People come into the office, people call up on the phone, who are angry and emotional because they feel quite deeply about issues on which my actions have an effect. I also have to deal with colleagues who don't always take kindly to my actions. It's a difficult situation. Dealing with people who are upset at you is just an integral part of a politician's life."

Technique helped you in this regard?

"It did. I've noticed a stabilizing of my feelings over a period of time. I find I'm not running on adrenalin so much. I'm not so bothered by outside events and also I'm not fighting myself so much."

"I find that I'm less uptight. I'm a little more orderly with my emotions.
There's a saying about Transcendental Meditation, 'Work less and accomplish more,' and I really find that to be true."

What do you mean by fighting yourself?

"I just find that I'm less uptight, I'm a little more orderly with my emotions. There's a saying about Transcendental Meditation, 'Work less and accomplish more,' and I really find that to be true. I seem better organized in my efforts. I'm not fighting my worries or anticipations of what might go wrong. If I have a project, I think out what the logical steps are to take and then I just go about them in the best way I possibly can. It's not that I don't anticipate problems—I do—but somehow problems don't become emotional problems to me now. They are just objects, things that have to be dealt with in an orderly way."

So the main benefits you have noticed have been in the area of increasing efficiency.

"That, but also in the area of my feelings. I have a much better sense of awareness about my staff, for instance. We all seem to be much more able to work together. In fact, many of my staff do Transcendental Meditation themselves, by now."

Why do you think this level of feeling increases?

"Your mood is just better. I've even seen it with my family. It's a difficult life for a politician because you are away from your family a lot. My first two years in the legislature were very hard on my family. I wasn't home a lot and then, because the tensions were so great, when I got back home I usually wasn't in the mood to reach out and do the loving thing. I'd still be reacting to the pressures of legislative work. But since I've started Transcendental Meditation I feel much more able to be loving, to have better feeling and understanding in all aspects of my family life."

Do you think that if more legislators were doing the Transcendental Meditation Technique, the quality of government would improve?

"I've talked to some of my colleagues about it, told them how it helps to dissipate the stress we face all the time. But government is not just a problem of legislators. I've thought about it a number of times and I really believe that if a significant number of the citizens were meditating, the democratic process would work much more effectively."

Why do you say that?

"Because I feel that the people aren't making their governmental institutions work. This has probably been my fundamental effort since I came to the legislature—trying to reform the political system. Right now a lot of people have no great trust in the government, they believe that public institutions are just beyond them. It's difficult to get them interested in looking at the long-run consequences of what we are doing, and when that happens you have serious trouble."

How can the Transcendental Meditation Technique affect this?

"One thing about it is that it seems to give people more perspective on what they are doing. It brings about some kind of heightened awareness of the impact of what you're doing, opens up a vision of the long-range consequences. We need that. I think that it would mean that the people wouldn't stand for the same nonsense from their government. They would become more conscious and aware of the fact that so much we do as a society just makes no sense, and then they'd get involved and help bring some order to what's going on."

Some reform has already been going on the past several years. Maharishi's not afraid to give some of the credit for that to the fact that there are a million meditators in America already.

"I don't know how we could know that for sure, but I think it's clear that much has to do with the threshold of public tolerance—how much has to go wrong before the public reacts—and I'm sure that with Transcendental Meditation we can lower that threshold. You see, I believe the institutions we have in this country are good ones—*if we have an informed, aware citizenry.* But I don't think it's fair just to blame the people, either. They have been dropping out, but it's because society has been hard on them. Everything has become so impersonal. The relationship between government and the people is just not working at the person-to-person level. And I think this is an area where Transcendental Meditation can have an impact."

"I know TM can help people be more human to others. And when you start spreading humanity around, that has to have a good effect on people and their attitude toward their government."

It could improve relations between government and the people?

"I'm sure it could, because it can help bring back that sense of humanity, that good feeling at the personal level. People who have themselves together have a good effect on other people. That's obvious even for people who aren't meditating, and I know Transcendental Meditation can help people in this way. Then we would see more people being human to other people. And when you start spreading humanity around, that has to have a good effect on people and their attitude toward their government. If people feel that they matter,that they are being treated with respect, then you'll see more people being involved in the process. And as far as I'm concerned, that's where the problem is, getting people involved in the process. That's why I feel that a technique like Transcendental Meditation may be one of the few ways we can save the democratic system."

To have this effect, won't the government have to step in and support the Transcendental Meditation Program?

"We are working on that. The only way you could get such a program adopted, I believe, is to prove that the government could save money by supporting the program."

But there is already so much research proving the benefits of the Transcendental Meditation Technique.

"Yes, but none of it is directly tied to financial savings. Many of the people in the legislature, at least in California, are quite skeptical. But if you could prove to these people, who are responsible for the taxpayer's dollars, how those dollars could clearly be saved by a Transcendental Meditation program, then legislators would have to support it."

So what steps can be taken?

"We are already working on a demonstration project. It seems that the area where we could have the best study with the greatest possibility for control is in the area of corrections. Then, if the results in this area are positive, we should be able to get funding for a more widespread approach."

203

Science

Dr. Brian Josephson
Nobel Laureate, Physics

Professor Brian Josephson is one of the world's most eminent theoretical physicists. A Professor of Physics at Cambridge University in England, Dr. Josephson is also a Fellow of the Royal Society. In 1973 he was awarded the Nobel Prize for work that seems, somehow suitably, to verge on the impossible. He outlined theoretically what has come to be known as the "Josephson Junction," a sub-atomic "switch" that works because electrons will sometimes go through barriers that, by normal calculations, they should not be able to go through. This "impossible" tunneling by electrons through an impassable region allowed Dr. Josephson to develop an extremely sensitive junction between two "super-conductors" (a super-conductor is metal frozen so close to the absolute zero point in temperature that it loses all resistance to electrical current). The variations in current through this sensitive junction can be used to measure electrical, magnetic and atomic properties, and is now being used in the design of the next generation of computers. Dr. Josephson, who has been practicing the TM Technique for five years, frequently consults with the faculty of Maharishi International University on theoretical issues.

"I learned the Transcendental Meditation Technique in 1971," says Dr. Josephson. "I was on sabbatical from Cambridge at the time, working at Cornell University."

Was this before or after you won the Nobel Prize?

"It was three years before. However, I had completed the work that was considered for the prize before I took up TM."

Then we can't say much about the relationship between the Transcendental Meditation Technique and the fact that you won the prize?

"No, but I do feel TM has helped me in a number of different ways. I feel better, my general health is better, and I do feel I can better accomplish the particular things I want to do now."

Do you find that it has helped you with your studies in physics?

"Actually, with most of my time now I'm working on the question of intelligence and how the brain works—and also with the general question of how the individual develops. This is why the process of Transcendental Meditation is of some interest to me. The question of how it works fits naturally into my overall interest in intelligence and development."

In what direction have your studies of the TM Technique taken you?

"It's important to understand those special characteristics of the Transcendental Meditation Technique that distinguish it from other things people might do. Many people think that TM is just a form of relaxation, for instance. They think that other things might be as good. This is why it's important to know exactly what the Transcendental Meditation Technique does."

How would you define the process?

"The most useful description is that it allows a person to go beyond the frame of reference of his previous experiences. When one is starting off the process, there are some particular thoughts. But then the process allows one to bring the attention away from any particular area, to go outside those areas, beyond them."

And this a useful experience?

"It allows one to go beyond the limits of everyday experience, beyond the limits of the past. This tends to develop whatever abilities a person has. And two particular aspects of this are quite important, I believe. In the first place, the experience is not directed in any particular direction. It is not a technique that has purely physical effects or purely psychological effects. Whatever problems might be dominant in a person—physical, emotional, whatever—they are accessible to the technique. And the second point, related to this, is that the technique, unlike many procedures for self-development, does not proceed through a process of building up a picture of what one ought to be.

What do you mean by "building up a picture"?

"Let me give you an example. Suppose somebody wants to stop smoking. Normally, he would do this by thinking, 'It would be a good thing not to smoke.' Then his mind contains two ideas. The first one is the original idea, that he would like to smoke. The

---

"The TM Technique allows one to go beyond the limits of everyday experience, beyond the limits of the past. This tends to develop whatever abilities a person has."

---

second one is the new idea, that it would be beneficial not to smoke. Hopefully this second idea will have a powerful effect, but the problem is that nothing has been done about the first idea. Any process of personal development based on building up ideas of what a person should be like doesn't affect all the old ideas that are still there. Thus, there is always the danger of being pulled back toward the old ideas."

What is the difference with the Transcendental Meditation Technique?

"This is based instead on changing a person's *attitudes* to a situation, especially those feelings of dissatisfaction which lead a person to engage compulsively in activities such as smoking. One of the ways in which the process of Transcendental Meditation allows this to be accomplished is that it produces a state in which a person views his dissatisfactions objectively, from the outside as it were."

Maharishi talks of going "beyond boundaries". He says that during the process of meditation, the mind experiences a state of "unbounded" awareness. Does this make sense to you?

"I think so. In everyday activity,

whatever one is doing one is guided by some mental description of what it is that one is doing. The narrower that description is, the

> "People who meditate will tend to have a much more positive approach to life and this kind of feeling, distributed among enough people, may well tend to spread to many of the non-meditating public."

more one's abilities are restricted. But when the mind is allowed to experience things beyond the boundaries of any particular problem, this loosens the restrictions. This would be the importance of unbounded awareness. The point is that the brain functions a lot through inhibitions. One is inhibited from doing certain things, and this is necessary so that one will not act on faulty ideas. But inhibition can be a problem in itself. In the meditative state, the mind need not inhibit its own processes."

When can inhibition be a problem in itself?

"When it is excessive. This can be considered to be an emotional situation. If there is a feeling of anxiety, some aspect of the personality can feel compelled to stay in a particular restricting situation. One feels anxious, and therefore keeps trying to find an answer by going in only one direction, even if logic dictates that the direction is wrong. At this level, one is not handling much of the available information, not seeing the situation in a wider context."

And the Transcendental Meditation Technique can help increase the perspective?

"It provides a way to rid oneself of these compelling anxieties. This seems to have the effect of allowing one to get out of a situation during activity that is somehow static and restricted. The mind increases in its awareness of possibilities."

Can you foresee any positive results for a society as a whole if many of the members of that society are meditating?

"Yes, in two ways. Firstly, I think it is very likely that people meditating will tend to be in a considerably better state of health than the general population is at the moment. This aspect will of course benefit only those who meditate. On the other hand, people who meditate will on the whole tend to have a much more positive approach to life, dwelling less on its dissatisfactions. This kind of feeling, distributed among a substantial number of meditators, may well tend to spread to many of the non-meditating public."

The Arts

Francesca Moss
Painter and Lithographer

In the last several years Francesca Moss has emerged as one of America's respected young artists. Based in Chicago, and working often in collaboration with her husband, Dusty, Ms. Moss has produced works that are part of the permanent collections at UCLA and the San Diego Museum of Art. Her paintings and lithographs are displayed by galleries from coast to coast, including Rizoli's in New York, The Art Institute in Chicago and the API Gallery in Los Angeles. Ms. Moss is not only gifted artistically, but also has the facility for making verbal sense from the experience of non-verbal creativity. She begins a discussion by pin-pointing the extremes of feeling often associated with art.

"Before I started the TM Technique," says Ms. Moss, "my relationship to my art sometimes was exhilarating, almost ecstatic. And sometimes it was frustrating, just plain miserable."

What accounted for the changes?

"I think any artist knows this experience. Sometimes it's all so easy. You set up your clean, white canvas, you stand back and look at that pure surface. And then an image comes, an impulse, almost a vision. It's just like a force hits you, an energy flow in your mind. Then the next step comes, the connection between your head and your hand. You find yourself manifesting your image through your hand onto the canvas. That's all art is—just manifested thought. And when it's right, it's a spontaneous flow. You don't even seem to be doing it yourself."

But art isn't always this way?

"Not for most artists, and certainly it didn't used to be for me. Suddenly the flow just cuts off. Everything that was easy before is suddenly impossibly hard. One moment you are in connection with the level of creativity, caught up in that lively flow. The next you are disconnected, out of touch. Dirty dishes are everywhere, the rent is due. Life is suddenly miserable."

It sounds like riding a roller coaster.

"It's like that. Highs and lows. And this is very common to artists. You can see it in the letters Van Gogh wrote to his brother. He would get in the flow and just keep going no matter what. He writes about standing in the fields during a tornado, at dusk, with candles fastened to his hat, painting in a fever of exaltation. Then suddenly that happiness would be cut off, and the contrast was just overwhelming. And not only is it depressing to be out of touch, but it leads to a great sense of tension and pressure. An artist has a need to *do,* a desire to create, and when you can't get it going, the tension builds up to horrible levels inside."

And this was your experience before you began to meditate?

"It definitely was. On and off. And sometimes the dead spots would last for months. It was really painful. I started to get bitter. And the experience became entangled with my struggle to get my work on the market, and the problems I faced as a woman artist. The world of art is one of the last frontiers of male supremacy. For centuries people were convinced that women just didn't have it as serious artists. I had great difficulty finding any support for my work. The flow would cut off and I would become bitter, and then very angry. I became something of a raving women's liberationist. I was so angry I couldn't do anything else. Whatever positive impulses did come up were choked off by the anger. I blocked my creative flow altogether."

This was your frame of mind when you began the Transcendental Meditation Technique?

"It was. This was four and a half years ago, and I had stopped painting altogether. So when I started meditating, the results first showed up in a surprising way. Since I wasn't painting, I didn't notice a sudden rush of brilliant creativity. What I found instead was that I was enjoying small, everyday aspects of life. Sweeping the floor, gardening—simple things brought me pleasure. I hadn't realized before that I could

experience joy outside my art. I used to consider activities like these as mundane interruptions to my real purpose. But I found as I continued to practice the TM Technique that a feeling of wholeness began to develop in my life, that I would enjoy whatever I was doing."

And what happened when you went back to your art?

"At first I was a little worried. I thought I might have lost something from the layoff, that I would have retrogressed. But when I started in, I found that actually I was far ahead. It was like I has taken a quantum jump in my abilities. I had learned a million things without knowing it on the conscious level."

Maharishi sometimes explains the TM Technique as a method for opening a pipeline to a reservoir of creative intelligence within us. Did you find that you seemed to be more in touch with your creativity once you started meditating?

"There's no doubt of it. I found that more and more of the time, the flow would be there. And now, for the last couple of years, it seems there is never a moment when it's not there. I can sit down at any time, day or night, and just begin. And my work is so fast now. I

"As I continued meditating, I found I wasn't getting into problems any more. I was getting into solutions. My work was so strong and clear, and I felt so good, success seemed automatic."

---

have something of a reputation as one of the fastest workers in the field. Whether my work is better is hard to say, of course, but I know that *I* like it better, and I also know that my results in the marketplace have increased enormously, so other people must like the work better, too. It's a good feeling to know that your paintings are being sold in some of the best galleries around the country."

So you broke through into that male dominated world. Was it much of a fight?

"In fact, I didn't struggle in that area at all. As I continued meditating, I simply found that I wasn't getting into my problems any more. I was getting into solutions. All of a sudden, my work was so strong and clear, and I felt so good about it, that success just seemed to come automatically. If I had to speak to somebody, to deal on the level of business, I found that I was getting respect just naturally because of the way I felt about myself. It's something that's difficult to talk about, the change was so total."

So you are enjoying your art and your life now?

"Definitely. I didn't know these feelings were possible."

But what about the theory that an artist must suffer to create great art? Is great art possible without pain?

"Oh, of course. When an artist is in the flow of creation there is no suffering. It's a joy. If many artists have suffered in the past, it's not because of their creativity. Often it's for other reasons associated with the artist's life style. Usually there is not much money and getting enough to eat and drink can be a problem. Many times great artists are ahead of their time, and that means they have a difficult time finding an audience for their work. And this can cause suffering because art is designed to communicate. Unless your work can move out away from you into society, you feel incomplete, unfulfilled. And then the other reason artists suffer is that they are not strong enough to handle the forces of creativity inside them."

What do you mean by that?

"An artist has to be open to the passion of creativity. It's a powerful force, like a huge flow of electric current. It's very intense. And if an artist is not strong, then it's not possible to transmit this flow without being burned, so to speak. The personality goes out of balance and the experience makes you

---

"The TM Technique gives you strength, and also it gives you a way to dip inside yourself, to pull from the source of life that's deep within and then spread it out in front of everyone."

---

weaker and weaker. This is one of the reasons why the Transcendental Meditation Technique is so important to artists. The TM Technique doesn't weaken that level of passion and commitment to your art. What it does is strengthen the system so you can be grounded and stable while the flow is coming out. It gives you a little distance, an increased balance, so you can transmit that creativity without being knocked off balance. Practicing the TM Technique gives an artist such a great advantage. It gives you that strength, and also it gives you a way to dip inside yourself, to pull from that source of life that's deep within and then to spread it out in front of everyone. Artists are used to working from subtle levels anyway, and the TM Technique just gives them a systematic way to make those levels available all the time. It's like a bee line to the source. It brings a total connection between you and the work. And then every aspect of your art expresses that fullness. The art becomes so powerful. The whole work is soaked in that creativity."

So an artist has a very clear way to see the progress that is coming from the practice of the Transcendental Meditation Technique.

"It's so clear. You can see the growth of consciousness in every brush stroke. It's a beautiful experience."

Education

Dr. Sidney Reisberg
Educational Communications

Dr. Sidney Reisberg is a respected leader in the field of educational communications. His qualifications have made him much in demand as a consultant to private companies and in such capacities as Executive Director of the New York Kidney Foundation and Deputy Director of the Mass Media Study for President Johnson's Commission on Civil Disorders. Most recently he was Associate Dean in the Center for Educational Communications at the State University of New York. As this book goes to press, Dr. Reisberg is in attendance at a teacher training course for the Transcendental Meditation Technique being conducted in Livingston Manor, New York. Dr. Reisberg begins a discussion on the role of the Transcendental Meditation Technique and the Science of Creative Intelligence in modern education by talking about student needs.

"It won't come as any surprise to anyone in education to say that there is a big gap between what the students say is important and what the schools say is important. As a matter of fact, that was the theme of a keynote address by the incoming President at the National Conference on Higher Education several years ago. Dr. Patricia Cross had done a study that showed that students thought that their schools gave highest priority to the acqusition of knowledge. The students themselves, however, placed academic development fourteenth on a list of twenty goals.

What did they place first?

"A category labeled student development. That means helping students to identify and pursue their personal goals, to develop a sense of self-worth and confidence, to achieve levels of self understanding and develop open and trusting relationships."

What do you think is the conclusion to be drawn from this by an educator?

"It's a problem, because we can say that the major concern of students is with self identity. And education has been in a bind because the one skill that we have not been able to provide in our schools is how to enable a student to be in touch with himself, how to make contact with his internal state of being and to achieve deeper levels of self-understanding."

And you feel that the Transcendental Meditation Technique is useful for this purpose?

"Yes, it provides precisely the skill for enabling students to get in touch with themselves. The results have been shown in the research—students who meditate improve their grades, get along better with people, and go off drugs. The same thing happens with teachers, too. Meditating teachers communicate better with their students. In fact, when you present these results to educators, it can sometimes be a problem."

Why is that?

"You frequently get an incredulous response, something like, 'Come on, are you saying this is some kind of miracle cure that's good for everything that ails you?' And I think that's a perfectly reasonable reaction. It was the reaction I had when I was first introduced to Transcendental Meditation."

The broad range of the research on the Transcendental Meditation Technique can seem to be a little much.

"It can as long as we are caught up in an allopathic concept of the nature of problems."

Can you define allopathic, please?

"It means the method of treating specific symptoms with specific cures, usually drugs. You take this drug for this symptom and that drug for that symptom. But Transcendental Meditation rests on an entirely different view of the organism. It looks upon the person not as a series of parts, to be treated separately, but as the single organic entity that it is. And the point is that all of these integrated parts, and also all of the behavior patterns of the whole, are largely affected by the state of the nervous system. When the roots of thought and action in the nervous system are nourished by creative energies, then I think it is perfectly under-

standable that the whole organism will respond positively."

And how do you relate this to education?

"If a student does not get along well with his peers or his parents, if he is tense and distracted, if he uses drugs and alcohol as some form of release, then learning may

---

"When the roots of thought and action in the nervous system are nourished by creative energies, then it is perfectly understandable that the whole organization responds positively."

---

come very hard. No matter how well the teacher may present the material, he will have a difficult time getting through because the student is just not available. He is not ready, he is just not prepared for learning. And similarly, if a teacher has his channels blocked, his antennae dull—if he finds in his work little joy and self expression—then he will have an equally rough time. So the answer to the question is that Transcendental Meditation can provide a base to the entire curriculum, that it can provide an activity which at once prepares the student for learning and the teacher for teaching. I don't think Transcendental Meditation should be seen as just one more subject to be squeezed into this or that department. It is an experience that provides the availability, the readiness, the openness which is so profoundly needed to join teacher and student in the joy of learning."

This should mean that the Transcendental Meditation Technique will spread rapidly in the educational field. Do you see any reason why it shouldn't?

"I think some educators may still ask this sort of question: Why does Western education need Maharishi and Transcendental

Meditation to solve its problems?"

You don't share that kind of concern?

"I think the question has been largely answered by the research that has appeared recently that indicates that the two hemispheres of the brain operate in very different ways. One of the hemispheres is verbal and has to do with language and analytic ability, and the other one has to do with artistic and musical ability and spacial perception—the more synthetic abilities."

What does this have to do with education?

"Only one of these hemispheres heavily dominates Western thinking and education. That is the verbal, analytic hemisphere. This mode of knowing the world is treated as if there were only one path to learning, one way of using the mind. We are so used to this way of thinking that many of us don't even suspect the existence of another way. But now researchers have provided some evidence that this other hemisphere of the brain is the source of a different form of learning, a kind of spacial, holistic, intuitive thinking. Unlike the linear, orderly form of language processes, this hemisphere processes information all at once, simultaneously—in a holistic manner.

"What Maharishi has done is to make this knowledge available in a systematic way so we can see it clearly and make use of it in our on-going education."

Can you express this difference more clearly?

"It's difficult because the very categories of our language are inadequate for expressing this information well, for talking about different forms of directly experiencing knowledge—not· talking about it, but experiencing it. And although this path of understanding derives from Maharishi's culture—and has therefore been considered to be outside the frame of our educational theory and practice—the fact is that knowledge such as this has threaded a path through the whole history of Western culture."

What do you mean by that?

"What we are talking about are non-ordinary forms of experiencing reality—intuitive, subjective means of gaining knowledge—and this sort of experience is found in William Blake and Tennyson and Samuel Butler. It's found in Walt Whitman, Rainer Maria Rilke, Robert Graves, D. H. Lawrence, Carl Jung, Martin Heidegger, William James and Doris Lessing. Gustav Fechner, Edward Titchener and Wilhelm Wundt, the early researchers of modern psychology, were all engaged in the systematic analysis of introspection and subjective states of sensation and feeling. These ideas are brilliantly developed as the spearhead of evolution in the work of the French Jesuit paleontologist, Teilhard de Chardin. This complementary joining of intellect and intuition has also been expressed by many great scientists, such as Poincaré, Huxley, Jeans and Einstein. The fact is that this ancient wisdom has always been a part of our culture."

Then what has been Maharishi's contribution?

"The knowledge has existed in the recesses of our culture, but has never really become a part of the mainstream. It has generally been hidden from view. What Maharishi has done for us is to make this knowledge available in a systematic way so we can see it clearly and make use of it in our on-going education."

When this systematic technique is used in education, when the Transcendental Meditation Technique is taught as part of the curriculum, what do you feel is the most important contribution it makes?

"We have to talk about Transcendental Meditation and the theory behind it, the Science of Creative Intelligence, and what they do, I feel, is to provide a perspective on knowledge and reality whereby the apparent diversities and irreconcilabilities of life can be understood and unified."

What do you mean by the phrase, "diversities and irreconcilabilities"?

"If we look at education today, what we find is that the accelerating rate of information and knowledge is almost beyond our comprehension. Even more importantly, we have no way of tying all the knowledge together, of viewing it as a unified whole. The Science of Creative Intelligence gives us perspective on this problem. The point it makes is that absolute values are not to be looked for in the objective world. They just aren't found there. The Science of Creative Intelligence directs us to look rather to consciousness, to the self, as the continuum in which expanding knowledge can be stabilized and unified. It presents the opportunity for us to rediscover for ourselves the knowledge that the objective world in which we experience relative values is not the whole of life—that it is really within the other part of life, the subjective world, that we come to know absolute values. If I may read to you something from Robert Browning, lines I love that speak to this issue:

'Truth is within ourselves; it takes
   no rise
From outward thing, whate'er you
   may believe:
There is an inmost centre in us all,
Where truth abides in fulness . . .
   and, "to know"
Rather consists in opening out a way

Whence the imprisoned splendor
   may escape,
Than in effecting entry for a light
Supposed to be without.'

While there is nothing new about this understanding of reality, 'know thyself,' it has never been anywhere near the usable center of Western education."

If, despite all this, an educator asked you why he should implement the Transcendental Meditation Program and the Science of Creative Intelligence in his curriculum, what would you tell him?

"There are many people today who say that humankind is in the midst of an enormous and historic transformation. There is a strong feeling in many quarters that we shall *have* to achieve higher levels of consciousness to meet our evolutionary challenge. So my answer would take the form of a question: Considering where we seem to be in our evolution, can we afford to miss any serious signpost that might guide us into the future?

Health

Dr. Hans Selye
Director, Institute of Experimental Medicine and Surgery
University of Montreal

Dr. Hans Selye is one of the most eminent men in the medical sciences. More than thirty years ago, Dr. Selye broke totally new ground in his field by identifying the medical concept of stress. Through a series of experiments he determined the exact physical effects of stress, and in the process made a number of important discoveries about the biochemistry of the body. He has written thirty-two books, including the highly influential works, *The Stress of Life*, and *Stress Without Distress*. He has served since 1945 as Professor and Director of the Institute of Experimental Medicine and Surgery at the University of Montreal. The sum of Dr. Selye's work has helped make doctors aware that they must not only treat specific diseases, but also help their patients handle the overall effects of all types of stress, and Dr. Selye is now recognized as the leading authority on the subject. His interest in the use of the Transcendental Meditation Technique as a method to handle stress began several years ago.

"It is my good fortune to have spent almost an entire day with Maharishi Mahesh Yogi at one of his international symposia on the Science of Creative Intelligence," Dr. Selye says. "Ever since then I have felt it would be extremely fruitful to explore in detail the obvious physiological and psychological influence exerted by Transcendental Meditation on stress in the body."

You do feel that the TM Technique is of value in combatting stress?

"Research already conducted shows that the physiological effects of Transcendental Meditation are exactly the opposite to those identified by medicine as being characteristic of the body's effort to meet the demands of stress."

Since we are having a chance to talk to the inventor of the stress concept, we should probably find out exactly what you mean when you talk about it. Perhaps you could tell us how you first developed the idea.

"Well, actually, as far as I can remember it, it was when I was a second-year medical student. There was a class where the professor first showed us how to ask questions of a patient in order to arrive at a specific diagnosis. You see, classical medicine is based on the fact that you have to know what the patient is suffering from specifically. You have to find what we call the pathogen—the disease producing agent—so you can prescribe something against that particular pathogen. I remember being very impressed by the way the professor could diagnose these various diseases by mere questioning, and looking at the various signs and so on. But when he was through, an afterthought came to me. It seemed curious that he never spoke about those aspects of disease which even I, who knew nothing about medicine at the time, could see very well."

What sort of things are you speaking about?

"The professor had deliberately selected the patients he was using to be quite different. They all had very different diseases in order to show how to arrive at different diagnoses. Still all these patients had one thing in common."

What was that?

"They all looked *sick*."

Sick people looked sick? Isn't that a pretty obvious thing to say?

"It is, isn't it? When I say that to audiences they usually laugh, because it seems such a silly thing to say. Naturally, if people are sick, they look sick. But the word to question there is 'naturally.' Why naturally? We are used to the fact that, whenever you are sick, you are kind of pale, you feel weak, you have no energy, and so on. If it lasts a longer time, you lose weight, you become nervous and irritable, and you exhibit other such signs. These are general signs but often they aren't self-evident."

Why not?

"The main concern of a doctor is to look for a specific syndrome characteristic of a specific disease."

Could you define syndrome?

"A syndrome is a set of symptoms or manifestations that go together. For example, the syndrome for scarlet fever includes the skin rash, the temperature, and so on. They always go together. Well, people knew about specific syndromes—how you can diagnose tuberculosis, for instance, and tell it from

"They all had very different diseases, leading to very different diagnoses. Still all the patients did have one basic thing in common. They all looked sick."

leprosy or anything else. But it was never mentioned that there is a syndrome of just disease in general, and, as a second-year medical student this made such a deep impression on me that I have spent the rest of my life working on that syndrome."

You have been talking about disease, about a general syndrome for disease. But isn't it true that the concept of stress includes more than just the effects of disease?

"That's correct, but it wasn't until a little later, when I was an Assistant Professor of Biochemistry in Montreal, at McGill University, that I ran into this same syndrome in a more scientific way and the idea developed further. I wasn't using the word stress at that time."

You were doing experiments at McGill?

"Yes, using rats. You know I am an endocrinologist, so I am interested in hormones. The procedure I used was to make extracts of various glands, which contained hormones, and inject them into the rats. Just as with diseases, one extract did one thing and another extract did another, but they all also produced a common syndrome. I was able to characterize this syndrome exactly by killing the animal and looking at its organs. And the syndrome was the one of just being sick."

What were the signs of this syndrome?

"Several were important. I saw, for example that the adrenal glands—the two glands which are above the kidneys—had become very large and hyperactive. I saw that lymph nodes had shrunk, and this was important because the lymph nodes look after the body's immunity and defense reactions. Also gastric ulcers developed, duodenal ulcers developed. All these changes went together. It was a syndrome, and it was one quite independent of what caused it."

This is the syndrome of being sick, but you had caused it with hormonal extracts rather than disease.

"That's right. And then I tried not injecting any extract, but just exposing the animals to stress—what I would later call stress—that is to say, any kind of demand on the body which deranges its normal equilibrium. I did this by inducing nervous tension, for example, or pain, fear, or chemical defense. And when we looked at these animals we found that all these measures would produce the same syndrome. Gradually this way, we had an experimental model on which to work out the biochemistry of stress, to determine which hormones, which nervous functions participate in producing it, and what it's manifestations can be."

Speaking in the context of the Transcendental Meditation Technique, we say that stress is some impression left on the body or nervous system, some form of dysfunction, that results from an overload on the system. What definition of stress did you come to from your experiments?

"Well, the scientific definition of stress, the one used in medicine now, is a little different. Officially, it is defined as the non-specific response of the body to any demand made upon it."

Non-specific?

"That is to say, the common response, the response that happens all the time. If you ask me to lift a weight, make a demand on a particular muscle, that is a specific demand. If you are making a demand on my ability to adapt to cold, that's also a specific demand. But adaptation just in general, to function, that's a non-specific demand. And stress is a non-specific response to any demand. The demand may be to fight an infectious disease, to fight an unpleasant social situation in your family or your job. Or it may be to create something and have an outlet for your energy. And whatever responses the body has in common to all of these demands, that is stress as it is officially defined."

And so when you say that the effects of the Transcendental Meditation Technique are the opposite of those resulting from stress, you mean that the results are the opposite of those produced when demands are made upon the body?

"Yes. The research shows this for metabolism, breathing, skin resistance, blood lactate, brain waves and the cardiovascular system. The same way, the therapeutic effects of Transcendental Meditation on

---

"The therapeutic effects of TM on bodily derangements is most evident in the conditions known as 'diseases of stress'—especially mental, cardiovascular and gastrointestinal ailments."

---

bodily derangements is most evident in the conditions known as 'diseases of stress' or 'diseases of adaption'—especially in mental, cardiovascular, gastrointestinal and hypersensitivity ailments—ailments caused by inappropriate responses to the stresses of everyday life."

Maharishi says that if we continue to meditate, the system dissolves stress progressively and cumulatively, and that eventually it is possible to live life free from stress altogether. Do you also see this as a possibility for the human system?

"Well, we are talking about different definitions of the word stress, and I think that even though this conversation is meant for nonmedical people, we should keep it absolutely correct scientifically. And if we use the medical definition of stress, then it isn't the object of Transcendental Meditation or any other technique or medicine to annul all stress."

Why not?

"Without some level of stress, we couldn't even be talking now."

It takes stress to talk?

"The definition of stress is the response to *any* demand. Even while you sleep, even while you are under anesthesia, you have some stress, because you are using some part of your body—your heart pumps, your respiration goes on."

So talking about it simply, the difference in the definitions is that when Maharishi uses the word stress he definitely means something negative, but the medical definition can mean something either positive or negative.

"Yes. You see, when I created the concept I didn't think of this difference, so I called it all stress. But then there was often confusion. The general public uses stress and distress as synonymous, but they're not. The stress of pain, of sorrow, of nervousness, of suffering—that's bad stress, distress. But the stress of creation, or the stress of being able to achieve by taking things in a resilient way, you don't want to eliminate that. So there is

good stress (technically "eustress") or bad stress ("distress") but the response to any demand is stress. There is always stress, so the only point is to make sure that it is useful to yourself and useful to others."

"The TM Technique is a method which so relaxes the human central nervous system that it can live with stress better, that it doesn't suffer from stress."

So then, using these terms, how would you define the usefulness of the Transcendental Meditation Technique?

"I would refer to it as a method which so relaxes the human central nervous system that it can live with stress better, that it doesn't *suffer* from stress, without losing all it's useful effects. The Transcendental Meditation Technique prepares the nervous system for all activity. It's the nervous system, after all, that is the major source of pleasant stress or distress, of satisfaction or dissatisfaction. And I think if you can influence the nervous system through Transcendental Meditation so that it can really relax, really be at it's best in responding non-specifically to any demand, that is an ideal solution."

Business

Blue Cross/Blue Shield
Chicago

The field of business is one of those that has taken to the Transcendental Meditation Program most enthusiastically. Business shares with the world of athletics a high level of stress and intense pressure to perform at full potential. For these reasons, implementation of a TM Program in a business setting brings rapid and obvious results. The experience at the Blue Cross/Blue Shield office in Chicago has been typical, where more than fifty people have been involved in a large pilot program that began in the fall of 1975. Four of those people, all of whom occupy important executive positions, are Paul Miller, Vice-President and Director of the Systems Division; John Ryan, Director of Training and Development; Mrs. Mary Alice Smith, Manager of Systems Support; and George Graham, Manager of Supervisory Training and Management Development. Paul Miller was the one who began the TM Technique first, and it was he who first stimulated interest at Blue Cross.

"I had noticed clear benefits from the practice of the TM Technique myself," says Mr. Miller, "and I felt that since it would help improve business performance the corporation would be willing to pick up the cost."

So the initial program was just in the Systems Division?

Ryan: "Paul checked in with us in Training and Development, to get some involvement from a relevant corporation department. Several of us sat in on the two introductory lectures. When the course began we decided to start."

Smith: "I think there were thirty-two people at those first meetings, and we all started the program."

And what have the results been?

Ryan: "About six months later we did a quick 'pencil survey', and we found that about seventy percent of that first group were still meditating and enjoying the practice. And even most of the ones who were not meditating at the time said they intended to get back to it, that they liked it. So in that sense, at least, you would have to call the program very successful."

Have people talked about any benefits they see coming from the practice?

Graham: "I know that I, personally,

have noticed many benefits. I have greater energy now. The quality of my sleep is much improved. I seem to be more in touch with myself, with what's going on inside me, and I think this has led me to have greater control over events going on around me."

Smith: "I certainly feel I am more efficient in my job. I do much less unproductive fretting and worrying. Something may have happened badly yesterday, but today I don't feel so emotionally enmeshed in that problem. I feel now that I live more in the present."

You don't worry so much about past actions?

"Or about the future. It used to be that when I had a busy day coming up, I'd just go over and over things in my mind—four times, five times, ten times. It was unnecessary, unproductive. I would get entangled in worries. Now I feel much less tension connected with my life. I prepare myself and do the job. I take things less personally."

Graham: "I can support that very strongly. I feel the TM Technique has been very helpful in my ability to apply myself effectively to any given task. It seems to take me less time to do things. I've heard most people in the program comment on this. It seems to be mostly because of increased clarity of thinking. There is less useless material in the way of productive thinking. There is less time wasted having to corral thoughts and purposely *direct* them a certain way. It's just easy to apply yourself to the task of the moment."

Ryan: "Something I've noticed since I started meditating is that I have felt much more open to things around me. I feel more alert and aware, more absorbed in my activities. It's not just that I cope better, but that there are more positive contributions I can make. And I can see the change in others,

too. Just about everybody in our department who started the technique says he feels better, and in some cases the changes are marked. I have one instructor who used to have great difficulty handling two or three projects at once. Now his load is up to eight and nine, and far from complaining, he's thriving on it."

"The TM Program encourages cooperative, open information sharing and problem solving. I think it leads to a tendency to move toward what is good and positive."

Besides benefits such as these at the individual level, have you noticed any positive changes coming in your business interactions?

Ryan: "I'll tell you something interesting. Most of the people who started the TM Program were either with us in Training, or with Paul Miller in Systems. I don't know how Paul feels, but I think the contrast in the working relationship between the two departments is 180 degrees."

Miller: "Without question I have noticed a change in our attitudes. The stresses and pressures of the job are still there, but I feel we are better able to put them in perspective and deal with them."

Ryan: I think we should point out that the Systems Division is one of the divisions in this corporation that is under the most pressure."

Why is that?

Miller: "Our division has responsibility for all activities that support our computer systems everywhere in the corporation. And from my perspective, the job does entail a great deal of pressure. We are a service organization, and we are asked to do things for others the way they want them done. And our time frames are usually very tight. I know that before beginning the TM Program I personally felt a great deal of pressure, both from those who asked things of us and also from the corporate structure."

Have you noticed an improvement in this situation, especially in relations with other departments?

"I have. I think before there was a tendency in our department to get defensive. The job seemed to be a one-way street. When we would do well, there would be no feedback. When we made a mistake, we really heard about it. So we started to feel sorry for ourselves a little bit. 'No one appreciates what I'm doing'—that type of outlook. And then we'd get agitated because we couldn't afford to let the people we worked for know about that attitude. If we did, then *they* would get defensive, and they would be more likely to throw barbs at us for non-performance. It was this type of stress I thought the TM Technique could help us with, and I know it has worked, at least for me. I'm much less defensive now. I'm more inclined to address the issues that are at hand, and to forget about personalities. This means I'm more liable to take the correct angle in any given situation. And my peers have told me they have noticed very significant changes in the way I can cope with stress—that I can respond now without raising my voice, without getting overly anxious and agitated."

Ryan: "I know this. The Systems Division is now one of the most open and cooperative groups we deal with in Training. I was talking about this with one of our managers the other day, and what he said was this: You come out of a meeting with those people and you actually feel like a human being. It's not like being in a battle."

Isn't that a usual feeling after a business meeting?

220

Ryan: "Not always, that's for sure."

Smith: "The world of business can be a pretty run-for-your-life type of existence. There can be a lot of game-playing."

Ryan: "There's so much stress in a business environment. It leads to a lot of counter-productive behavior, especially in

---

"Most of the people who started the TM Program were either in Training or in Systems. I think the contrast in the working relationship between the two departments is 180 degrees."

---

meetings. You get a lot of blocking behavior, and a lot of head-to-head confrontations. You can come out of meetings all bruised and bloody. The trouble is that everybody gets a 'win-lose' attitude, instead of a 'win-win' attitude, and it can make the business world a lousy place to be. And more than that, it absolutely cuts into productiveness."

What do you mean by "win-lose" attitude, or a "win-win" attitude?

Ryan: So often the interpersonal dynamics in a business setting are aggressive. People try to move ahead at the expense of other people. The attitude is that if I want to win, I have to make the other guy lose. But that's not the most productive approach. The better way is for two people, or two departments, to realize their mutual needs and to look for ways both sides can come out looking good. This is the 'win-win' approach—the recognition that there are many ways that both sides can profit. And based on our experience, I believe the Transcendental Meditation Program helps foster this sort of attitude at a very basic level. It seems to lead to the kind of values that bring about positive behavior. It encourages cooperative, open information sharing and problem solving. Basically, I think it simply leads to a tendency to move toward what is good."

Graham: "That description parallels my experience. I feel I have much more tolerance when I'm in an interpersonal setting. I find myself overlooking a lot of personal differences that used to bother me. I simply orient more to the positive now."

Smith: "I think the TM Program can help straighten out business values in another sense, also. There's a lot of quite insane activity that goes on. There's a great tendency to pretend, to fool ourselves."

How do you mean?

"So many times, people don't really try to solve problems. They just go through a charade of problem solving. You see this in government, too. People set up a study committee, go through a lot of work, put out a report. But everybody knows—even to start with—that nothing is going to come of all that motion. That's why it's a game. But it seems that when people begin the Transcendental Meditation Technique, it tends to put them back in touch with themselves, and therefore with a sense of reality. Action becomes more productive. It leads people to deal more in realities—at least in the experiences I've had."

Ryan: "We can bring it back to the meetings we have with your department now. Not only are they positive in tone, but we find that your people have done their homework. They ask good, sharp questions. Things get accomplished."

Miller: "I think that sort of progress is only to be expected. If people don't have so much tension and stress, then it's just easier to take an objective look at problems. It's easier to come to a decision about what the best approach is in a given situation."

To sum up, then, what do you think is the most important contribution the TM Program can make in a business environment?

Miller: "The stress angle is so important. And it's more important the higher you go in management. One of the measures of a manager's performance is how he performs under stress. If he gets so flustered he can't perform, he hurts himself and his company."

Ryan: "To be very basic, if the technique did nothing else but help people sleep, lower their blood pressure, relieve drinking problems—it would be worth it. Executive health is a big problem in any business."

Graham: "If we look at it from the side of management, we can make a very compelling case for the TM Program. The individual people in an organization are, to borrow a manufacturing phrase, the 'units of production.' If you can enhance either the rate or the quality of production by these individual units, then the organization is closer to its goal. And if you can get both rate *and* quality, then you've caught the brass ring. And now we can say there is a practice that can be applied to these 'units of production' that will not only increase their production in the short run, but also—and this is the clincher—it will increase their developable potential on the job. In a sense, it's a way people can re-make their capabilities in a very holistic, general way. This is not just a way to teach the nitty gritty of one specific task, but a way to increase a person's ability to handle all people, all situations, all tasks."

Ryan: "I believe this is the key, too. The TM Program transcends all specifics. It infuses all activities. It's an underpinning for success because it increases energy, openness and creativity. People absorb more, do more, take on more, look for more."

Graham: "Human resources are the basic asset of any organization. And if you have a technique that can upgrade the quality of these human resources in a holistic way, then you've got yourself a winner."

"The world is as we are."
—Maharishi

Maharishi Mahesh Yogi
Inauguration Speech—January 12, 1975

Jai Guru Dev. It is a very great and joyful time for us all to be recognizing the dawn of the full potential of the human race on earth—full potential in terms of unbounded happiness, harmony, peace and fulfillment.

We are realizing this on the basis of the scientific validation of our teaching in the world for the last eighteen years. We have been teaching the knowledge we received from Guru Dev, our Master, and by now all the waves of joy we were feeling in our humble efforts to spread the light of his knowledge in all parts of the world, the waves of joy we have been experiencing during the process of teaching the Transcendental Meditation Technique to single individuals here and there, all these different, innumerable waves have gathered together to form a tidal wave of hope—hope founded on the basis of the verifiable results the knowledge has produced in the lives of more than one million people so far. It is on that basis we see the onset of a better society, the onset of a better world, the onset of a happy age, the onset of the age of fulfillment, the onset of the age of wholeness in life, the onset of the Age of Enlightenment.

We started out eighteen years ago on the basis of the experience given to us by Guru Dev, telling the world, "Life is bliss" and "No man need suffer any more." It was a surprise to the world how we could dare to say this when everywhere life was suffering and struggle. But we knew that bliss was unbounded, deep within, so we advised the people to turn their attention inward, to experience that unbounded wholeness of life and bring the mind out, fully saturated with that. The people, even not believing our words, started. And once they started, the experience was there. Like that, from individual to individual the experience spread in the midst of those expressions, "Life is bliss" and "No man need suffer any more."

"The people, even not believing our words started the TM Technique. And once they started, the experience was there."

225

All that is necessary is to close the eyes and fathom the depths of unboundedness within one's own consciousness; realize that fullness of life, that level of enlightenment which is kindled deep within everyone's heart; unfold that experience that is enough to make the whole life more orderly; life in orderliness, life in accordance with all the laws of nature.

And now great information has come to us about the effects of the Transcendental Meditation Technique on the whole society. Before this, for eighteen years throughout the world we have been asked by people concerned with our society, "Your meditation is all right for the individual, but what about society? A man meditates and he may become a better individual. But what about the whole society?"

We have been giving the logic that the individual is the unit of society: if individuals become better the society will become better. We felt confident; the logic is self-sufficient. But now, today, has come this new finding of the statistics on whole cities—when the number of people in a city practicing the Transcendental Meditation Program reaches one per cent, then the crime rate falls. What we find now is that just a few orderly people moving around change the trends of the whole society. This evidence produced by science is much greater than the logic we have been furthering so far.

And when we find that the crime rate decreases, that means the most intense area of stress in society is influenced by one per cent of the people meditating and moving around. So when the most disorderly area of society is influenced, how much greater will be the influence in the other ninety-nine per cent of the people, where the stress is not so much? This brings the possibility of a better world very near.

And the whole thing is so natural. One man, having a desire to evolve, having a desire to progress, having a desire to grow by nature, will take up the Transcendental Meditation Technique. On that basis, he will start producing a harmonious influence around him. Without knowing how he does it, without knowing the mechanics of how the radiations go from a more orderly mind to influence the less orderly minds around him, invariably he'll be producing a harmonious influence in the whole society. Then the whole society will find a trend in the direction of progress and evolution.

The personal advantages of the Transcendental Meditation Program are so enormous, as now validated by the scientific experiments, that any intelligent man will not be able to resist it for very long. And there are enough intelligent people in the world to start the TM Technique for their own individual benefit. Then their influence will radiate in society and the whole society will become better.

And this declaration of the Dawn of the Age of Enlightenment is an expression of a phenomenon that is already happening. When I reviewed the statistics, I found that we should have said this sooner, because there are cities in the world that now have three per cent, five percent, of their populations meditating. This we should have caught two or three years ago, when those cities had only one per cent meditating. So we are late, but it doesn't matter. We are being dragged on by time. The Age of Enlightenment is going to drag us out of the darkness of the age of ignorance and into the bright sunshine.

I give credit to the scientists today who have, through their knowledge and procedures, contributed so much to this Dawn. And at this very precious moment for the whole world, I feel highly emotional toward my master, Guru Dev. The age-old knowledge was there, but it needed Guru Dev to whisper it out and make it available to the world.

I feel so full of feelings of gratitude.

On this auspicious, highly momentous occasion for the whole world, we can only say, "Jai Guru Dev."

Acknowledgments

In a sense, of course, all the credit for this book could go to Maharishi Mahesh Yogi. It is his expression of an ancient knowledge that gives substance to the work, and it was with his kind permission that I went along to report on the 1975 tour.

During the actual writing and production of the book, however, I have received gracious assistance from scores of other people. Recording my gratitude is one of the pleasures of this project.

Priority of place goes to my parents, who both made important contributions at every stage, from concept through expression to punctuation. Similar help came from Jerry Jarvis and Vesey Crighton of the International World Plan Executive Council, who deserve special thanks for two qualities: sensitive guidance and gratifying promptness. A special thanks is due to Lisa Locke whose crucial assistance in research, editing and production made the mechanics of the book much more enjoyable and efficient.

In terms of the writing itself, the largest contribution was made by Bob Roth, who combined relentless logic and functional sympathy (in the German sense of "feeling-with"). After his critique of the first draft, there was a book. Jack Forem also supplied important insights in two separate readings. Many other people read the manuscript in whole or in part, and their help far exceeds the gratitude I can express in this simple listing of names: Allen Altman, Charlotte Arnell, Caroline Arnell, Meg Cowles, Doug Duda, Ursula Freer, Laurie Glass, Marv Goldschmidt, Margaret Hill, Suzanne Howard, Susan Levin, Diana Major, Rick and Amy Moss, Gail Parmet, Janie Schechter, Steve Taylor, Hal Sutter, Barry and Bonnie Uslianer, John Wiebusch and Frank Zachary.

To many others, I owe a pleasant debt for assistance of other kinds. Thanks are due to Michael Skoletsky, Michael Goodman and others for research assistance in the film and tape library at Maharishi European Research University; to Victor Raymond and Fred Den Ouden for help in photo selection (most of the color photographs of Maharishi in this book were taken by these two); to Lawrence Sheaf, Steve Benson and Pat McKee for help in design and production; to David Johnston for important design contributions; to Kathy Oldenburg for rapid, accurate production work; and to John Huntley for invaluable go-between assistance on two interviews.

Special thanks are due to two more people. One is Bob Cobb, who put up with my endlessly escalating demands for production quality in this book, and made them all come true efficiently and economically. The other is Herbert Alexander whose important contributions far exceeded, both professionally and personally, the vital guidance he gave me through the uncharted world of publishing.

Production Notes—Typesetting for this book was done by Computer Typesetting Services in Glendale, California. The printing is by R. R. Donnelley in Indiana. Printing and production coordination were handled by Cobb/Dunlop in New York.